Conversation, Risk, and Conversion

Conversation, Risk, and Conversion

THE INNER AND PUBLIC LIFE
OF SMALL CHRISTIAN COMMUNITIES

MICHAEL A. COWAN

BERNARD J. LEE, S.M.

ORBIS BOOKS

Maryknoll, New York 10545

The Catholic Foreign Mission Society of America (Maryknoll) recruits and trains people for overseas missionary service. Through Orbis Books, Maryknoll aims to foster the international dialogue that is essential to mission. The books published, however, reflect the opinions of their authors and are not meant to represent the official position of the society.

Manufactured in the United States of America

Library of Congress Cataloging-in-Publication Data

Cowan, Michael.
  Conversation, risk, and conversion : the inner and public life of small Christian
communities / Michael A. Cowan, Bernard J. Lee.
    p. cm
  Includes bibliographical references and index.
  ISBN 1-57075-149-8 (alk. paper)
  1. Christian communities—Catholic Church. 2. Basic Christian
communities—United States. 3. Sociology, Christian (Catholic)—
United States. I. Lee, Bernard J., 1932- . II. Title.
BX2347.72.U6C68 1997
250'.973—dc21   97-18566
                 CIP

To those whose faith in God and in each other
generates the energy and the passion
to build communities
determined
to redeem our histories and renew our earth

We say that we "conduct" a conversation, but the more genuine a conversation is, the less its conduct lies within the will of either partner. Thus a genuine conversation is never the one that we wanted to conduct. Rather, it is generally more correct to say that we fall into conversation, or even that we become involved in it. The way one word follows another, with the conversation taking its own twists and reaching its own conclusion, may well be conducted in some way, but the partners conversing are far less the leaders of it than the led. No one knows in advance what will "come out" of a conversation. Understanding or its failure is like an event that happens to us. Thus we can say that something was a good conversation or that it was ill fated. All this shows that a conversation has a spirit of its own, ... that it allows something to "emerge" which henceforth exists.

—Hans-Georg Gadamer
Truth and Method

Contents

ix

CHAPTER ONE

Conversation, Risk, and Conversion

The Inner and Public Life
of Small Christian Communities

INTRODUCTION

Talking happens a lot. It is often monologue. Conversation is rarer, by far. It is always dialogue. No one takes leave of a real conversation the same as when one entered into it. Our conversations create us. Conversation and risk and conversion belong together. Conversation is dangerous, therefore, to anyone unwilling to embrace or at least to accept transformation.

When we first addressed the experience of small Christian communities [SCCs] in our book, *Dangerous Memories: House Churches and Our American Story*, we borrowed the expression "dangerous memories" from the work of Johannes Metz. When we remember that things were other than they are now, and that they were holy and right when they were like that, we suddenly realize that they could also be different than they are now, and be holy and right. Those memories often feel like a danger because they make us face the fragility and mutability of the world we know well and in which we are relatively comfortable. That realization relativizes the present moment—any present moment. Metz says that such memories are dangerous because

> they break through the canon of the prevailing structures of plausibility and have certain subversive features. They are like dangerous and incalculable visitations from the past. They are memories . . . with a future content (Metz 1980, 109-110).

The notion that small Christian communities are rooted in memories with a future content that endangers the status quo was appealing to our readers and our friends in many workshops and retreats, basically because it rings true.

There is some drama in the expression "dangerous memories," but it is more than a showpiece. We squirm with the demands it makes, and we smile at the invitation to remake the face of the earth, a vocation we have because we are children of Spirit. As we began to use the metaphor of conversation to think once again about the character of the small Christian community, we recalled that Hans-Georg Gadamer, who pressed "conversation" into metaphorical service in that way, also reminded us that only those who are willing to put their presumptions at risk can engage in true conversation. We may not change our minds, but we cannot have genuinely confronted otherness and remain utterly the same; and we don't know ahead of time what the difference might be.

We are continuing the intuition, laid out in *Dangerous Memories,* that small Christian communities are a piece of very important conversation in the church today, where participants are taking some risks on behalf of the reign of God and the people of God. There is risk indeed. We who know that we live in a world at risk and a church at risk belong in this conversation. What we risk by participating is conversion.

There are some very important conversations about life and faith that happen in small Christian communities—that happen often, in fact—but which occur far more rarely in the more traditional forms of gathering that have characterized Catholic life. It is the dynamic of the small group, and especially of the small groups that are communities, that makes this important kind of conversation more likely to happen. There were conversations in the early house churches that have not occurred regularly since Christian communities lost their marginal status with the assimilation of Christianity into the dominant culture. The conversations that constitute us are the daily interactions between friends and family members and community members. They are conversations between Christian communities and the larger worlds that constitute their social environment. They are conversations between God and the people of God. It should be clear that conversation is for us a metaphor for our relationality, at least for the kind of relationality that makes us become the particular people we are. Becoming is relentless both in conversation and in conversion. The two words have the same etymological parents.

CONVERSATION AND CONVERSION:
SOME TELLING ETYMOLOGY

It is no etymological fluke that conversation and conversion have the same Latin roots from which we have pressed both words into English. Throughout our lives our conversations change us, move us, and often convert us. The root connection between conversion and conversation is more than fun with words. The etymological connection tells some important truth. It tells us a story about our humanness. And our divinity.

Verto, vertere, versi, versus is the Latin verb for "turn." Adding *con* makes the verb mean "to turn with … " or "to go in a new direction with … " It takes on a dialogic sense. We say in English, for example, that our friends "were conversing with each other."

In Latin when a noun is made out of a verb, that final part of the verb, *conversus*, provides the base. The noun from *conversus* is *conversio*, or in English "conversion." Conversion always involves interaction with another or with others. It is not a simple, individual "turn around." It is a turn we take in the company of others.

Latin has a way of turning a verb into a more intensive meaning of the same verb. Once more, the last part of the verb, *conversus*, lends itself to forming a new verb. The new intensified verb is *converso, conversare, conversavi, conversatus*. And when you once again make an intensified noun out of an intensified verb, the last part of the verb, *conversatus*, is pressed into service, and the new noun is *conversatio*, or "conversation" in English. Intensified conversation and conversion are connected at their roots.

That conversion and conversation are related in meaning and etymology is no superficial intuition. Hans-Georg Gadamer says that true conversation always puts conversants at risk, because you cannot truly converse without risk of conversion. Gadamer is the contemporary thinker who has most helped us understand the dynamic energy of conversation. Put people together in genuine community where conversation allows them to participate in one another's lives (*koinonia*), and throw the Christ event in as a conversation partner (*kerygma*), and *ekklesia* is born. Church happens.

Conversation is our root metaphor for the way of living which lies at the heart of both the inner and public life of SCCs. Conversion is what happens whenever authentic conversation occurs. Community is the place where conversation continually provokes conversion.

It is important to unpack our root metaphor—conversation—as a prelude to our overview of the book.

THE METAPHOR OF CONVERSATION

A metaphor is a way of telling the truth, when something about one thing is truly like another thing. We are all familiar with the literal use of "conversation" in our culture: two or more people speaking and listening to each other with some degree of genuine mutuality in their dialogue. Now we stretch that meaning in metaphor to talk about our interaction with a book (as conversation with the text), or with a tradition, or even with a social system.

It is a metaphor to talk about our conversation with a text, since conversation usually means something that goes on between people. But we often find that a metaphor which took us in one direction, turns around and surprises us with a new metaphor when it comes back. We usually think about reading a text, but we can also tell some metaphorical truth by noting that we learn to "read" each other's lives. We read our tradition. We read our social systems.

Let us begin with some of the most obvious literal meanings of good conversation, meanings that we then expand further to illuminate the life of a community.

Every act of human communication involves reading and being read. We interpret and we are interpreted. We never have unmediated or uninterpreted access to the experience of others or even of ourselves. Every perception of others or ourselves is an interpretation. In our lives together there are no uninterpreted facts. Dialogue between people is but one instance of the back-and-forth movement of questions and answers. We dialogue with our church, with our community, always interpreting as we do. And this is a political act, because it is about how people live and work together in the same city (or same church, or same family, or same friendship). *Polis* is the Greek word for city, the place where people come for common purpose. Here they have to work things out, often in compromise, to achieve some common purpose. Being political is always part of being human, no less in church than in the city.

The meanings for "conversation" just described are operative whether we address the relationship among community members, or between the community and the larger church, or the community and the neighborhood or city, or the community and the nation's economy.

We are all familiar with tensions that arise from the encounters between experience and tradition; for example, when young adults argue with the inherited wisdom of their forebears, or when Catholics argue with the inherited wisdom of their tradition. Sometimes we dislike it when the inherited wisdom calls our current interpretation into question, and we know the challenge is right. Other times the inherited wisdom fights off the challenge from experience to learn a new wisdom from a new experience for a new time. The dialectic between tradition and experience is as fierce as it is transformative.

The practical fruit of mutual meetings is the difference they make for the subsequent directions of our lives. Possible futures, ways that our lives might unfold, inevitably surface in authentic dialogue, in the form of invitation and confrontation. Those possibilities then await our response. They may appear as a result of momentous, once-in-a-lifetime meetings which later seem to have changed the shape of our lives. Even more important for most of us are our ongoing exchanges with the conversation partners named friend, spouse, neighbor, and community member—and even (or especially) enemy. Within the dialogical web of these sacred everyday relations, possible futures are always taking form.

We will return often to the metaphor of conversation, risk, and conversion, but this has been a start.

WHAT LIES AHEAD

Chapter 2, "The Wider Context," is a framing chapter for the rest of the book. We are giving an initial account of the small Christian community and the growth of SCCs during the recent dozen years. We have also named some features of U.S. society and Catholic culture that are particularly relevant to the life of SCCs.

Because SCCs are a relatively new phenomenon, albeit with some features of the church of the first centuries, it is important to pay attention to their churchhood. And that is the focus of chapter 3. We want to engage ecclesiology, but we also want to use extrarational assistance from images and models, because new work of the Spirit elicits poetry as well as logic.

Chapter 4 expresses our conviction, rooted in both theology and sociology, that a community is both gathered and sent. As gathered, it attends to the conversation of its inner life. As sent, it carries on a conversation with the larger world beyond its immediate constituency. We offer an understanding of practical theology as a privileged mode of conversation in the small Christian community. Practical theology gives configuration to both its inner and public life.

Healthy conversation always involves a concern for ways of finding or making consensus, and for creative ways to respond to conflict. Chapter 5 addresses these issues in a community's inner life. We think of the many ways in which Paul reminded the early communities how people who were members of each other were expected to comport themselves toward each other. There is a behavioral logic in being the Body of Christ.

Chapter 6 is about the public life of SCCs. It takes its theme, the *shalom* of the city, from Jeremiah 29, in which the prophet requires God's faithful, even in the terrible circumstance of living in a city of exile, to work for the good of the city and to pray to God for the city, since people cannot find individual salvation (*shalom*) apart from the salvation of the city.

Chapter 7 is the closing witness of the authors of this book to the preciousness of community, and to our valuation of SCCs as an adventure in community. But it is not the final word.

We have invited a number of our colleagues, women and men with long experience of and animated commitment to the life of small Christian communities, to name their realistic but adventuresome dreams of where SCCs could be ten years from now. And we have invited them to describe what needs to happen in the meanwhile for those dreams to become church. Their futuring is chapter 8, the epilogue. And those are the book's final words.

CHAPTER TWO

The Wider Context

Small Christian Communities, American Society, and Church Culture

INTRODUCTION

This is a lengthy chapter, speaking to three areas of concern: small Christian communities, their U.S. cultural environment, and their U.S. ecclesial environment.

In part I of this chapter we are indicating what we mean by "small Christian community" throughout the book, even though more detail gets filled in throughout the book. We also want to name and document the growth in SCC activities over the past dozen years. It has been formidable.

In parts II and III we continue to do some sketching in broad strokes on the contexts in which SCCs operate: those in the U.S. culture and in the U.S. Catholic church. We are not implying that most small communities are self-consciously interacting with all of the contexts we name, and we acknowledge that our description of them is both partial and selective. But these are major contexts, and they provide us with insight into the world as it is, and sometimes into the world as it could be. How the world *is* now shapes SCCs, and how the world *might be* represents possible mission for SCCs.

In part II we are looking at American society from three perspectives: individualism, economics, and racism.

We examine the individualism that sociologists have long named as a tenacious component of our cultural identity. Individualism simultaneously makes us wary of the commitments needed to form community and also makes us hunger for community, because we need it and yet avoid it.

We then focus on the economic system that prevails in this nation (and in much of the world beyond). It tends to move resources relentlessly out of the fiscal bottom and middle and into the fiscal top, from which not much at all trickles down (as supply-side rhetoric would have it). Robert Reich, in fact, speaks about the secession of the successful, the top 20 percent that "is quietly seceding from the rest of the nation." Their largesse "does not flow mainly to social services for the poor ... [but] to the places and institutions that entertain, inspire, cure, or educate wealthy Americans" (Reich 1991b, 42). While the reign of God is certainly not exhausted by an economic system's functioning with justice, neither does it get very far without it. Justice is the equitable distribution of power as well as of goods, i.e., the power to participate in decision making that affects our lives. Coalitions between the bottom and middle could have immense transformative power with respect to economic justice, and this might well be a task for SCCs to confront explicitly.

We are also naming racism as a cultural presence in the United States, especially since its contemporary virulence is once more becoming very visible. Because the two of us are closest to relationships between the Black and White communities in New Orleans, that will be our focus. SCCs are not often racially or socially mixed, which leaves them in danger of being gatherings of the like-minded, what Robert Bellah calls life-style enclaves. Our experience here with the involvement of SCCs in a broad-based community organization has been a solid experience of community activity that is heterogeneous, though not easily achieved.

In part III we will address some features of the ecclesial environment as a context for the post-Conciliar emergence of small Christian communities. One of the most obvious features is the conflicted state of affairs in our church today. No anthropologist or sociologist would be surprised at so much conflict during a period of fundamental systemic change; knowing it, however, does not ease the pain of it. Our way of naming some of the deeper impulses of our conflicted church will be with the metaphor of a church that has two different birth certificates.

A birth certificate is an accounting of one's origins. Each birth certificate validates power arrangements that differ in both the location of power and in the character of how power functions. Power is certainly among the most volatile issues in the contemporary church. We will be naming that as a feature of the contemporary ecclesial context.

We will then speak to pluralism, which we are learning is a normative situation, not just a temporary condition on the way to shared agreement. Finding ways to affirm both some normative pluralism, and also some possibility of genuine community that embraces it, is an ecclesial vocation to which small Christian communities might offer some wisdom. It is easier to grapple with pluralism in smaller systems, in communities like SCCs, than in huge, expansive institutional structures like the larger church. Bringing this off in small communities is certainly not easy, but it is a bit more manageable. Our hope is that small communities might experiment on behalf of the larger church and that some transfer of learning might become viable.

We conclude part III with a look at people's religious hungers, especially in the context of Catholic life. We are sacramental people. Bread and wine; water and oil; movement and song; lights and aromas; beauty; devotion;

Mary: these things matter to our relationship with God, with the things of the world, with ourselves, and with one another. Ritual has traditionally meant a lot to Catholics.

Church attendance is way down for Catholics; a recent study has regular church attendance at about 27 percent. It seems fair to conclude that institutional church life, overall, is not attending well to the nature of these religious hungers in their contemporary contextual setting—above all in respect to youth and young adults.

Insofar as membership in small Christian communities requires additional time and energy on the part of members, we can presume that these are religiously motivated people in search of more than they are getting in traditional expressions of Catholic life. We would like to pay some attention to what is happening in Catholic piety and to what seems to be some of the religious attraction of SCCs.

PART I: THE NATURE OF SCCs AND THEIR RECENT SUDDEN GROWTH

THE SMALL CHRISTIAN COMMUNITY

Joseph Healy, a Maryknoll missioner in Africa, has collected more than a thousand names and expressions for what we call "the small Christian community" in this book. The fact that we have so many names indicates a richness of experience that is not easy to pin down. When we were writing *Dangerous Memories* a dozen years ago, it wasn't clear what terminology we should use to describe these groups in our country. Language about them was (and is) still developing. Some preferred "intentional Christian communities" [ICCs], which we tended to use in *Dangerous Memories*. Others used "basic Christian communities" [BCCs] after the Latin American phenomenon, or similarly, "base ecclesial communities" [BECs]. Some communities use the language of the early church, "house churches" [HCs]. While the language remains fluid, there is a growing tendency in our American context to speak about "small Christian communities" [SCCs]. We will, therefore, use that language often but not exclusively.

The Institute for Ministry at Loyola New Orleans is currently undertaking a detailed empirical and theological study of the SCCs, funded by the Lilly Endowment; and the planning stages have already provided some initial information (the full study will appear later in a book). Here is a profile:

1. Most SCCs have between six and twelve adult members. There are more women members than men. Some SCCs include children because families are members.
2. Most SCCs meet biweekly or weekly, some less frequently.

3. Leadership is nearly always lay leadership, and it tends to function in very collaborative, participative ways.

4. The majority of SCCs have some kind of parish connection, most often as a result of the impact of the parish Renew Program, or from the model of "Restructuring Parishes into Communities," developed by the Reverend Arthur Baranowski, and used in parishes throughout the United States. Some SCCs are not parish-connected in any formal way, even though they function more or less within the parish, and members attend parish Eucharist and parish activities. Their instigation was from themselves, not from parish initiatives. They want more community and/or mission than is offered by parish life.

5. There are several kinds of SCCs that have no parish connection at all.

   a. There are groups that call themselves intentional Eucharistic communities. They regularly have Sunday Eucharist, either because they have ordained members among them, or because they make contacts with priests who will celebrate Eucharist in their communities.

   b. There are communities that find their inspiration in the charism of religious orders, like the Jesuit Christian Life Communities and the Lay Marianist Community network. This is a growing group.

   c. The most marginal of the communities are composed of people who are disaffected with or have been wounded by the institutional church, but refuse to stop being church, though they do it differently. The voice of their sanctified anger is as important as it is painful and difficult to hear.

CONVERSATIONS THAT CREATE US

In his influential book, *Philosophy and the Mirror of Nature,* Richard Rorty says that he does not understand philosophy to be an articulation of timeless, indisputable principles, but rather an ongoing conversation in any culture about what matters most. And he says that such conversations are so vital that they in fact contribute constitutively to a society's character. They help make it be what it is. We are making a similar claim for SCCs: conversation is a root metaphor for the interpersonal interchanges that are, in fact, a community's concrete reality. We would make the same claim for theology that Rorty makes for philosophy, that it is a conversation of such importance that it contributes to the reality of a community's life and its faith.

We proceed now in our characterization of SCCs to name some of the major conversations that constitute their life and their conversions, and all the risks that occur between conversation and conversion.

Conversation with God

All SCCs embrace prayer in some form. Sometimes the leader (of the community or of that week's ritual) will pray in the name of the community, sometimes all members contribute to the praying, sometimes both. SCCs are a place where people pray out loud together and, in doing so, find encouragement for their personal prayer lives throughout the week.

Many communities have the breaking open of God's Word as the centerpiece of their regular gathering. The happy rediscovery of the Bible is familiar to SCCs. They usually follow the lectionary, and they often use materials that provide some commentary. Sometimes they incorporate readings from other sources. We call our scriptures God's Word because of the belief, embedded in the Judeo-Christian tradition, that God not only spoke once, which those texts record, but speaks still and again through them. When our contemporary encounter with Word puts our lived experience under requirement, our grappling together as a community and our actions are our speech back to God. We hear, take our stand, make decisions, and speak with our lives. We are conversation with God. It constitutes us as community.

Conversation among Community Members

The quality of relationship and support within and among community members is very important to today's SCCs in this country. In contemporary U.S. culture, we have a hunger for support groups. These needs also animate SCCs where they well up further out of the inexorable logic of baptism. We are, after all, members of one another. We were that already before baptism. In baptism we become by grace what we are through nature, an interconnectedness that becomes Christ's Body, the grace of new being which exacts new behaviors. Paul sometimes tells the house churches in quite specific ways what their conversation together should be like because of who they are.

We do not exist and *then* have relationships. We come out of relationships in the first place. We are interdependent and interconnected family members who share the earth as a common home. Christians share the reality of the Body of Christ—they are members of one another. We must be intentional about this. The intentionality is called commitment, and its object is genuine mutuality.

Conversation beyond the Immediate Community

Members of SCCs are generous and committed. They would not be doing this something extra were they not. "Extra" perhaps names the perception that no one has to belong to an SCC—it is chosen because it is needed. For many SCC members, the community does not seem extra anymore, but essential. Whether extra or essential, community requires time and energy—in a word, generosity. It is no surprise, therefore, that members of small Christian communities tend to care about social issues.

Many members already have social commitments of one kind or another. They brought these with them when they came to community, and they are appreciated for them. Our experience of SCCs tells us that social energies tend to be present, but that they are rarely named as a community expectation, or organized as part of the community's group life.

To be a genuine ecclesial community, a group must be both gathered (attentive to the dynamics of their inner life) and sent (attentive to the dynamics of their mission). SCCs in this country find the dynamics of being gathered easier than the dynamics of mission. This, we believe, is not a matter of generosity, but fallout from U.S. culture, and from the rather mistaken presumption that middle-class America is doing well. Hispanic SCCs tend to be more aware of themselves as sent than Anglo SCCs. Culture and economics make the difference.

Overall, only a small number of SCCs have explicit commitments to social agendas as a group, or as a shared expectation for individual members. Intentional Eucharistic SCCs, the SCCs that attend Call to Action, and the SCCs that checked into the Loyola research through notices in the *National Catholic Reporter* are more likely to be engaged in activities beyond the immediate group and its concerns. Most of these are not parish-connected.

In our experience communities that try to pick a common project rarely find anything that engages the common energies of the whole group. What works best is a conversation that is sustained over time between our faith and our social worlds, so that issues and priorities become clear through dialogue—often difficult and tedious dialogue. The projects that engage a community profoundly are those that, over time, well up out of the community's sustained conversation between its faith and its culture.

While concern for mission does not characterize the majority of SCCs in this country, our experience in workshops, classes, and network gatherings across the country seems to indicate that social agendas are getting more and more explicit attention. Informed biblical interpretation and skilled social analysis bring an essential framework to this conversation. They need not be scholarly, but they must steer wide of biblical fundamentalism and simplistic guesses at social systems (however well intentioned).

Our judgment in this book, for Gospel reasons and for sociological reasons, is that SCCs in this country will be a blip on the screen of ecclesial history rather than an engaging, strong narrative, if communities do not have proactive conversation with the world beyond their community membership as well as effective mutual conversation with each other. Gathered *and* sent. The gathering does the sending. The sending calls for gathering.

Conversation with Other Ecclesial Groups

People sometimes ask, "Do small Christian communities not invite elitism and factions?" That clearly is a possibility. While there have always been factions ("heresy" is the Greek word for "faction"), the more small groups there are, the greater the possibility. That needs to be said up front. Paul had to remind the house church communities in Corinth that they didn't belong to Cephas, or to Apollos, but to Christ.

Becoming an idiosyncratic group, floating more or less loosely, is antithetical to the reality of church. Part of being truly church is that each church community is in communion with other churches. *This* church's conversation is in touch with *that* community's conversation, and with *those* other churches' communication. Marginal groups especially need lines of communication, and the church's need to hear marginal voices makes cross-conversation fiercely important. At the level of large church, the conversations that bishops have together is essential to church. The great councils, like Nicæa, Ephesus, Chalcedon, and Vatican II are worldwide megaconversations.

Practically speaking, the regular gathering of SCC animators or leaders helps parish communities stay in touch with each other's experience, both to teach and learn from one another. Membership in some of the national network organizations is another way of staying in touch. The names and addresses at the end of this chapter indicate networks as well as resources.

A DECADE OF SUDDEN AND GREAT GROWTH

Our book, *Dangerous Memories,* was written in 1984-1985, and published in 1986. We were members of a small Christian community in Minnesota, and we knew that there were others around the country. Articles were beginning to appear. The movement was served by the *National Catholic Reporter*'s periodical, *Gathering,* although that publication was discontinued after a few years. The basic Christian community movement in Latin America was becoming increasingly familiar.

The amount of new activity in the recent dozen years is really quite amazing. In the final chapter of this book, futuring will be done by people with extensive experience of small Christian community life, many of whom will be named in the paragraphs below. Practically none of the organizations, activities, and resources we are naming below even existed a dozen years ago.

In 1986 a few people interested in small Christian communities met in Buena Vista, Colorado, to ponder some kind of network that would be useful to SCCs. Mike and Barbara Howard, from Arvada, Colorado, were prime movers. The organization now holds an annual convention that draws several hundred people. It publishes a newsletter, *Buena Vista Ink,* that reports on community experiences at home and abroad, evaluates resources, and communicates news about events.

The North American Forum for Small Christian Communities was organized largely as a network for diocesan personnel with special responsibilities to assist SCCs. A recent interest, promoted by the Reverend James Dunning, whose early death in 1996 was much grieved, is the catechumenal possibilities for parish SCCs with regard to the Rite of Christian Initiation for Adults. Instead of forming an RCIA team to journey with catechumens during the initiation rites and disbanding afterwards, catechumens could be apprenticed to already existing communities with which membership could continue after initiation. This is a new process, but full of promise, and profoundly consistent with the dynamics of RCIA.

Fr. Art Baranowski, a priest of the Detroit Archdiocese, took his own successful experience with restructuring a parish into small communities on the road, and has given workshops in many dioceses throughout the United States. He makes clear that he does not mean for small communities to be another program that a parish makes available, but rather a new way of being parish. He works only with parishes in which the pastor and staff are on board with the project. The National Alliance of Parishes Restructuring into Communities nurtures this parish development.

These three organizations named above jointly sponsored a first national gathering of small Christian communities at the University of St. Thomas, St. Paul, in the summer of 1992, with more than five hundred people in attendance. A second gathering is planned for the summer of 1997 at Loyola University in New Orleans, with expected attendance above the one thousand mark.

The Renew program, which originated in Newark with the support of Archbishop Gerety and the program development of Msgr. Thomas Kleissler, has been a remarkable stimulus to the formation of SCCs, though that was not the original intent. It happened often, however, that when the formal program had been completed, the group experience was so positive and so much personal bonding had occurred that people often opted to continue gathering. Since then a Post-Renew program has been developed, with video and print material, to encourage and nurture SCCs.

When the office that supported SCCs in the Seattle Archdiocese was closed, a group of lay women and men initiated the Ministry Center for Catholic Community to provide workshops and resources for SCCs. Their booklets on the church's social teaching, on special topics, and on the seasons of Lent and Advent have been marketed nationally. The center has a mailing list of several thousand.

The Pastoral Office for Small Christian Communities in Hartford, Connecticut, is a model for what can be achieved in a diocese. The Director, Bro. Robert Moriarty, S.M., is also a scripture scholar who oversees the publication of *Quest,* a seasonally published, lectionary-based program for SCCs. Originally prepared for the local church, these materials are now used widely across the nation (each printing is about 15,000).

The Sisters of St. Joseph in Minneapolis-St. Paul publish a lectionary-based guide for SCCs, *Sunday by Sunday,* edited by Sr. Joan Mitchell. Like *Quest,* it is a widely used resource.

An office for Latin American/North American Church Concerns (LANACC) was initiated and is directed by the Reverend Robert Pelton, C.S.C., at the University of Notre Dame. This important project keeps the experience of the two Americas in touch with each other and reaches out as well to the larger international scene. The first international convocation was held in 1991, the second in 1996.

Sr. Rosemarie Jasinski, of the Bon Secours community in Marriottsville, Maryland, organized a network of religious communities that make concerted efforts at forms of associate membership. These include SCCs that live out of the power of a religious life charism; some are self-consciously engaged in a specifically lay appropriation of that charism. A regular newsletter has very recently been initiated.

SCCs among Hispanics in the U.S. Catholic church have less formal structures and connections, and are, therefore, less easy to track in research. Culturally, however, Hispanics are much more open to community and commitment than are middle-class Anglos. There are some five to six hundred Hispanic SCCs, for example, in the Rio Grande Valley in South Texas, especially in the Brownsville diocese. Hispanic pastoral planning at the national level has placed a high priority on the small Christian community, and a bishops' pastoral has recently been issued to give guidance to the continuing development of small church communities, which is the bishops' preferred nomenclature. Sr. Ninfa Garza has been a key pastoral agent in the development of these communities.

The Loyola Institute for Ministry in New Orleans offers a Master of Pastoral Studies degree which has Basic Christian Community Formation as one of the possible specializations. Special courses in leadership and other dimensions of SCC life are offered at Loyola's Institute for Pastoral Studies in Chicago. A number of other Catholic university programs are now offering pastoral courses relevant to the life of SCCs.

In this list of activities relevant to SCCs, not one single item was in place during the year when we undertook the writing of *Dangerous Memories*. (Renew was active, but Post-Renew hadn't been invented.) While the phenomenon is young in this country, what has been documented above is an incredible and rather sudden evolution for a mere decade's worth of life!

This book continues the analysis we undertook in *Dangerous Memories* because so much has happened in the U.S. Catholic church in the intervening decade. We hold strongly to the intuition described on the opening page of *Dangerous Memories*:

> Earthquakes reshape the foundations of the world upon which our human constructions rest. They are part of the shifts the earth must make to keep its energies and counter-energies in balance. Something of earthquake potential has been rumbling through the Roman Catholic World for a generation now. Some dangerous things are being remembered (Lee and Cowan 1986).

Our collective memory of the house church as a normative form of Christian life in the early centuries is helping to fund new imagination. Such memories are experienced as dangerous because they call parts of the settled order into question. They feel dangerous to whatever part of the status quo is interrogated by some memory of how it was once different than it is now. The interrogation is carried on with an interest in a new future. Dangerous memories always remind us that something else might be the case.

At the end of this chapter we offer names, addresses, and phone numbers for many of the organizations, networks, and resources that might prove helpful to small Christian communities in the U. S. Catholic church.

PART II: THE CONTEXT OF U.S. SOCIETY

INDIVIDUALISM AND THE NEED FOR ITS SOCIALIZATION

In the November 1996 issue of the food magazine *Bon Appetit,* the Ad Council ran a full-page statement praising volunteerism in U.S. culture. A coffee cup that takes up two-thirds of the page has the following text printed on it:

> In America, you are not required
> to offer food to the hungry.
> Or shelter to the homeless.
> There is no ordinance forcing
> you to visit the lonely, or comfort
> the infirm. Nowhere in the
> Constitution does it say you have
> to provide clothing for the poor.
> In fact, one of the nicest things
> about living here in America
> is that you really don't have
> to do anything for anybody (193).

Then, in small print at the bottom of the page, there is praise for Americans who volunteered to do the above things, even though they were not obliged to. This is a remarkably clear (and for many of us, painful) statement of American individualism: we are not connected in ways that obligate us; any connection is voluntary, no matter what the need. This same advertisement appeared also on public television.

In his well-known essay on "Self-Reliance," Ralph Waldo Emerson echoes the same sentiment:

> Then, again, do not tell me, as a good man did today, of my obligation to put all poor men in good situations. Are they *my* poor? I tell thee, thou foolish philanthropist, that I grudge the dollar, the dime, the cent, I give to such men as do not belong to me and to whom I do not belong (Emerson 1983, 262).

The message here is the same: we do not belong to each other in any way that obligates us. We can, of course, choose to become connected, either because we like each other, or because it is useful.

In the 1830s an astute visitor to the United States from France, Alexis de Tocqueville, described a kind of individualism in this national culture that ran the risk of incarcerating people within themselves. A series of sociological analyses of U.S. culture in recent decades has continued that critique (Riesman 1950; Sennet 1970; Slater 1970; Bellah, et al. 1985). In *Habits of the Heart*, Robert Bellah and his colleagues said that the very individualism that tends to close us within ourselves also has the effect of creating a loneliness within us as a cultural characteristic. Our individualism makes us hanker for community, but it also stands in the way of the kind of commitment that community requires.

Habits of the Heart recommends that we look for some practical historical memories to help us use the resources of the American tradition to redeem it from its excesses of individualism, while retaining the goodness we have culled from our experiment with individualism. Bellah names two memories: the small religious communities (biblical communities he calls them) that have been part of U.S. life; and republican approaches to social issues, in the root sense of *res publica*, or concern for public issues. Republican instincts ask that people address public issues as close as possible to where the issues exist.

Robert Wuthnow's research, published as *Sharing the Journey* (1994), documents the upsurge in interest in belonging to small groups, which 40 percent of Americans now do. While he seems to feel that this is a good development in U.S. culture, he names two reservations. The first is that because the emphasis on mutual support is so strong, these small groups often tend to avoid tough issues, even among themselves. The penchant for smooth relations often domesticates groups, and, consequently, when they invoke God, they tend to domesticate God as well. They also tend to be preoccupied with their own internal issues, and relatively few of the groups he researched have a constitutive concern for issues beyond their own confines.

Small Christian communities in any location need to be in conversation with their culture from the perspective of their faith. Individualism is a critical context for SCCs in U.S. culture. We believe that theological reflection is a privileged mode of SCC conversation. Under the rubric of practical theology, theological reflection can help us with a two-fold religio-cultural task: to preserve what we have learned about the dignity of each individual life; and to resocialize our interpretation of the individual as connected not by mere option but by obligation to the common good.

The hunger for community is real and well documented. But groups can also take on the individualistic characteristics of the lone person. SCCs stand a chance of participating in the resocialization of individuality without losing the beauty. As our book unfolds, that is part of the context for the importance of mutuality in our inner life and concern for the commonweal in our public life. The SCC has some important redemption to mediate, perhaps not alone, but as one place of grace in American religion.

Paul was a genius in knowing how to seize a moment. He stood upon the Areopagus, a great mound of rock just outside the entrance to the temple complex on the acropolis in Athens. "Your genuine religious aspirations," he told the assembled crowd, "are expressed in your devotion to the unknown god. I know you care. I am here to tell you that I know that god's identity. Let me introduce you to God." And for a lot of those gathered there, Paul's strategy worked.

Those who understand the full power of the small Christian community are positioned to enter the marketplace of American society and say, "Your genuine hunger for community is expressed in the fact that 40 percent of you now belongs to some kind of small group. But there are groups and groups. Let us tell you about one called 'the Body of Christ,' that both gathers people in and sends people out, and the world is better for it." This is truly good news.

ECONOMICS AND COMMONWEALTH

We who write this book live in a city where hope is hard to come by. There are thousands of homeless street people and thousands of empty houses in New Orleans. Public education is in crisis. Poverty is deep and haunts the lives of African-Americans more than any other group. The murder rate is high; the largest percentage is black-on-black homicide in areas where drug traffic thrives. Violence is so omnipresent that most people think twice before walking just about anywhere after dark, and they usually don't if they can help it. Our house in middle-class New Orleans has been broken into, and we have been mugged in our own driveway. This city, sadly, is not an isolated phenomenon in the United States. This is becoming the accustomed narrative of urban sites.

Underneath and driving the violence is a widespread and deepening poverty. In an article in *America* (June 17, 1996), William Quigley reports on the most recent data (1994) from the U. S. Census Bureau. The share of the nation's income that went to the top 20 percent of households rose to 46.7 percent, an average annual income of $105,945. The bottom 20 percent averaged $7,762, about one-thirteenth of the top 20 percent.

"Net worth" is another kind of gauge. This figure includes property, cars, investments, and bank accounts—all of this minus outstanding debts. The 1994 data are as follows in table 1.

This is not just a recent phenomenon. Steadily over a two-century period of U.S. history, resources have steadily been relocated out of the bottom and the middle into the upper 20 percent. See table 2 (Osberg 1984, 44).

TABLE I

	Percentage of Nation's Wealth	Average of Net Worth	
Lowest 20 percent	-00.64	–$ 7,075	[debt]
Next Lowest 20 percent	+01.58	$ 17,503	
Middle 20 percent	+05.56	$ 61,777	
Next Highest 20 percent	+12.77	$ 141,778	
Top 20 percent	+78.47	$ 871,463	

TABLE II

Distribution of Nation's Wealth by Percentage

	1776	1976
Lowest 30 percent	2%	0%
Middle 50 percent	30%	15.4%
Top 20 percent	68%	84.6%

We are not economists, though we try to be decently informed amateurs because, as an obnoxious old proverb says, "War is too important to be left to the generals." We do feel confident in our grasp of a biblical guideline. As simplistic as it may seem, a biblical understanding of creation and of the human community holds that the earth is the shared home of all of God's creatures, and that God's people have a right to the necessities of life. Once everyone has enough, anyone can have more than enough. All people also have the right to a voice in decisions that impact upon them. We agree with the critique of John Paul II that no version of either socialism or capitalism has thus far proved up to the biblical guidelines. Whether some other economic system is needed, or whether one of the two named is revisable so that it becomes able to serve the commonweal, or whether some combination could succeed, we do not pretend to know.

The first question that people must address together is what kind of life they should build for themselves and their children—what do they want human community to look like? This is the commonweal. Human community/society is the overarching system. All of our other systems are ancillary to the good of the community.

We will state the issue a little more theoretically. We are giving centrality to the question, what do we want our world to look like? For Christians, the same question is about God's intentions for our world and our collaboration with God's intentions. All of the subsystems in our lives should serve the needs of the human community. Economics is one such subsystem. Economics, however, has been emerging as the overarching system rather than a subsystem. As such, it asks what kind of community serves its purposes best. (NAFTA is an example.) In his book *Competing Gospels*, Robert Simons addresses this central question about human nature and the social systems at our disposal. He proposes "the radical need to move from viewing social relationships as embedded in an existing economy, to holding economic systems accountable to already existing sets of human relationships and communities" (Simons 1995, x).

We confess that addressing this situation in any way that stands a chance of altering the system is daunting. The gap between rich and poor is larger in the United States than in any of the other dozen and a half industrial countries in the world. The aggregate control of the economy by multinational corporations does not seem susceptible to much external influence. So why raise this as a context for the life of small Christian communities? Partly, at least, because our voice, however small, is still a voice. This was certainly an operative conviction at the Fourth Congress of European Base Communities, held in Paris in 1991. The agenda for the congress was formulated through consultation with base communities in many countries of Europe. Economics was at the top of the agenda. Profound concern for the impact of an emerging European Economic Community was named again and again at the Paris meeting.

In this country, as we have indicated above, the same basic dynamics that drive the economy are responsible for worsening the overall situation of both the middle class and the very poor. (Some make it better, of course, but that is not the fundamental story.) We believe in the possibility of effective alliances and coalitions between the poor and the middle class, and their potential as a Catholic voice and motivator of the larger church. We would like to address this possibility.

The Middle and the Poor: Alliances and Coalitions

One of the large differences between Latin American base communities and U.S. small Christian communities is that the large majority of base community members are very poor. In most Latin American countries, in fact, there is no large middle class comparable to that of the United States and Canada. In Latin America, therefore, the power for social change resides largely among the poor, once they are conscientized and organized. Some of the important leadership for conscientization and organization in base ecclesial communities has come from the church, often sisters, brothers, priests, theologians, and sometimes from bishops as well. But parts of the church, both locally and in Rome, have also resisted the development of base communities. In many Latin American countries (notably Brazil), base communities have been responsible for significant social programs and social changes that benefit the poor. Members have also been persecuted by military and police; some have lost their lives.

In the United States the majority of small Christian communities are middle class, although the minority of Hispanic communities is not small, and most of them are among the poor. If middle-class membership differentiates U.S. communities from Latin American communities, there is also an essential similarity: there is immense power for social action and social change in the middle class in the U.S. context. The role of middle-class leadership and middle-class activity was/is demonstrably present in the peace movement, the civil rights movement, the lettuce boycotts in support of the Farm Workers' movement, boycotts of both Nestle and Campbell soup products because of policies, the Greenpeace movement, etc. Probably no single group has been as effective in leading the U.S. Catholic church into a post-Conciliar age than women religious, whose membership is mostly middle class.

We are convinced that if the middle class and the poor form effective alliances and coalitions, their prophetic voice and prophetic action can matter a lot more. What underlies that persuasion is our conviction that the middle class is being steadily disempowered, that poverty is deepening, and that the causes of both phenomena are fundamentally the same economic policies.

The following analyses depend upon a cluster of studies, and the picture is painted from their reflections as well as some of our own experience. These are helpful resources that we want to name here and recommend as resources for social analysis as part of the exercise of practical theology in SCCs, to be discussed at length in chapter 4: Harry Boyt's *Commonwealth: A Return to Citizen Politics*; Catholic Bishops of the U.S., *Economic Justice for All*; Eric Clark's *The Want Makers*; Benjamin DeMott's *The Imperial Middle*; J. Kenneth Galbraith's *A Journey through Economic Time;* William Greider's *Who Will Tell the People*; John Haughey's *The Holy Use of Money*; David Hollenbeck's *Claims in Conflict: Retrieving and Renewing the Catholic Human Rights Tradition*; Paul King, Kent Maynard, and David Woodyard's *Risking Liberation: Middle Class Powerlessness and Social Heroism*; John Kavanaugh's *Still Following Christ in a Consumer Society;* Walter Owensby's *Economics for Prophets*; Kevin Phillips's *The Politics of Rich and Poor* and *The Boiling Point*; Robert Reich's book *The Work of Nations* and his article "The Secession of the Successful"; Barry Schwartz's *The Battle for Human Nature: Science, Morality and Modern Life.*

"Middle class" is a cultural classifier. When both of us were children, our middle-class families lived on the income of one person (the father). Our parents bought a house (not fancy), owned a used car, and paid tuition for children in Catholic schools. Our parents worked hard to become respectable self-made people, who were better off than their parents, and whose children would be better educated and more affluent than they were. There was a small amount of surplus. They felt relatively secure about being in charge of their lives. They could count on retirement and social security, and did not worry terribly about the future. That middle class is over!

While it may not have been all that easy, the 1950 middle-class family lived on income from forty hours a week of work. Today it takes double that amount of income; two wage earners are necessary for most middle-class American families today. Both parents must work, which alters family life in radical ways. There is a decreasing sense of economic security. Middle-class people often feel relatively little control of their work space or their political reality. Health care and education costs have soared so quickly that middle-class people are chronically nervous about the future. They no longer presume that their children will be better educated, more affluent, or more secure. The middle class is led to believe that welfare programs are responsible for their plight; but in fact, the shift in tax burdens is a far larger cause. Between 1977 and 1989 the federal effective tax rates for the lowest 20 percent of families in this country increased by 0.1 percent, and for the next 20 percent increased by 1.4 percent, while for the top 20 percent the tax burden dropped by 5.8 percent, with a 13.5 percent decrease for the top 5 percent, and 24.7 percent for the top 1 percent (Phillips 1993, 282).

Three characteristics of today's middle class are that they tend to be patriotic, to be religious, and to behave in consumerist ways. Pecuniary envy, the incessant desire to have more money, drives consumerism. Advertising invites all Americans to dream upward, but the spending that middle-class Americans presume will get them there has in effect impoverished them and often burdened them with things they rarely use. How often do most middle-class families use a formal living room and dining room when they have a large family room and a sizable dining area adjoining the kitchen? But middle-class dwellings are regularly built with that rarely used space.

Clark's book on advertising details how VALS, for "Values and Life Styles" sizes us up. VALS, a typology for classifying potential consumers, was developed by social scientists for SRI Research Center in Menlo Park, California (Clark 1988, 163-171). VALS serves AT&T, Avon, Coca-Cola, General Motors, Proctor and Gamble, Reynolds Tobacco, Tupperware, and other corporations. They have analyzed the spending propensities of nine categories of people gathered into four groupings:

Group A   — Need Driven
   1.   4% — survivors (very poor and elderly)
   2.   7% — sustainers (edge of poverty, younger people)

Group B   — Outer Directed (they respond quickly to signals about what
                   they should do/have)
   3. 38% — belongers (they want to fit in, not eager to stand out)
   4. 20% — achievers (competitive, eager to stand out)
   5. 10% — emulators (upwardly mobile, very ambitious)

Group C   — Inner Directed (try to live according to values)
   6.   3% — people on the move from outer to inner directed
   7.   5% — mature, willing to experiment
   8. 11% — socially conscious, very responsive to social need

Group D — Integration of both Inner and Outer Motivation
   9. 11% — balance of inner and outer, can be appealed to on both counts,
        self-determinative

When VALS worked with Timex to enter the health-care market (the products included digital thermometers and blood pressure monitors), they targeted #4 (achievers) and #8 (socially conscious), and within one year, three of Timex's products were top sellers nationally. We in the middle class are easy prey to the advertising that first makes us want, then turns our wants into needs.

In the best of circumstances it is very difficult to refuse to get caught up in the dynamics of a consumerist culture. What makes it easier for most of us in the middle class to take a stand is to have connected in some substantial personal way with the poor of the world. What we learn through social analysis is that for us to give up things (cut back on our consumerist behaviors) will not change the system that disempowers both the bottom and the middle. Token sacrifices do not alter a system unless they are powerful enough to alter consciousness.

Those of us who work for the church know that the least attended classes, workshops, and lectures are those about social justice. Middle-class guilt is paralyzing. What is mobilizing is to take seriously what Abraham Heschel says about the basic message of the prophets, that while all are responsible, few are guilty. We believe that Yahweh would rather have all the people of God enjoy sufficiency. The elimination of middle-class sufficiency would not of itself create an equitable world. There is systemic dysfunction that worsens the plight of the bottom *and* the middle. Our recommendation for small Christian communities is that we find ways to form effective coalitions with those whose poverty and need are severe. We agree with the conclusion of King, Maynard, and Woodward's *Risking Liberation,* that individual efforts can do little, but that social heroism has some potential. Connections between the bottom and the middle could be fertile ground for social heroism. Addressing critical, unmet human need is a noble motivation. Knowing that coalitions between the middle and the poor stand a better chance of addressing the disempowerment of the middle as well is perhaps less agapic as motives go, but is not without noble qualities. On the surface, middle-class folks may find it easy to get satisfaction from "helping the poor." But, in fact, we learn quickly that interactive conversation with poor people is a stronger gift to us from our poorer brothers and sisters than we normally make to them.

In his book, *Christ in a Pluralistic Age,* John Cobb reminded Christians that a christological function of Jesus is to end poverty. We should not find Christ, therefore, simply "in the poor," but rather in our identification with everything in the poor that wants to stop being poor.

We have already named the serious issue it is when profit-driven market economics becomes the overarching system served by other systems, rather than a subordinate system that serves the overarching common good. While it is important not to be naive about this and about the possibility of significant transformation, we want to acknowledge not only for socio-economic reasons but for gospel reasons that coalitions which pressure systems are important expressions of faith's public life. The resources named above include Harry Boyt's book, *Commonwealth,* and William Greider's book, *Who Will Tell the People,* because both authors sound a call for a society that knows how to keep its officials and its systems accountable. We also believe that profit motives can indeed be a moving force in a system that takes the common good seriously.

We dwell at length in chapter 6 on broad-based community organizations because that has been our best experience of finding essential common ground between the poor and the middle.

RACISM

We are addressing the issue of racism from our own social location. We are white, and we live in New Orleans where the most palpable expressions of racism involve Whites and Blacks. *Mutatis mutandis,* there are many versions of racism alive in our nation. In our social location, our best sustained experience in multiracial community has been in a broad-based community organization in which Black and White members of religious congregations work together to build a more just world. The collaboration is not always easy. As White women and men, we are challenged to confront our own complicity in racism. We also want to ponder the redemptive potential of SCCs in this regard.

Division along racial lines is perhaps the most significant challenge to the survival, decency, and well being of public life in the United States today. In urban America the unhealed wounds of racism lurk beneath the surface of ongoing conflicts about education, jobs, housing, and public safety. In national debate on public policy, the issues of affirmative action and immigration may stretch the nation's civility to its breaking point. In these circumstances, as our colleague the Reverend Dwight Webster of Christian Unity Baptist Church insists, "color blindness" is just another name for blindness.

At this juncture in our history there is no prospect for a livable communal future unless explicit, honest, and respectful public conversations about race can be deliberately initiated and sustained within a web of lasting relationships grounded in shared action in the pursuit of mutual interests. The healing of racism and its associated devastations is imaginable only if we are able to participate in difficult exchanges. We need to engage one another in dialogue across the now-paralyzing boundaries of racial separation, endure the necessary tension of such engagements, and develop powerful interracial instrumentalities for acting in good faith to bring about the transformations of our common life which such exchanges will demand of us. Talk about race which is not wedded to the power to act collaboratively for the continuing transformation of racist institutions and attitudes is of limited value.

We must work so that a seasoned and tested ability to engage one another across lines of race in direct conversation and joint decision making about our common life gradually becomes integral to the public culture of the United States. Otherwise, the divisions among us, of which race is only the most potent instance, will continue to cripple and may eventually destroy our capacity to strengthen the peace of our common life.

Action-oriented conversation across such barriers requires a context, a place in the real world within which it can happen. In our judgment the best instance of such a place today is to be found in broad-based community organizations like those affiliated with the Industrial Areas Foundation network, which we will discuss in chapters 4 and 6. In these organizations citizens and people of faith join together through their congregations, schools, and civic associations across lines of race, creed, and class. They work together to develop a practical agenda for the well being of their diverse communities based on mutual interests and respect for differences, and to build a power base for making that agenda felt within the arena of public decision making. In more than sixty communities throughout the United States, as well as in the United Kingdom and South Africa, such organizations have been making a difference in public education, law enforcement, job training, economic development, home ownership, medical care, and a variety of other critical issues of public life for the past twenty-five years.

The significance of broad-based community organizations rests not only on their formidable political astuteness and effectiveness, but on their potential as crucibles for the reconstruction of civic culture in a pluralistic world. A crucible is a vessel which will not melt when the ingredients it holds are heated to a point where they are transformed. The conversation about race which will be required if we are to be healed personally and collectively is one that will generate serious heat, including rage, shame, and anxiety. It needs a container that will not melt when such intense emotions arise. By deliberately and patiently building and sustaining relationships across the usual barriers of race, creed, and class—relationships characterized by authentic public conversation—broad-based community organizations may become those crucibles. Our experience in one of these organizations—The Jeremiah Group in New Orleans—over the past five years leads us to conclude that it is in learning to act together for the common good within such carefully cultivated public relationships that Blacks and Whites have our best opportunity to create the conditions required for reconciling the devastating racist history which continues to burden us all.

Risking engagement in public conversation for the common good across racial lines, including a critical examination of ideological "whiteness," is how we might heal the divisions of racism. Sociologist Frank Wright once observed that "most of us perhaps owe more to violence done on our behalf than we realize" (Wright 1987, 269). Violence historically done to others in public life—in the arena of politics, economics, and culture—must be publicly reconciled. New promises must be made and kept in the pluralistic public square of our time. Denying America's race problem means allowing the redemptive possibility of a culturally diverse public life to sink beneath the weight of slavery and racism. Through the vehicle of participation in broad-based interracial organizations, SCCs now have the opportunity to participate in the creation of a truly inclusive public life in which no privilege is granted or withheld because of gender, race, or social class. The motivation for Christians could not be clearer: "For those baptized into Christ Jesus there can be neither Jew nor Greek, there can be neither slave nor freeperson, neither male nor female—for all of you are one in Christ Jesus" (Gal. 3:27-28).

PART III: THE CONTEXT OF ECCLESIAL CULTURE

THE METAPHOR OF "BIRTH CERTIFICATE"

In the contemporary culture of the Catholic church there are deep divides, deep enough to become a chasm if we do not come to terms with them. Joseph Cardinal Bernardin's plaintive cry for dialogue in the months before his death responded to the pain and dividedness we experience.

One way of assessing an important aspect of the conflict is to reflect on the church's self-understandings under the metaphor of "birth certificate," meaning the church's interpretation of how it came to be. But this is no minor matter: our memories of where we came from drive the anticipations out of which futures are created. Not only are there alternative futures, there are alternative pasts. Perhaps, more truly, there are alternative futures *because* there are alternative pasts.

A community's collective remembering does two things: it adds more completeness, and it often pulls out things that trigger connections. But collective memory, for all of that, is no less selective. Although it is fuller, it may also be more unbalanced because it can concentrate the force of selectivity, and thus bury excluded memory more deeply.

There is an archaeology of memory. If we begin digging, we bring more to the surface. Archaeology also uses methodological tools like cultural anthropology, sociology, and economics to interpret the meaning and function of what has been recovered. Memory does this too.

As we continue to interpret and nurture small Christian communities in the U.S. Catholic church, how church itself is interpreted matters greatly. We do not want to exaggerate the two churches that claim variant birth certificates. But neither do we care to be naive about the dialectic that exists between competing claims, usually around power issues. Our hope is that small Christian communities can be nurtured under both ecclesial rubrics, and, even more, that they might help constitute the conversation that needs to happen out of both forms of remembering the origins of church.

Nietzsche's well-known observation that there is no such thing as an uninterpreted fact applies to memory as well. Every memory is selective, as we indicated in the introductory chapter. No one remembers anything perfectly and in its entirety. Our present location is one of the factors that shapes selectivity. We are learning, for example, that poor people remember their history differently than affluent people; that black Americans remember U.S. history differently than white Americans. The feminist historical critique includes a women's memory that differs from a men's memory. People in every social location have vested interests in how a past gets remembered. By this we do not mean consciously manipulated memory, but rather, that our interests inevitably shape even unconscious retrievals.

The two birth certificates are in fact two memories about how we began as church. For shorthand, we will call one a doctrinal birth certificate, the other a biblical birth certificate. The doctrinal birth certificate has been long in the making. Augustine's sense of the church would be an example. There are already seeds of it in the later documents of the New Testament, like the pastoral letters to Timothy and Titus. In the defensive ecclesiology of the Counter-Reformation, and in subsequent centuries until Vatican II, this doctrinal version of church origins has been the centerpiece of Roman Catholic imagination.

The second we are calling a biblical birth certificate, though more than scripture is included. This is a much newer birth certificate. Or perhaps better, this is in fact the older birth certificate that has been recently rediscovered, and it is even now still being unfolded. Critical biblical scholarship during the twentieth century has hugely reshaped our conversations with our early texts and our early history. Biblical hermeneutics (a theory of interpretation) has taught us both the intricacies of memory and the performative or transformative character of the texts we create.

Differing memories about where we came from spin out different understandings of who we are now, and how our future narrative is to be written. That is why emotion runs high around these issues: they are not just about a past, but about essential present identity and about the allocation of energies and resources for the church to whose upbuilding we are committed.

A Doctrinal Birth Certificate

The church is founded by Jesus, in fidelity to his Father's intentions for him and for the world. Because most Jews do not elect to become followers of Jesus, this New Covenant replaces the Old Covenant, whose purpose, we now know, was to prepare for the New Covenant. The use of Old Testament texts in Matthew's Gospel, for example, makes this clear.

The Apostles provide the basic paradigm for the later development of the church. They are an apostolic college which provides the nascent church community with the leadership that Jesus wills. The college of bishops is the direct successor of the college of Apostles.

Peter is the pre-eminent Apostle to whom the leadership is entrusted in a special way. The popes are the successors to Peter. In earlier church history, the popes are called "vicars of Peter." It is a later tradition in which they are called "vicars of Christ." To safeguard the faith of the church, infallibility is conferred upon Peter in Matthew 16:18-19 and upon the college of Apostles in Matthew 18:16.

When, during the Reformation, the sacramental system of the Catholic church is called into question, the Counter-Reformation's Council of Trent affirms that there are seven sacraments, that this has always been the case, and that each sacrament is individually and specifically instituted by Jesus Christ. Theology, then, speculates on the moments of institution. Baptism and Eucharist are the easiest to document in the New Testament. The ordination of the Apostles as priests of the New Testament occurs at the Last Supper when Jesus charges them to "Do this in memory of me."

While the church has continued to elaborate its understanding of Christian life, the deposit of faith closed with the completion of the New Testament. The deposit of faith and the structures and teachings of Jesus are non-negotiable.

The Holy Spirit has continued to direct the church and to assure its faithfulness, especially in the guidance of the pope and the college of bishops in their roles of governing, teaching, and sanctifying the faithful of Jesus Christ.

The existence of religious orders of men and women does not begin in New Testament times, nor even soon after. But they are founded in the evangelical counsels of celibacy, poverty, and obedience given the church by Jesus in his lifetime.

It is worth noting that ecclesiology, such a standard branch of Catholic theology today, did not become a specific discipline until after the Reformation, when the church's institutionality was called into question in many areas. In the *Summa*, for example, Thomas Aquinas does not have a tract on church. He moved directly from christology to the sacraments. Much of this birth certificate's articulation, therefore, develops from the sixteenth century onward.

It is only in more recent times, especially beginning with Leo XIII, that the teachings of Jesus regarding social justice as belonging to the essential character of the Reign of God have become more explicit teachings of the church.

The Biblical Birth Certificate

"Biblical" is shorthand for the kind of historical research that begins to show up already in the late 1700s with Hermann Samuel Reimaurus. He wrote an essay to the effect that the aims of Jesus and the aims of his disciples were not identical. This initiated more than a century of biblical studies that attempted to use the same historical methods that were developing in secular history writing. Albert Schweitzer's criticism of this quest for the histori-cal Jesus at the beginning of the twentieth century helped redirect historical research, not only about scripture but also about the very early period of Christian history. These methods, which continued to refine themselves, met resistance in Catholic thought until well after Vatican II, notwithstanding Pius XII's approval of historical methodology in scripture study.

The biblical picture that is emerging with contemporary historical and hermeneutical methodologies has begun to affect the church's self-interpre-tation. The historical tools and methodologies that have emerged largely during the twentieth century were simply unavailable to the church's self-interpretation for most of 1,900 years. But there has, in fact, been a fierce resistance to some of the self-reinterpretation that modern scholarship pro-poses. The regrettable modernist controversy in the late nineteenth and early twentieth centuries documents a stubborn ecclesial resistance to his-toricized self-interpretation.

The immense amount of historical research carried on in the twentieth century about the church and its origins has begun to impact upon the doc-trinal birth certificate. This influence is clear, for example, in the Second Vatican Council's document on liturgy and the restoration of the Rite of Christian Initiation for Adults. Historical and biblical retrievals are responsi-ble for the priority given to the people of God ecclesiology in *Lumen Gentium.* One of the lesser-explored but far-reaching testimonies of Vatican II about Christian origins occurs in the church's affirmation in *Nostra Aetate* that "God does repent of the gifts God made" to the Jews (foremost among them, Covenant), that Jews remain "most dear to God," and that they have not been repudiated by God (§4).

We have barely begun to reflect on what we mean by "New Testament" once we affirm God's continuing Covenant with the Jews who remain most dear. It appears very unlikely that Jesus' self-understanding included the founding of a new religious community outside of Judaism. The early commu-nities, as Acts clearly reflects, honored the Jewish feasts and holy places as well as their own eucharistic table community. *Nostra Aetate* makes it diffi-cult for Catholics to interpret the Jesus movement as a termination of God's Covenant (the "Old" Testament) with the Jews, and its replacement by a new one (the "New" Testament). It calls some of the doctrinal birth certificate into question and cries out for a permanent relationship between the syna-gogue and the church.

The biblical birth certificate requires critical re-evaluation of parts of the doctrinal birth certificate. It is not the church that is called into question, but how it accounts for itself and for the proactive presence of the Holy Spirit in its formation through time.

We will offer a brief birth certificate of church origins that reflects the historical methodologies alluded to above. Probably no one scholar has described it exactly as we do, but the interpretations are all to be found in current respected scholarship.

Jesus initiated a reform movement within Judaism. He was a lay Jew who did not step out of Judaism to be who he was or do what he did. His repeated insistence in Matthew's Gospel that he came for the House of Israel is probably an accurate memory. At the close of Matthew's Gospel, Jesus tells the Apostles to baptize all nations in the name of the Father, of the Son, and of Holy Spirit. Most Matthean scholars agree that this ending is added on to Matthew at a later time, and reflects in its language the baptismal liturgy that has developed.

No follower of Jesus in the Christian scriptures is called a priest. That language for interpreting the role of the leader of Christian communities does not become prominent until the third century. In the Letter to the Hebrews Jesus is called our High Priest, but this is a metaphor which interprets the christological meaning of Jesus. As an essential metaphor, it discloses the christological meaning of Jesus, but it does not disclose biographical information. Jesus was a lay Jew, not a priest. He is from the kingly family (David), not the priestly family (Levi). And we know the name of the high priest during Jesus' time.

There is no textual indication that Jesus ordained anyone. As Raymond Brown long ago concluded, there was no need for priesthood in Jesus' time because his followers were all within Judaism, which had a functioning temple priesthood (Brown 1970, 13-45).

The church structures that have become familiar to us developed over time and were influenced by the structures of civil society. The Spirit has guided the church in its development, working through (not around) the normal ways of social life within various cultures and ages.

Restoration/Refounding

It is commonplace today, partly helpful and partly not, to distinguish between a restoration impulse and a refounding impulse. Probably no one's approach is all one kind and none of the other. The two categories are a typology. Typologies reflect clear tendencies. Typologies offer real but partial insight.

These two approaches to change are not identical to the two birth certificates, but there are some similar impulses at work. The restorationist inclination tends to rely on the doctrinal birth certificate. It remembers a settled time when seminaries were full and religious orders thrived; when Mass was well attended; when ritual was high and beautiful; when the sense of tradition was esteemed; when authority was rarely questioned by Catholics; when church order was accepted because what comes directly from Jesus Christ is and must be "the way it is." This was not a begrudging acceptance, not a hesitant, questioning acceptance. The restorationist impulse wants as much of that back as we can reasonably reassemble within today's circumstances, because it was and is right. This is not a desire merely to repeat, but to retrieve what has been lost, and to do it in ways that are faithful to the church's self-interpretation under a doctrinal birth certificate.

The refounding impulse, because it tends to rely on the biblical birth certificate, feels that its memory leaves it freer than does the doctrinal birth certificate to imagine alternative futures. The danger that hovers around it is to become biblicist in ways that ignore development under the Spirit. One can't just leap over 1,900 years of tradition. Its strength is in a refusal to absolutize historically contingent forms of church, because a Spirit at work in earlier institutionalizations of church can be a creative power in new institutional forms as well. Discerning the Spirit now, as discerning the Spirit then, is no simple matter.

The small Christian community has not been a normal, common form of Christian community since the early centuries, unless one counts communities of religious orders. Community movements have sprung up in church history, like a rash of them in response to Joachim of Fiore. But these have been very localized. In the last few decades, small Christian communities have become a phenomenon on all five continents, in a great variety of forms, and for many reasons. Sometimes embraced by the hierarchy and sometimes decried, even when embraced they were not simply the brainchild of the hierarchy. They more easily claim a rationale for themselves from a biblical than a doctrinal birth certificate. However, because so many in the U.S. Catholic church are also parish connected, they are perhaps in a position where dialogue between the churches with the two birth certificates can fruitfully occur, less at the theoretical level of discourse, though that too, and more at the grassroots level of experience.

PLURALISM AND DIALOGIC COMMUNITY

The two birth certificates and the contrasting impulses of restoration or refounding are but two examples of the deepening pluralism within the Catholic church, a situation likely to remain normative. We should, therefore, address pluralism as a key contextual feature of Catholicism in this country. To be sure, pluralism is a church experience throughout the world, but we have our own particular appropriation of it within American Catholicism.

Announcing the Common Ground project in a press conference in August 1996, Joseph Cardinal Bernardin, Archbishop of Chicago, said,

> I have been troubled that an increasing polarization within the church and, at times, a mean-spiritedness have hindered the kind of dialogue that helps us address our mission as a church and our concerns as a church. As a result, the unity of the church is threatened ... the faithful members of the church are weary and our witness to government, society and culture is compromised.

He said these things in the context of a paper, "Called to be Catholic: Church in a Time of Peril," prepared by a group that included bishops, priests, religious, women, and lay Catholics. The paper is an invitation to find forms of dialogue that allow us to confront differences honestly and directly.

There are many reasons why these deep differences exist and many forms of uneasiness about them. Some feel that genuinely honest discussion will result in unanimity. There are indeed forms of difference which, if our conversation is good and our minds and hearts are open, we can transcend. When this is possible, we should pursue it. But not all pluralism is subject to resolution.

We want to speak to one particular form of difference and suggest a possible contribution to this situation from SCCs. Our focus is on a normative kind of pluralism and the need to learn new forms of community that are able to assimilate pluralism. Is community possible, based not upon agreement about content, but upon commitment to a respectful (even loving) form of dialogue that keeps relationship intact?

Historical consciousness is the awareness of all the ways in which our experience, understanding, and articulations are conditioned by experience, history, language, education, and temperament. There is no such thing as being unbiased. We are all biased; it is important to acknowledge bias as a condition for interpretation. There is no uninterpreted fact. There is no way to transcend entirely all of these conditioning factors in order to arrive at "untarnished" objectivity. We have to live with all of the ways in which our differences are embedded early on in our presuppositions and the ways they leave unsolvable remainders. This is what we mean by normative pluralism: the kind that does not go away. That is the most serious kind with which church needs to come to terms. Assent to normative pluralism does not imply that all interpretations are equally valid or that we may not dispute—only that we recognize its probable permanence and know that we must still remain together in human community, or in church.

We applaud the effort to engage in serious respectful dialogue. To expect to return to an earlier kind of consensus, based upon a shared understanding of church teaching, is not realistic. Besides that, we probably romanticize the unity we once had. Catholic thought has always had some unruly propensities, whether adventures toward new insight or new heterodoxy; and it is not possible to have one without the other. The pressures today, however, arise peculiarly from our historical consciousness. In the preface of his book, *Plurality and Ambiguity*, David Tracy writes:

> What the "essence of Christianity" might be after Christians seriously acknowledge first, the plurality within their own traditions, second, the import of the many other religious traditions for Christian self-understanding and third, the profound cognitive, moral, and religious ambiguity of Christianity itself is, to put it mildly, a very difficult question (Tracy 1987, 10).

It will probably be easier in SCCs than in the larger institutional church to experiment with a form of community called "dialogic." When dialogic community succeeds, it is a stellar example of true conversation at work. For this form of community to work, there are some conversational commitments that members must make:

1. When I speak I will do it in a way that gives you the best chance at understanding exactly what I hold and why I hold it. I am speaking so that you will understand me, not in order to convince you.
2. When I listen my sole intention is to hear you in order to understand you. I will have to let your words mean what they mean to you, not what they perhaps mean to me. I will not listen in order to refute, but to understand.
3. I promise up front that I will not withdraw from the conversation, no matter how difficult it might become. I won't go away.
4. It will be OK for us to disagree, to argue, and to challenge. But not until our achievement of the first three points is accomplished.

This is not the way church has handled differences, because its habitual modes were developed during nineteen centuries before historical consciousness began to condition our self-understanding. It is clear that we do not yet have widely disseminated skills in ecclesial culture for this kind of conversation. That we experience some kinds of pluralism as normative is new. Skills in the dynamics of dialogic community are not likely to enter ecclesial culture from the top down. They probably have to be experimented with and developed at grassroots levels.

We are suggesting that SCCs are at least one place where we can explore whether dialogic community is a possible gift to the Body (politic) of Christ. Skills in consensus building and conflict resolution with which we deal in chapter 5 are important for more reasons than the challenges created by normative pluralism, but they are critical for the success of a dialogic community response to pluralism.

We are proposing that small Christian communities are a place where the church can experiment with dialogic community as an ecclesial model— when they do this, they *are* the experimenting church. New possibility rarely—perhaps never—appears first in a society's center. Possibility gets its first credentials in the margins.

POWER

Words like "power" and "politics" badly need to be rehabilitated. They are features of human interaction any time people are together. We will focus here on broader issues around power. It is our sense that SCCs are experimenting with some models that are pertinent to the larger ecclesial body as well.

Jesus did not give to his community of followers any specific structure for the function of power. He offered root metaphors instead: how shepherds function (especially their penchant for the stray); how stewards function (they do not "own" the community; they try to make it work well on someone else's behalf); and servant (they do not create the agenda, they serve it). How power functions is a major issue in the contemporary church. In his Letter *Ut Unum Sint,* Pope John Paul II recognized that even the exercise of papal power needs to be assessed (not whether, but how). Our reflections here refer particularly to the servant metaphor for how power functions.

Mark's Gospel recounts that when Jesus and the disciples are on the road, John and James approach Jesus and ask him for a special place above the others (Mk. 10:35-44). When the others hear of this they are miffed with John and James. Jesus takes them all to task, saying that power must be understood very differently in the reign of God on earth. Leaders mustn't lord it over others, as pagan leaders do—they want to make their authority felt. Rather, the leader is at the lower end of the traditional power structure, where the servant is found.

The disciples in Mark's Gospel are usually very slow to catch on. When Matthew recounts the same story, he rescues the disciples by having the mother of James and John, rather than those two themselves, ask Jesus for privilege for her sons. The message is the same. Servanthood, not prestige or naked power, is the name of the game in Christian community.

In Luke's Gospel no names are mentioned (Lk. 22:24-27). We are only told that a dispute arose among "them"—presumably the Twelve. It is stunning that Luke places the scene at the Last Supper, immediately after the treachery of Judas is foretold. We can only speculate why. Power issues must have arisen in community for the instruction about servant leadership to be placed in such a precious setting. The text suggests that Jesus himself was serving them at table: "Who is greater, the one at table or the one who serves? The one at table, surely? Yet here I am among you as one who serves!"

That the issue has moved from discourse to drama is clear in John's Gospel (Jn. 13:2-16). The scene once again is the Last Supper. Jesus removes his outer garment and dresses as a servant, towel around his waist, and washes his disciples' feet. "Now copy my example," he tells them. He whom the disciples rightly call "Master" and "Lord," does the dirty work.

Power issues are once again urgent, tedious, and volatile in the church. Process theologian Bernard M. Loomer has a remarkable analysis of power in a lecture in social ethics delivered at the University of Chicago (appears as an appendix in Lee 1995, 169-202). It offers substantial insight into servant leadership. One kind of power, the kind most celebrated in dominant U.S. culture, is unilateral. Effects move in one direction. The more a person can have influence while remaining free of influence, the greater the power. Having effects is power in the unilateral model.

The alternative—relational power—defines power as the capacity to receive effects as well as to have effects. The servant should respond effectively and strongly, but only after having learned what needs exist, only after having received the story of those served. The servant leader is there for the community. The community is not there for the leader.

Leadership in SCCs tends to be collaborative and relational, often as a reaction to the experience of unilateral power in the institutional church. In these small churches the dangerous memory of servant leadership is often full of future content, for themselves, and perhaps for what they offer the larger church.

RELIGIOUS HUNGERS

Gallup research over quite a number of years steadfastly documents the religiosity of Americans. Within Catholic culture, workshops and classes in spirituality attract many takers. There have been numerous publications over the last dozen years about lay spirituality and about spirituality in the marketplace. There is keen interest in learning more about the Bible. But church attendance is very low, and younger people are not a large part of those who do show up. This is a painful reality for Catholicism because "Mass" has been an utterly central experience in Catholic culture.

It is not our intention to try to offer a sustained analysis, only—again, with some quite broad strokes—to sketch the religious landscape. In the chapter which follows we will speak further about religious practices in SCCs, when we name *leitourgia* (familiar public worship) as belonging to the experience of churchhood. Liturgy is familiar ritual that has elements of utter predictability as well as of freshness in each expression. The dance of predictability and freshness is tenuous in times of upheaval. We probably all tire of hearing that we live in an in-between time, when many familiar ways of being Catholic have largely disappeared, and when familiar new ways of being Catholic have not really congealed. Consider the language familiar to those of us "of a certain age":

"What Mass are you going to?"

"I heard the 8:30 Mass."

"Who said the Mass?" or "Who had the Mass?"

The fact that for centuries Mass was "said" in Latin, while for most of those centuries the people in church neither spoke nor understood Latin, made it clear that the priest who spoke the Latin was the one who "said" the Mass. From back to front, people saw only the backs of people who were in front of them, except for the priest who saw no one. There was nothing that any person "attending Mass" was expected to do liturgically except to be there.

Contrast this picture with the directives of Vatican II on Liturgy that there should always be "full active participation" on the part of all of those present. Full active participation means a ritual behavior that is entirely in opposition to the behavior of hearing mass. It takes time to develop a different ritual history. In fact, the expression, "ritual history," is redundant. Ritual works because people have lived into it and have it embedded in their instincts. That happens only through thick historical time. A congregation with six hundred people does not suddenly—perhaps not even in a single generation—create a new instinctive behavioral history of full active participation. Size is not the only drawback (history is the most significant), but it does make a huge difference. One of the most consistent patterns in SCCs is the full active participation of all of the members when the community gathers. A new history is accumulating.

Full active participation does not mean merely participating in what the presider does. That still falls short. The liturgical subject is the community. In fact, in the early church, community leadership came first, and whoever presided in the community's life also presided in the community's Eucharist, for that was part of its essential life. (This was affirmed in two memoranda sent by the Central Theological Commission to the bishops working on *Lumen Gentium* in Vatican II.) SCCs do not perhaps think out consciously the nature of community itself as liturgical subject, but their behaviors are moving in that direction, especially in celebration of the Word. A black pastor here in New Orleans often says to the congregation: "You are not the audience. You are the performance." That can and does happen far more easily in an SCC than in a traditional parish. It can happen in parish liturgy as well, and as we are creating its forms, we might do well to consult the lived experience of SCCs.

What is at stake here in Catholic culture is a reclaiming of the centrality of the community as people of God. In the Rite of Christian Initiation for Adults [RCIA], for example, it is clear that responsibility for forming new members into a Catholic faith belongs above all not just *to* the community but *in* the community. There is fruitful exploration afoot, especially in the North American Forum for Small Christian Communities, about the catechumenal possibilities of SCCs, since the initiation model is based upon the dynamics of socialization rather than indoctrination (though initiation into a belief structure is important as well).

The emphasis in the Tridentine Eucharistic ritual was upon the transcendent majesty of God, a sense of deity reinforced by the soaring, eye-lifting lines of Gothic church architecture. With liturgical reform came a rearrangement of liturgical space. The altar is once more also called the table and is placed *in* the community, rather than against a wall. Community members greet and speak at the kiss of peace. The language of the entire celebration is familiar, i.e. the vernacular. Communicants take the cup, hold the consecrated bread in their hands. These changes place more emphasis upon God as immanent.

There has been some strong disruption of community over this retrieval of immanence and its relation to what many feel has been a loss of transcendence. Battles over the removal or retention of the communion rail have been commonplace. Removing that structure changes the relationship between sacred space (where altar, tabernacle, priest, and altar servers are) and profane space (where the community gathers). The line of demarcation is lowered. The communion rail battle is about an interpretation of who God is and where God is to be found. Is God more likely to be encountered in sacred space, or does space become sacred when God has been encountered there?

When it registers for David that he lives in a magnificent palace while the Ark of the Covenant is simply shaded under an awning, he decides to build a lavish temple for Yahweh. But Yahweh balks at this, and has Nathan remind David that Yahweh always chooses to pitch a tent wherever Yahweh's people pitch their tents. Yahweh is content to continue traveling with only a tent. "Holy" is wherever the people are and Yahweh is with them.

The theological task for the church today is to affirm that "with us" (immanence) and "beyond us" (transcendence) are coordinate experiences. We can only experience God on the basis of God's being with us in some way. God is always more than we experience, but the only clues we have to the "more than" are those intimations that glimmer through God's being with us. It is our surmise that SCCs might provide the faith experience that can fund a new theological understanding of the internal relationship between immanence and transcendence in religious experience.

We have named the religious context of Catholic culture in the United States in two ways. The first is the transformation that recentralizes community and recognizes the whole community as a liturgical subject. The second is a serious question about religious experience: who God is and, thus, where and how the encounter between God and us takes place.

In the ritual life of small Christian communities, there is usually a transparent experience of full active participation. And the fact that they tend to meet somewhere else than on church property also makes a statement about sacred space. "House church" is a healthy reminder about the breadth of the "where" of God.

CLOSING

Understanding how we understand is the business of hermeneutics. We always understand where we are from, who we are, what our history is, what our language is, and what our loves and hates are. As Clifford Geertz has helped us see, all knowledge has some local character to it (Geertz 1983). *Constructing Local Theologies* is Robert Schreiter's development of the same theme in respect to our faith interpretations (Schreiter 1985). While it is always possible for us to transcend local limitation in some measure, we can never fully take leave of the local situations in which we live and move and have our being.

Small Christian communities are a worldwide phenomenon. Through international consultations, such as those at the University of Notre Dame in 1992 and 1996, we recognize how diverse are the regional, national, and continental appropriations of this form of church experience. Thus, we have chosen to open this book on small Christian communities with some clear indications about the local situation called "U.S. Catholic church." From a huge panorama of possible topics we have selected several about U.S. society and about the Catholic church in this country—in a word, we are trying to explore SCCs with a keen awareness of the implications of our local situation, for these frame our scope and our limitations.

NETWORKS, ORGANIZATIONS, RESOURCES

Buena Vista
P.O. Box 5474
Arvada, CO 80005-0474 Phone: (303) 657-9428
Buena Vista began as a network for parish-based communities; it is now much more inclusive in membership. Newsletter. Annual meeting. Resource materials (print and video).

International Office of Renew
1232 George Street
Plainfield, NJ 07062 Phone: (908) 769-5400
Post-Renew was developed especially for groups that want to continue as communities when the formal Renew program has been completed, but its videos and printed resources have a wide application. SCC resources (videos and printed materials).

Latin American/North American Center for Church Concerns
215 Hesburgh Center—Kellogg Institute
University of Notre Dame Phone: (219) 631-8528
Notre Dame, IN 46556
The center fosters church dialogue between Latin America and North America, with a special concern for SCCs. It has sponsored two international conferences, and published *International Papers in Pastoral Ministry.*

Loyola Institute for Ministry
6363 St. Charles Avenue
New Orleans, LA 70118 Phone: (800) 777-5469
The Institute for Ministry offers a Master of Pastoral Studies with a focus in Basic Christian Community Formation. It is conducting a three-year research project, funded by Lilly Endowment, Inc., on Small Christian Communities in the U.S. Catholic Church.

Ministry Center for Catholic Community
540 N.E. Northgate Way, Suite 141
Seattle, WA 98125 Phone: (206) 763-6222
Lay founded and lay led, this Center has SCC resources for scripture, for liturgical seasons, and for topics of special interest.

National Alliance for Parishes Restructuring into Small Communities
c/o Carrie Piro
P. O. Box 1152
Troy, MI 48099 Phone: (810) 637-1830
The alliance serves parishes that work to include SCCs as a structured form
of parish life. The printed resources and videos are useful in wider contexts
as well.

National Forum for Small Christian Communities
Joan Cunningham, Membership Coordinator
Office of Evangelization
1935 Lewiston Drive
Louisville, KY 40216 Phone: (502) 448-8581
Intended originally as a network for diocesan personnel with responsibilities
for nurturing SCCs, it still functions that way, but it is also open to a more
inclusive membership.

North American Conference of Associates and Religious
Bon Secours Spiritual Center
1525 Marriottsville Road
Marriottsville, MD 21104 Fax: (410) 442-1394, e-mail: JSonnen954@AOL.com
This new organization facilitates networking and communication among
associate communities sponsored by religious congregations. It publishes a
quarterly newsletter.

Quest: A Reflection Booklet for Small Church Communities
The Pastoral Department for Small Christian Communities
467 Bloomfield Avenue
Bloomfield, CT 06002 Phone: (860) 243-9642, Fax: (860) 242-4886

Sunday by Sunday
1884 Randolph Avenue
St. Paul, MN 55105-9934 Phone: (800) 232-5533
Published under the auspices of the Sisters of St. Joseph of Carondolet, this
lectionary-based liturgy of the Word, prepared for small Christian communities, is a four-page guide for each Sunday. It is available by subscription.

CHAPTER THREE

The Churchhood of Small Christian Communities

Claiming Ecclesiality

INTRODUCTION

We ended the last chapter by saying that churchhood is important to small Christian communities because it gives their participation in the conversation called church a constitutive role. It could perhaps be told as well in the opposite direction: being a voice in the constitutive conversation confirms small Christian communities' churchhood.

In the early years of the Latin American experience with small Christian communities, they were often referred to simply as base communities (*communidades de base*). It soon became important, for the reason just mentioned, to rename them base ecclesial communities [BECs]. Base communities in Latin America claim to be not just part of a church (like part of a parish), but actually to be church, church in embryo. There is an analogy with the redevelopment of local ecclesiology. Dioceses are not administrative units of the Vatican. Each is church. The authority of the Bishop is not delegated from the Pope. The authority of the Bishop derives from the Bishop's legitimate leadership of a local church. Churches being in union with each other and with Rome is also constitutive of churchhood, and is not arbitrary. Both official practice and popular perception have a lot of catching up to do.

Now "church" is not an easy word to pin down, partly because for so long it has named something so precious, because it is so laden with emotion, because even its earliest uses disclose some ambiguity, and because in our time of great change it is both battleground and solace. Our quest is not for an exact definition, but more, perhaps, for the poetics of being church. For that reason, we are using the language of churchhood. The question we want to broach is not whether, but in what ways churchhood can truly be claimed by a community. In *The Four Quartets*, T.S. Eliot reminds us that we only find adequate words for the things we no longer have to say. But in the meanwhile, for the things we do have to say, we must make a raid on the inarticulate, for which poetry, image, and metaphor are well suited. We will, of course, use some theological and sociological assistance in making the raid.

As a word, "church" shares a history similar to that of "synagogue." The most recent archaeology in Galilee, while it discloses much about village life, has not identified a single synagogue building that dates to the time of Jesus. Every village had public space where it gathered to attend to its religious and civil life, though that distinction would not have made much sense at that time. Behind the Greek word we know as "synagogue" stands the Hebraic word "qahal," meaning simply a gathering of people. When the Gospels say that "Jesus went into the synagogue," we should probably say in English that Jesus went among the people who gathered to observe Shabbat (Sabbath) in the village's public space. And they that gathered were the Covenant people of God.

There were no church buildings for centuries in early Christianity. Communities met in people's homes (house churches). In his Letter to the Romans, for example, Paul greets Prisca and Aquila and sends his greetings also "to the church at their house" (Rom. 16:5). In his Letter to the Colossians Paul asks that his greetings be given to his "sisters and brothers in Laodicea, and to Nympha and the church which meets at her house" (Col. 4:15). The Greek word *ekklesia* which usually comes into English as "church" names the people gathered in discipleship to Jesus.

The Greek word only occurs several times in the Gospels, all of which are in Matthew 16 and 18. In *The New Jerusalem Bible* translation, Jesus says to Peter in Matthew 16:18, "on this rock I will build my community," i.e., "Peter, you have the key role to play in the community of disciples formed by my proclamation and initiation of the reign of God." In terms of meanings that "church" tends to carry today, "community" is a more responsible translation of *ekklesia* in Matthew 16:18.

For many Catholics the word "church" signals either the institutional church, or, at the level of image, a church building. Neither of these is surprising. Beginning with the Constantinian era (313 C.E.), when Christianity was state-recognized, its institutional character received increasingly more attention. Yet even through the great medieval period of scholastic theology, ecclesiology was not a distinct branch of theology. That development awaited the Counter-Reformation. In the decades before Vatican II, important historical work (e.g., biblical scholarship that addresses Christian origins), and theological reflection (like Yves Congar's work on the laity), laid the foundations for the recovery of a people of God sense of "church." When the Second Vatican Council affirmed that "church" and "Kingdom of God" are not interchangeable (the kingdom of God is wider and deeper) some new vistas began to open up.

In the Catholic imagination, it is also commonplace for "church" to signal a building. The imposing legacy of the Gothic cathedrals put the church building visually at the village center, with steeples that reached toward the heavens, towering above every other building in the town. The Renaissance put classical architecture at the disposal of church buildings, with the addition of the artistic and engineering genius of people like Michelangelo, da Vinci, and Bernini.

The small Christian community, or house church, is a new conversation with those two instinctive senses of church. The initiatives from SCC members that make SCCs work is an expression of church experienced as people of God. The new Code of Canon Law, for example, affirms that all Catholics have the right to assemble and form associations. SCCs are not oblivious to the church as institution, but they have convictions about their sense of churchhood because they are a gathering in discipleship of the baptized. They aren't just borrowing church identity from the larger institution. They exercise the indigenous ownership of the baptized.

The fact that most SCCs do not meet in the church building also helps intervene in the instinctive connection between the word "church" and an image of a building. SCCs often meet in members' homes (as did the house churches of the early centuries). While today's SCCs have some things in common with the house churches of the early centuries, they are certainly not a mere repetition. House churches were the only option in the beginning. They were the normal form of ecclesial life. They made use of social forms current in Mediterranean first-century life (the "household"), but nonexistent in most nations in the twentieth century. House churches exist now in a new time for many new reasons. They reclaim "gathered people" rather than "gathering place" as a fundamental meaning and image for the word "church." How they claim churchhood is an enriching phenomenon for the entire People of God.

One of the surprises at the Fourth Congress of European Base Communities in Paris in 1991 was the representation from countries that had been behind the iron curtain. During those long, dark decades, house churches once again became the central experience of church for many people. We know now that Catholic bishops ordained married men and women in these communities, a pastoral response to the apostolic right of a church to Eucharist. It was a conversation with exigency that was not without risk. It also a conversation that is not over. That is not a theological judgment. It is just a fact that the conversation continues.

In part because some familiar meanings of church are in the process of being modified, the issue of churchhood is important and pressing. If church as institution should not be the centerpiece of ecclesial perception, neither is it arbitrary. And if church does not first and foremost name a building, sacred space is no less important. The network of small churches needs a gathering place as much as any individual community.

Churchhood, therefore, is a vital discussion. Raising the issue of the churchhood of the small Christian communities springing up all over the world is not without problems. The New Testament advice about not putting new wine in old wineskins applies. There is new wine. "Church" has never been a univocal word. It is polyvalent, rich in abundant significations. We should be thankful for the polyvalence, for it houses some blessed ambiguity about church that prevents us from blithely packaging its mystery.

In each of the churchhood frameworks that follow we are attempting to be descriptive. It is not a matter of saying that when these models or conditions are fulfilled, you are church. Our starting point, rather, is that when you find what most people recognize as church, you can use these categories to describe what you find. Categories are typological—but typing never does justice to any concretely existing reality. We bristle personally at being typecast, and so does (or ought) church. Mystery is not susceptible to being tamed by typological categories, especially the works of God.

We will first re-examine a typology which we offered in *Dangerous Memories* that many have found useful: *koinonia, diakonia, kerygma,* and *leitourgia.* Then we will recall the extremely helpful "models" framework articulated by Avery Dulles: herald, community, servant, sacrament, institution—although our laying out of these does not exactly follow his use of the models.

Finally, we will pay some attention to the difference between mainstream and marginal church life and to SCCs that reflect such differences. The two categories are not two possibilities, but two ends of a spectrum with countless possibilities between them, and probably no pure type.

FOUR DESCRIPTORS:
KOINONIA, DIAKONIA, KERYGMA, LEITOURGIA

For some reason it has become commonplace to cite these descriptors in anglicized Greek, perhaps for easy reference, and perhaps because such usage makes it easier to remember that these are technical, interpretative categories. We'll look at them one by one.

Koinonia

The word itself connects with meanings around the notion of participation, and that is a good place to begin. The Gospel is a revelation of God's plan for God's people, and of the redemption of human life that comes to all people who are God's people. Redemption itself, as we were reminded in *Lumen Gentium,* has a fundamentally participative character.

In many places, but especially in the latter chapters of 1 Corinthians, Paul reminds Christians that they are members of one another, that they are all parts of the same body. They don't become connected when they choose to behave in certain ways. Through baptism they are already connected. The only question is how powerfully they will honor all the ways in which they participate in each other's reality. SCCs are a place where lives rub up against each other in near enough ways that this truth stands a solid chance of capturing human consciousness behaviorally.

We want to offer a short aside about our use of the social sciences in theological reflection. When David Tracy says that Catholics have an "analogical imagination," he names our tendency to emphasize how the world is like God who made it, and how the world mediates our experience of God. We know that sin is there too, but we have confidence that the analogical connections are superabundant. He contrasts this with a "dialectic imagination," which is preoccupied with the great gulf between the world and God and dwells upon how unlike God is to our soiled, creaturely experience. He says there are no pure types, no one who is only analogical or only dialectic, but that these are marked tendencies. Because of our analogical imagination, sacrament is especially important. A world which, in Gerald Manley Hopkins's words, "is charged with the grandeur of God" is a world able to mediate religious experience.

Contemporary Catholic theology is often disposed to have the human sciences as partners in reflection upon religious experience. Marriage is already an Old Testament metaphor for God's relationship with Israel. By the end of the first Christian millennium, Catholic experience has begun to reckon marriage as a sacrament. We would add that a solid, loving marriage mediates our experience of God's love for us. A poor marriage is less good at that. We can describe a good marriage in religious language, and we can also use the language of the social sciences to say what is healthy and functional and what is disabling and dysfunctional. We can use the language of organization and management to describe healthy ways for power to function in human community, or we can use metaphors that Jesus uses for leadership (servant, for example). The conversation between theology and the social sciences is particularly important to people who are at home with an analogical imagination.

As we speak about *koinonia* in this book, we can use the language of being members of one another, as Paul does, or we can speak about relationships where mutuality thrives, where reconciliation—never easy—is expected to occur. We can talk about wounded conversation or upbuilding conversation. Having these two languages for religious experience helps to elucidate history's mediation of God's presence. In this book, therefore, there is a lot of moving back and forth between these two languages (a reflection, surely, of the primary disciplines in which the interpretative instincts of the two of us have been incubated!).

Chapter 5, for example, puts at the disposal of a community's inner life a lot that we have learned in our century about conflict resolution, about the qualities of good conversation, about the dynamics of consensus building, about the redemptive demands of mutuality. Chapter 6 puts at the disposal of a community's public life a lot that we have learned about how people are empowered to participate in history.

Koinonia is not only about the way in which community members partici-pate in one another. It is about how communities are connected, and how they participate in each other. Paul feels the need to scold house churches in Corinth for tending to become idiosyncratic, that is, off on their own. No mat-ter who starts the community or who leads it, it does not belong to Apollos or Cephas or even Paul (though Paul makes a special claim). It is especially important for communities that are not parish-based to maintain connec-tions so that they do not become Cephas's or Apollo's or Paul's. Forming net-works at the local level is one way. Becoming members of one of the national SCC networks and attending regional and national meetings are other ways.

Community is an extraordinary grace. Community is necessary and can be of incredible beauty. But no one has ever claimed that community is easy! The dynamics of disparate lives participating in one another is a fearsome task—not nearly so formidable, however, when the journey is walked out loud with many companions. With truly ample *koinonia.*

It is worth noting that the kind of Greek in which the New Testament was written is called *koine* Greek, that is, the kind of Greek that people spoke in their daily living as a way of being in each other's lives through their ongoing conversation together. The quality of our conversation and the quality of our community are of a piece. The quality of our conversation with God and with each other and our conversion are also of a piece. In both cases we often put ourselves at risk in the openness needed for genuine conversation. "Conversationriskandconversion" is a very large word.

Diakonia

Diakonia, which means service, comes from the same root as *diakonos,* which means servant. As we noted in the previous chapter, servant is one of the principal metaphors Jesus used for how power should function in com-munity. What a good servant does is respond to need. That presumes also that a good servant knows how to look and how to listen in order to assess need accurately. Empathy is one of the most necessary skills in knowing what needs cry out for service in the internal life of an SCC. The ability to engage in social analysis is one of the most necessary skills in knowing what needs cry out for service in the larger community in which the SCC functions.

Deep in the Judeo-Christian tradition is the advice that we are to be holy in the way that God is holy. The two recurring clues to the center of divine holi-ness are justice (*tsedeq*) and mercy (*hesed*). While justice includes many of the legal meanings that it tends to carry in our culture, it is a much more embracing concept in the Hebraic world view. There is an essential rightness about how the world should go, rooted in God's intentions for the world. This rightness sometimes makes an appearance when the Hebrew word *tsedeq* comes out in English as righteousness as well as justice.

Hesed names the tender mercies of God as they respond with immediacy to critical, unmet human needs. In the tradition we have sometimes called basic, mercy acts through corporal works of mercy and spiritual works of mercy. We are clearly obligated to respond swiftly to critical present need. But if that were that all we did, we would often be empowering an unjust system to endure even longer, since someone keeps picking up the pieces. Those who are committed cooperators with God's intentions for the world are under requirement to intervene in and work to alter unjust social systems responsible for the miseries which mercy must address.

It is easier to engage in works of mercy than in the dynamics of systemic change. For reasons that will be laid out in more detail in chapters 4 and 6, SCCs as mediating structures in society can be a front-line contact zone for the social justice energies of the church; but that requires some conversion of consciousness in a culture that likes to keep religion private, and in fact "pays" religion, through tax exemption laws, to keep out of public life.

Some SCCs begin their meetings ritually with "the news." For each gathering someone is responsible for a couple of minutes of news, using newspapers, news magazines, and religious publications to say: "Here are some events that happened since we last met: world events, national events, local events." Such a brief news time helps a community to have wider eyes. Some communities either add their own news on to this, making time for members to tell some of their own stories, or else alternate personal news and world news at different gatherings. The personal news gives community members a chance to share experiences that they feel are important since the last meeting. Sometimes a lot has happened. Sometimes a little. Sometimes someone says, "I pass this time. It's been a very ordinary week or two."

It is the obligation of any Christian community to service need within the community and beyond the community. A community needs to develop its own "listening devices" in order to assess need. *Diakonia* is a natural consequence of *koinonia*. If we are members of one another, the needs of the community and the resources of the community must connect.

Kerygma

There are nonreligious communities and organizations that take relationships seriously, and that are of service to each other, or to others beyond themselves. *Kerygma* gives small communities their essential definition as small *Christian* communities. The *kerygma* is the message of Jesus Christ, it is announcement of the reign of God, it is the Good News. And in one of its earliest names, it is simply "the Way."

If the *kerygma* was called the Way, or the Good News, there had to be reasons for the excited experience that did the naming that way. These are not the only names that the post-Easter communities came up with. New Testament scholarship generally agrees that "teacher" and "prophet" were probably used of Jesus in his lifetime, but that most of the christological ways of naming Jesus were conferred by the believing community after the Easter event. Each title reflects some community's particular experience of Jesus in their lives. In the Jesus event, God did something for them that they could not do for themselves.

The New Testament is something like Elizabeth Barrett Browning's sonnet to her husband in which she asks, "How Do I Love Thee?" She replies to her own question, "Let me count the ways." And then beautiful images pour out, one after another, to tell of her love. The titles of Jesus in the New Testament were not assembled systematically. They came to the surface of different communities' experiences of Jesus, perhaps even several parts of the several communities. They rose up out of particular concrete experiences of Jesus. "How do I love thee? Let me count the ways. Thou art the Christ, the Messiah. Thou art the Son of Man. Thou art the Son of God. Thou art the Son of David. Thou art Lord. Thou art High Priest. Thou art Second Adam. Thou art King of the Jews. Thou art Truth. Thou art Life. Thou art Light." This is christological poetry.

To call these names for Jesus "christological" is to reach into the Jewish experience of being anointed. The Greek word from which we have "Christ" in English simply means anointed, one who has had oil poured on one. The anglicized Hebrew word for the same thing is "messiah." Kings and prophets were anointed, special ones. Israel experienced something that it needed to be saved from, could not seem to save itself from, and relied on God's promise that an anointed one would do for them what they could not do for themselves.

Kerygma is about what God does for us in the Jesus event that we need done and cannot do for ourselves. *Soter* is the Greek word for savior, and soteriology is the theology that recounts our sense of what we need to be saved from, and how God works through Jesus in the Spirit to save us. Soteriology is at the center of christology. If Jesus is experienced as the messiah, what is it that he does for us that we need to have done for us and cannot do for ourselves? What happened to people's lived experience in those earliest years that made them call the Jesus event the best Good News they'd ever heard, so good they'd die for it as well as live for it?

A recent study by Notre Dame sociologists puts regular Catholic attendance at Sunday Eucharist at about 27 percent. If Catholics are absenting themselves from church participation in large numbers, is this not a matter of relevance? Time at church does not connect faith and lived experience in a way that is clearly good for lived experience.

We begin the next chapter by saying that SCCs are a privileged place for the doing of theology. Theology often has the ring of an esoteric, academic enterprise. But like orange juice that's "not just for breakfast anymore," theology is not just for the academy anymore, and never should have been. It is organized reflection on the experience of faith by people of faith in communities of faith. Because the small communities are such a primary contact zone with lived experience for church, they ought to be a home for theologizing a new soteriology out of their experience. Members of SCCs are showing up for (house) church, and something is addressing them that makes them turn up. *Kerygma* gathers them in the first place, but it is also taking shape anew at a time when old answers are often not interactive with today's questions—or if they are, not in traditional forms.

The issue is more of an existential soteriology: What difference does or can Jesus Christ make to me, to us? What formulation of the *kerygma* can make its soteriological relevance incandescent? We express our hope that SCCs might help Christian faith do some reshaping of its soteriology so that *kerygma* regains a reputation for being unrequitable Good News.

Leitourgia

In its simple original meaning, *leitourgia* named public activity in ancient Greek city life, or sometimes the public responsibility of wealthier citizens. In Christian life liturgy names the prayer forms that have grown up out of a community's experience, forms that are readily recognizable to the community. Because liturgy is owned by the community, it is one of the means by which communities feel they belong to a life larger than their own.

In the early centuries before there was any such thing as parish structures, "house church" was the normal way Christians gathered. In Greco-Roman life the household did not mean just the family of parents and children that lived in the same house, but a wider relational group of servants, clients, and close friends. When the bishops were working on the Vatican II dogmatic constitution on the church, *Lumen Gentium*, the central theological commission forwarded two similar memoranda to them reminding them that in the early church, those who led the community also presided over its Eucharist. Laying on hands validated a person's leadership in the community, by virtue of which that same person became the natural one to lead Eucharist. In later centuries the relationship was reversed: the laying on of hands conferred the power to preside at Eucharist in virtue of which the ordained person would lead a community.

It's either an exquisite irony, or else a work of God's Spirit, that as the numbers of small communities mount, the number of the ordained diminish. Christian communities regularly having Eucharist was no problem for the early centuries. But that is not where we are today! The dangerous memory of ancient eucharistic tradition, however, perhaps holds future content.

Since most SCCs in the U.S. Catholic church are parish-connected, members ordinarily participate in the parish Mass, but they do not regularly go together as SCC members. Their principal activity as a community is around scripture and prayer. A small number of intentional eucharistic communities [IECs] regularly have Eucharist, most often by inviting priests to preside, although a few IECs have the same priest as a regular presider.

Many of the SCCs that are not parish-based and do not have Eucharist will nonetheless have breaking of bread and sharing of a cup as part of their regular ritual, to maintain their orientation toward the Lord's Supper. Some will say it's eucharist with a small "e" so as to make clear that they are not confusing their memorial with formal Eucharist. Scripture plays the central ritual role in most of these grassroots communities.

In *Dangerous Memories*, under the topic of *leitourgia,* our reflections were upon Eucharist. Based upon emerging trends since that time, we want to note the very important role that liturgy of the Word plays in the life of SCCs.

We would like to allude to a position developed more fully in *The Future Church of 140 B.C.E.,* that Catholics have begun a retrieval of scripture since the mid-sixties that hints at a new experience of two real presences, not just that of Eucharist (B. Lee 1995, 151-155).

Real presence is redundant. Either it's real or it isn't presence. "Real" is a way of naming a privileged or most important or utterly central experience of God's immediate, active presence through Jesus Christ in Eucharist. Edward Schillebeeckx has enriched the discussion of presence with the idea of "density." The Christ event is there for human history all the time. It is never missing. The issue then is not presence or absence, but density of presence. Every presence of God is mediated by the world and by events. To call Eucharistic presence a "real presence" is then a testimony to the centrality of Eucharist, its density of presence, in mediating the Catholic experience of Jesus Christ.

Many Catholics recall that the three principal parts of the Mass were offertory, consecration, and communion. To fulfill one's obligation it was necessary to be at all three parts. If you missed the first part, you could stay that far into the next Mass, but if you missed two parts, you had to remain for the entirety of the next Mass. What is interesting in retrospect is that the liturgy of the Word did not even count! Sermons were expected not to exceed ten minutes, and they were rarely of the sort that were genuinely insightful into the biblical text or into that text's relevance to the concrete lived experience of those assembled.

Finding the Bible again, along with a veritable mine of scholarship that is becoming available at the popular level, is changing the piety and liturgical life of more and more Catholics. When SCCs give a central place to scripture, it is no longer a ten-minute version. Probing scriptures is a sustained and organized conversation between Word and world. It often takes place with the help of a good commentary, seldom takes less than an hour, and sometimes takes twice that. The probing has some kind of social analysis as a conversational dialogue partner: What has this story to do with our story? In what ways is our lived experience accosted by God's Word? The words of the sacred story are not there just for remembering a past event, but for chasing down present events. The words are not fully Word until they confront present events. We know at that point that we have been addressed by the living God, and that too is real presence. It is not interchangeable with the real presence of the Eucharist, and is not meant to replace it. Those who cannot have Eucharist but can have Word know they are not without real presence of the living God.

Because of Catholic culture's love affair with Eucharist, liturgy of the Word sometimes seems like a poor substitute for the real thing when there is no priest. And indeed, it should never be a substitute. It is, in fact, a different yet shattering experience of presence, not in its old ten-minute sermon form, but in its new form of sustained dialogue with experience. A positive benefit is that it takes the pressure off of Eucharist to be almost everything. In its origins, the Eucharist on the Lord's Day celebrated the power of Jesus' death and Resurrection within a community's life. It was the high point of the week. When Eucharist became a daily devotion rather than a central Sunday event, the specialness of Sunday could only suffer. It may be that a new kind of rhythm between liturgy of the Word and liturgy of the Eucharist is an experiment in the name of the whole church that is being carried on in small Christian communities.

In any event, liturgy of the Word belongs to Catholic *leitourgia*. When trying to understand their churchhood, SCCs now know that Word as well as Eucharist is a shared form of public liturgy, and, as such, expresses their churchhood.

Canon law affirms the right of all Christians to assemble and form associations. Our baptism empowers us to do that. Like Schillebeeckx's notion of "density" with respect to eucharistic presence, the four characteristics named above can help SCCs reflect upon the density of their ecclesiality.

MODELS OF CHURCH:
HERALD, COMMUNITY, SERVANT, SACRAMENT, INSTITUTION

Avery Dulles's book *Models of the Church* immediately captured huge Catholic attention when it was published in 1974. It was and is a useful way of approaching the mystery of church. It will be clear that many of the concerns expressed in the categories of *koinonia, diakonia, kerygma,* and *leitourgia* overlap with these models, but are not identical. Models are a very different take on church.

Dulles offers the models as a typology. The models are built on images that function metaphorically. They are ways in which the whole can be viewed. Imagine the church as a *herald* whose central sense of itself is that of proclaimer of the Gospel. Through the lens *community* we focus upon a church whose sense of itself is as God's people responsible for and to each other. The *servant* lens will frame the church as a Gospel responder to need, especially to need that is most desperate. How authentically and palpably church manifests in its daily life the message of Jesus Christ will show up under the lens of *sacrament*—here "convincing visibility" is the key feature. The *institution* lens shows up the church's character as a structured organization that works under God's Spirit to safeguard and propagate the community of Jesus Christ.

Now whatever is truly church (all of the above) is on stage all the time. A spotlight will show off one part more than the rest, but they are all there at the same time.

An SCC that cares about its churchhood cannot pick one model and say "we'll be that one," and then disregard the others (just as a community could not opt for *leitourgia* and disregard *koinonia*). But an SCC can say, "which models are most developed in our life, and where is our work most cut out for us?" A parish or diocese can (and should) do the same thing.

Herald

We referred earlier to the back-seat position that scripture had in the Catholic tradition. For most of us, the Protestant kids in our neighborhood could run circles around the Catholic kids when it came to knowing the books of the Bible, or identifying characters from Old Testament narratives. They learned those things in Sunday school, and sometimes in summer Bible camps.

The herald model has a sort of chronological priority in the formation of church. Paul frequently headed for the synagogue to begin telling the story of Jesus of Nazareth, the Christ. Street preaching was not foreign to the early church leaders, as the Acts of the Apostles makes clear. It is the proclaimed story that first gets people's attention and gathers them. It doesn't do this once and for all. The story's function of grabbing attention and gathering people and their energies belongs to the ongoing becoming of the church. Practical theology, which we address in the next chapter, is the kind of conversation with the story that keeps the church becoming.

Because scripture plays such a central role in the prayer activity of SCCs, we want to make two recommendations to the contemporary herald church. The first is the importance of using up-to-date commentaries. It is no easy matter in a face-to-face immediate conversation to hear another voice accurately. But when the voice comes from a different culture and from a different era, the conversation is far more demanding. Twentieth-century biblical scholarship has broadened and deepened our ability to access the culture and world view of first century Galilean culture. Archaeology has uncovered many aspects of the life and the times. Hermeneutics sensitizes us to the complexities of interpretation. A person doesn't have to become a biblical scholar to access much of this. There are accessible tools. Sr. Macrina Scott has published *Picking the "Right" Bible Study Program: Reviews of 150 Recommended Programs with a Listing of the Top 15*. Each resource is judged according the following twelve criteria:

1. Up-to-date scholarship incorporated?
2. Background information emphasized?
3. Application to personal and family life emphasized?
4. Application to the life and mission of the church included?
5. Application to broader social issues included?
6. Generic masculine avoided?
7. Guidance for prayer at group meetings provided?
8. Discussion questions provided?
9. Practical directions for group leaders provided?
10. Biblical background for group leaders provided?
11. Biblical background for group members presumed?
12. Participants required to prepare for each session?

We cite the criteria because they name some things that ought to be among the concerns of a herald church today.

Our second recommendation to the herald church is to make use of social analysis in our encounter with scripture. Herald church doesn't just proclaim the gospel, it helps the gospel address the particularities of people's lived experience, and it must understand them to address them. A justly popular resource is the 1984 book *Social Analysis: Linking Faith and Social Justice*, by Joe Holland and Peter Henriot. At Loyola's Institute for Ministry we have developed a shorter model, adapting an approach developed in the Iona Community in Scotland and presented in Ian Fraser's book, *Reinventing Theology*. The process can be described briefly, which we shall do. But, in fact, it may take weeks or months to carry out adequately. A community goes through these questions and clarifications and actions together:

1. Identify the social unit that will be the object of social analysis (e.g., a city's school system, a particular parish, a school, a corporation). Name one or two (several at most) of the most positive, creative, supportive features of that social system. Then do the same thing for the dysfunctional or destructive features of the same system.
2. It is important never to float in generalities. For each of the positives and negatives indicated above, describe some concrete specific way in which that feature of the system has been experienced. Keep the critique of good and bad grounded in actual experience.
3. In what ways does your religious faith help clarify what you believe is either good or bad about the system? It is important to be as proactive in support of what is good as it is to intervene proactively in what is not desirable. Praying for insight and honesty is a must, and prayer should accompany social analysis at every stage. It might even be more accurate to acknowledge that social analysis can itself be a form of prayer, flowing as it does from our passion about God's reign. We can lose our innocence easily when we critique what has caused us pain, just as we can lose our critical sense before that which favors and savors us. Our prayer doesn't absolutely guarantee us, but it surely guards us.
4. Behaviors in a social system happen the way they do because of the ideas and energies that drive them. Try to make your best guess at what kind of thinking stands behind both the healthy and the dysfunctional behaviors. It is very important to stay even-handed. We easily impute bad motives for what we don't like. Communities really need to challenge how the good and bad features are interpreted. This exercise is sometimes called ideology critique.
5. Who is doing the thinking that drives the system? Whose ideas are at work? Who believes in the things that are responsible for the good behaviors and for the bad ones? If we want to support the good or tackle the dysfunctional, we have to know where agency lies. Support for what is

good or intervention in what is not good must be applied where agency functions.

6. Jesus advised his disciples to be as clever as serpents and as innocent as doves. He gave examples of what not to do: don't build a building without a careful analysis of the terrain; don't engage in battle unless you sense there is a chance of success. A community that wants to help goodness continue or wants to end injustice must be realistic. In stark terms, we need to know what kind of a power base it takes, what kind of credibility we need to build to have helpful effects. Only then should concrete steps be taken to do what needs to be done. Intervening in a social system is a complex action.

Much of this discussion will taken up again in chapter 6.

Although this observation is more empirical than ideological, it seems that one of the gifts of SCCs to the larger church is how scripture is taking hold of the communities' conversation with themselves and their larger world. Scripture is becoming a source of energy unaccustomed until recently in Catholic culture.

Servant

In Catholic life a paradigm shift has been underway, since Leo XIII, from charity to justice. This claim needs to be nuanced. The need for charity never disappears, and the church's response should never be lessened. We are, however, recognizing more clearly how many charity needs are the result of dysfunctional systems. If the systems are not corrected, the charity needs continue and multiply. If all of the people out of work suddenly had full-time jobs, and worked forty hours a week at the minimum wage for 52 weeks, their income would still be below the poverty level. The fact that minimum wage still leaves a family of four below the poverty level is a social dysfunction.

Mark's Gospel has the narrative that most people recognize as "the widow's mite" (Mk. 12:38-44). Many rich people put large amounts of money in the treasury. A widow throws in two of the smallest coins in circulation. Jesus praises her, for she gave of her substance while others gave from their surplus. Too seldom is this passage connected with the immediately preceding passage. Jesus has just criticized the scribes for their fancy dress and their desire for recognition. Scribes devour widow's resources under the pretense of offering long prayers for them. Widows are not allowed to be estate executors when their husbands die. That is a social function which the scribes fulfill. They rake in a large take for their function, and are committed to pray for the widow. The monies help them sustain their status. This is a systemic way in which widows are kept poor and a wealthier class is enriched more (Myers 1988, 320-323). While the generous widow deserves to be praised, she is in fact putting even more money into the coffers of organized religion whose structures, in this case, have something to do with her poverty in the first place. In Jewish life in the time of Jesus, civil structure and religious structure were not separate realms—the same structures can be identified by either name. It is important that we not let a charity instinct (let us assist the widow today) deflect us from correcting a systemic abuse of power. The informed servant community does both.

The teachings of the U.S. bishops on the "Challenge of Peace" and on "Justice for All" are a remarkable servant response to critical human concerns. The challenge is to make them operative. Such documents have limited value unless they are studied, debated, and applied in local contexts all around the country. That could indeed be a servant role of SCCs.

There is yet another servant sense of things that is especially relevant to SCCs. In his life time, Jesus gave the church no specific order or structure. What he did provide, as we indicated in the previous chapter, were some striking metaphors for how power should function among them, whatever its structure: servant, steward, and shepherd. Servant is the most developed metaphor. The servant is there for the community, responsive to what is happening, assisting in every possible way. One way of putting it is that the servant leader does not generate the community's agenda but assists the community in every possible way to implement it. That does not mean that the servant leader has no input into the agenda, but that the input comes from community members (as well as the leader), and community membership is what validates its importance. A servant leader does not attach leader-prestige to her/his input.

SCCs are generally a stunning experiment in community leadership. SCC structures tend to be very participative and leadership very collaborative. We have found, in fact, that there is often such reaction to nonparticipative, noncollaborative exercises of leadership in the institutional church that SCCs can bend over backwards so far that leadership gets neutralized rather than transformed. The experiment of SCCs with participative leadership structures deserves to be an insistent piece of conversation in the larger church community.

Community

We have already focused upon community under the rubric of *koinonia* in an earlier part of this chapter. Community has long been a very high value in Catholic tradition. At least some of the reason has to be the presence of men's and women's religious communities in Catholic history. In some ways, Catholicism has maintained a double structure, a diocesan system which is hierarchical, and a vast network of religious orders, "which does not belong to the hierarchical structure of the church," but is nonetheless "devoted to the welfare of the whole church" and has "the duty of working to implant and strengthen the kingdom of Christ in souls and to extend that kingdom to every land" (*Lumen Gentium, §44).* The pastoral care of entire villages has often been largely the ministry of religious communities rather than diocesan structures. These two structures have worked well together. Sometimes the relationship has been tense, but usually it has been creative.

Pluralism, which we described in chapter 2, is a new cultural situation in contemporary history that is a challenge to community, one to which SCCs might have some experience to offer. In some sense, pluralism is not a brand new situation. There has always been a variety of positions in the church, and there has always been a sense that some positions are utterly inconsistent with community membership.

What is new, with the advent of historical consciousness, is the recognition that pluralism is not a temporary place on the way to agreement, if only we pursue truth honestly together. Pluralism is a normative condition, reflecting the conditioned and partial nature of all experience and all understanding, an historical contingency that is not transcendable. We are not talking about a soft pluralism that says, "Anything goes." We are interested in how people who experience and perceive very differently from each other can still form community.

We already named the importance of dialogic community in the second chapter, and we described some of its conversational rules. The emphasis is upon commitment to a communal process rather than upon shared convictions (B. Lee 1995, 160-168). In order to function these ways, skills of self-disclosure and empathetic listening are essential, as are the dynamics of conflict management and consensus formation.

The church at the level of institution is not likely to appropriate models of dialogic community. That experiment needs to occur at grassroots levels, and work its way up. SCCs are as good a place as any to search for authentic ecclesial appropriations of dialogic community. Because the Body of Christ is what it is, women and men who interpret the world very differently can still be members of each other, and need community forms that have room for them. The efforts initiated by Joseph Cardinal Bernardin and Fr. Philip Murnion at the National Pastoral Life Center to find (or perhaps create!) common ground is a move in exactly the right direction.

SCCs, because of the very nature of Christian community, need to pay attention to a certain heterogeneous character in their membership. Frankly, this is not easy to bring off. A certain like-mindedness tends to characterize community membership in this country—in fact, there is relatively little racial, educational, denominational, or socio-economic diversity in SCCs in the United States. In discussing the need for community in U.S. culture, Robert Bellah warns us not to count life-style enclaves as real examples of community. We want to be realistic about the power of similarity in gathering people, but resist becoming merely life-style enclaves. Some of our interest in SCC membership in broad-based community organizing is that it offers— even requires—heterogeneity among communities (if not within the community itself).

Sacrament

Luke's admittedly romanticized presentation of early Christian life in Acts recounts that those who beheld these communities were struck by how they loved one another. The early Christians shared all their goods. They prayed together and shared meals together. Their embodiment of the message of Jesus caused many others to join. Their numbers grew daily.

In a landmark book on sacraments, Edward Schillebeeckx calls Jesus the primary sacrament of our encounter with God (Schillebeeckx 1963, 47-89). The next level of sacramentalization is the church itself. If the church is faithful to Jesus, those who behold it can "read" the gospel in its behaviors. As sacrament, the church is, in Dulles's words, "under requirement to be a convincing sign" (Dulles 1974, 63). As a sacramental sign, the early communities convinced others of the power of the Good News so powerfully that their numbers grew daily.

In a word, as effective sacrament these early communities were clearly generative—their palpable presence elicited the formation of new communities. Because of communities' effective sacramentalization, church grew. In sacramental theology we say that sacraments cause the very thing they signify, and the act of signifying is where the power lies. In chapter 2 we documented the growth of SCC activity in the past decade. It is fair to assume that SCCs are visibly meeting felt need, and that they are effecting new communities.

The most obvious application to any SCC is that, as church, it must be a convincing sign. We would like to call the attention of small Christian communities to the generativity implied in sacramentality. If churchhood is true of an SCC, then the hope that others will form new communities will animate its life. SCCs, no matter how satisfying their experience, may not claim churchhood and remain self-contained and satisfied.

Institution

Sociologists of religion talk about the relation between charism and order. A charismatic figure brings brilliant new insight to bear upon the deeper yearnings of human beings, challenging the settled order, and initiating new forms of human life that break free from forms that were no longer life-giving. There is a fresh, wild character to charism. It breaks free of forms that no longer hold life, and it runs hard and clear.

People who are utterly captivated by charism want with all their energy to share it with others. Before long they want to get it down in writing to be able to hold on to it and communicate it. They want some control over interpretation of the charism to safeguard its authenticity. They want to choose spokespersons for the charism who can be trusted. They want to secure its future.

That's where the jousting between charism and order begins. Charism will be lost if there is no means for its locomotion into the future, and the carrier is structure, or order, or, simply, institution. On the other hand, there is no way for charism to maintain utterly intact its fresh, wild creation of new futures, and submit at the same time to structure. When the structure gets too tight, the charism breaks loose. When the charism gets too wild, the institution grabs for the reins. The engagement between charism and order is a contact sport! The contest is redemptive of both charism and order. In fact, they play off of each other. They need each other.

The parish that restructures as a community of communities is not just adding a program, it is trying a new version of an old order—there's something at least a little fresh and wild. That is clear from the institution's nervousness about it all. The more marginal experiments are looser. They are more resistant to order, but they also need to attend to their connections so as not to become wayside shrines rather than real church.

Let us say two interrelated things in conclusion to this section. The first is that SCCs must exercise initiative in remaining conversationally connected *in some way* with the rest of the church, and there are undoubtedly more ways than we have yet imagined. The second is that the institution must also exercise initiative in connecting with communities. Not all of the initiative for being connected belongs to the communities alone. Because priests and bishops were beginning to float free of their connection to real Christian communities, Canon 6 of the Council of Chalcedon said that if priests and bishops were ordained without a connection to some specific community, the ordination was invalid—not just that it wasn't a good idea, but that it didn't even count. While it is stretching beyond the Chalcedonian Canon to say that church leaders must connect with communities, we believe that it is in the spirit of ecclesial leadership to reach out to SCCs, whether they are "standard versions" or not. We express a hope that leaders of local churches will reach out with welcome to this new movement of community, to risk listening to its voice, and to give it room.

MAINSTREAM AND MARGINAL: A CONTINUUM

To begin with, we conclude that SCCs generally have some marginal characteristics. They are not the usual way that church has been done for centuries upon centuries. They are an alternative. Some are closer to mainstream; others are on the edges of wide margins. Mainstream and marginal are relative terms that constitute a spectrum. The experiences they name are part of any living social organism. These categories, like any, are misused if they are applied narrowly and without nuance. The categories do, however, name tendencies that include ideas, feelings, values, and related behaviors. In settled times in any institution's life these are not submitted to critical evaluation. Some amount of change is regularly needed in all institutions, and as long as it does not call its structures into serious question, organizational management normally negotiates the needed change ("we have structures for effecting change"). But when far-reaching structural transformation is needed, when people in central leadership would have their own organizational positions called into question, the push and shove for change, the experiment with alternatives, will come from below where the critical impulse has more freedom.

In his analysis of how cultural transformation occurs, anthropologist Victor Turner refers to the larger institutional structures and interests as *societas,* and the organized counter movements as *communitas.* Every healthy institution experiences the unnerving dialectic between the energies of *societas* and *communitas.* They threaten each other and need each other. The Turner categories are an anthropological way of addressing the dialectic between order and charism, but add some new institutional insight.

Change occurs as the experiments of *communitas* work their way into the innards of *societas,* sometimes causing major indigestion. William James described the three careers of an idea. When a large new idea appears, most people say, "It's dangerous, it's untried, it's not orthodox, it should be left alone." But if it hangs around and does well in the second stage of its career, people are less unnerved and say, "It's nothing that unusual, what's the big deal, take it or leave it"; but they are not fighting it tooth and nail. In its third career, when a new idea has in fact been found very interesting and fruitful, those who found it dangerous in the first instance now claim to have discovered it.

It is almost too trite and commonplace even to say it anymore, but the Roman Catholic church is in the midst of probably the most far-reaching transformation in its history. For about four centuries it fended off the disruptive and creative forces of modernity. Vatican II opened windows and doors. The great transformations and paradigm shifts that have occurred in Western and world culture have piled up high and are taking ecclesia by storm. It is no surprise to anyone who understands social change that the ecclesial *societas* and ecclesial *communitas* have exceedingly high passions around their respective projects.

In this present discussion, "mainstream" means closer to the energies of *societas* and order, and "marginal" means closer to the energies of *communitas* and charism. It must also be said at the outset of this discussion that the whole of the small or base Christian community movement, in its great variety of manifestations, runs counter to the way that ecclesial community has been understood and experienced in recent centuries. The parish that supports Post-Renew communities and the parish that is restructuring into a community of communities are both doing something structurally new, and therefore have some element of marginality. It is no secret that there is nervousness about this in the ecclesial *societas* even though cautious support is sometimes forthcoming.

By "mainstream" and "marginal" we are speaking therefore of tendencies, of being more or less one or the other, in short, of experience on a continuum, not either/or.

Mainstream

Mainstream SCCs, in this context, are those communities that are related in some way to parish life. The most integrally connected are probably those that are part of a restructuring process. The communities that are inspired by Renew also see themselves as functioning within the parish, much as Renew groups functioned within the parish.

There is a smaller number of SCCs that formed on their own initiative, and have no kind of recognition within a parish, but whose members continue to be active in a parish (members might come from several parishes). For all of these, parish is where their sacramental life is pitched, and parish is their center of gravity; yet these SCCs meet members' needs that parish life alone would leave unmet.

The strength of these mainstream groups is their support and inventiveness for changing parish life. They are a place where leadership for the larger parish emerges and is schooled. Because of members' attentiveness to need within the community, a lot of ministering occurs that does not require the efforts of the parish team. In this regard parish-based SCCs both reflect and initiate changing patterns in how ministry happens. To be sure, there are *communitas* issues that animate members of SCCs in the parish; the strong desire for something new, or dissatisfaction with how needs were met before. For such reasons, it is important not to make mainstream and marginal into unambiguously separate orientations.

At the October 1996 International Theological Consultation on Small Christian Communities, held at the University of Notre Dame, there was discussion about how SCC leadership should be named. One of the expressions that had support was "animator" (though the French original, *animateur,* carries more punch). In the course of that conversation, several people with parish-connected SCCs (on several continents) said that "animator" was also a good name, not just for community leadership, but for the function of SCCs in a parish. While they never constitute the majority experience, they are sufficiently active and engaged to provide some animation for the entire parish. At the same gathering we learned that in Tanzania there is a Swahili word for the person who does the spicing of food when it is being prepared. In the singular form, *mkolezati,* it has become one of the names for the SCC leader, and in the plural form, *wakolezati,* it names how multiple SCCs liven up the whole parish structure. These are examples of how SCCs are perceived in a parish structure to be something like a *communitas* to a *societas,* even in a more mainstream setting.

Marginal

These are more marginal contributions to the conversation called church, and they are vital.

We would like to cite Terry Veling's insightful description of marginal SCCs:

> Marginal communities recognize that there are many ways in which the center no longer holds in their experience of tradition and society. They challenge dominant orderings of patriarchy in their quest for renewed feminist expression; they seek more

inclusive and participatory structures over against hierarchical and clericalized structures; they turn their attention to ecological issues in the face of an overly technologized world; they are concerned with the causes of indigenous and Third World cultures in the face of dominant Eurocentric traditions. They are seeking alternative theologies, spiritualities, and practices, casting their "voice from the margins over the whole social-symbolic order, questioning its rules, terms, procedures and practices" (Veling 1996, 10-11).

Veling's *Living in the Margins: Intentional Communities and the Art of Interpretation* makes a convincing case for the institutional value of marginality. If the church as we have come to know it is like text on a page, and if there is a new text for church in the making but not yet in the book, the margins of the existing text are the place on the page where the unwritten text begins to interrogate the written text. What is important here is that the margins are *on the page*. Everyone who has ever borrowed a book knows that some other person's scribbling in the margins affects how we encounter the text. Margins matter.

Margins is a metaphor that comes from a page with a text and space around the text. We live in a church and a city and a nation and a world with a lot of history and story already on the page. The church and the world that we already know because they're here now—these are like texts that are already written. Marginal people rarely find their stories told or honored in the text the way it's already written. Lay people generally, and women in particular, have not found many significant parts of their story on the page of the text called church. So they are working to get the story written in a new way, convinced that the story is large and pliant for rewriting. A lot of these people live in what sociologists might call the margins.

In *Image on the Edge: The Margins of Medieval Art,* Michael Camille says that marginal art exists in the margins "in order to give birth to meaning at the center" (Camille 1992, 48). He examines the marginal art in manuscripts and the sculpture on the outsides of great cathedrals (the building's edges) in contrast with the sculpture and other art inside the edifice. The inside and the outside together complete meaning.

Camille illustrates his point from a page of a medieval manuscript of psalms in a prayer book. Whoever copied the manuscript drew a person in the margins who has climbed up the sides of the written text. With one hand he is pointing to a place in the text. In his other hand is a rope, and he is pulling something up. As your eyes follow the rope, you see that there are some lines of writing on the bottom of the page below the text—in the bottom margin. The marginal person is showing where in the main text the marginal text should be inserted, and he's going to pull it up with the rope and put it there. If he succeeds, he will have rewritten the story!

Sociologists tell us that any healthy organization must have marginal people who are challenging the written text and who have some variations of the story tied on to ropes, ready to haul in. That's the basic way that societies change and develop. Center has no meaning without reference to margins, and margins no meaning without reference to center. It is an interdependent relationship (J. Lee 1995, 30).

The Million Man March in Washington, D.C., was a well-crafted scribbling in the margins by black men, probably in permanent ink. Hispanics in California are not allowing their story to get eradicated from the page by hostile legislation. Both are adding new text to our story, by dint of their numbers, by dint of their insistent presence in the margins of the American page, and by dint of immense cultural beauty. During times of great transformation and upheaval, in the in-between times between deconstruction and reconstruction, marginal living is critical for the good of us all.

Not everything marginal is a good idea. On the other hand, most good ideas begin their careers in the margins. Like Christianity. The birth of Jesus was in Bethlehem in the Judean margins of Jerusalem. The death of Jesus was on Calvary on the edges of Jerusalem. The world's story has been altered because of these marginal events in Bethlehem and on Calvary. Already in the early months of the Christ event's gestation, Mary announced God's special love for those who live in the margins, and promised they would get God's privileged attention (Lk. 1:46–55). A recent study of Jesus by a renowned New Testament scholar, John Meier, is called *A Marginal Jew.* The politically correct were upset by the company Jesus kept. But Jesus kept on affirming that the tear-stained prayers of those who live on the underside of history are the first to reach the ears of God.

CLOSING

In the U.S. Catholic church, parish life has a long history that is solid, supportive and strong. Closely allied with parish life has been a vast system of Catholic schools in which the cultural identity of millions of Catholics has been formed. For most of their history, nearly all of those schools, whether parish related or private, have been under the sponsorship and direction of religious orders. In the 1950s, half of all the Roman Catholic seminarians in the world were in the United States. Parishes had many young priests with appeal to young Catholics.

Religious communities had many young members in their schools and hospitals. Because of that strong, good Catholic history, many of us remember church instinctively in those categories: vibrant parishes, strong schools, competent hospital care. However, during this period when many familiar, identity-forming structures are coming loose at the seams, we are thrown back upon our resources to re-imagine the meaning of churchhood.

To look through the vistas of *koinonia, diakonia, kerygma,* and *leitourgia* is a way of trafficking with the dangerous memories of an early time when there was indeed church, but few or none of its institutions were the forms of church life that later developed, forms familiar to most of us. There is future content in the sense that a past which differs from the present suggests the possibility of a future that differs from the present. These four descriptors are not prescriptive, like "one, holy, catholic, and apostolic."

The way that the models of community, herald, servant, sacrament, and institution are presented here is indebted to the 1974 work of Avery Dulles, but is not simply a replay of how he understood them. This format recognizes that paradigms shape human experience and human thought. There is overlap between the descriptors and models presented here, for example, in the concern of both with the role of sacred texts, one under the rubric of *lei-tourgia*, the other under the rubric of herald. One of the most important reminders embedded in the models approach is that while the model of institution can never not be an aspect of churchhood, it should never be the dominant model. It must be among them, but not first among them. The institution serves the community and its sacramentality.

Finally, we looked at the meanings of "mainstream" and "marginal." We must often remind ourselves that marginal does not mean irrelevant. No society can stay healthy without marginal activity which facilitates its own pattern of self-transcendence. Inasmuch as small Christian community structures have not been the way in which dominant Catholic culture conducted its churchhood in recent centuries, all of them, parish-connected or not, have some measure of marginality about them. By mainstream we have meant those SCCs that have a closer relationship with the parish. But, if one can speak of a sociological theology, we have also wanted to affirm the churchhood of more marginal gatherings of Catholics who are still on the page, because the margins are part of the page.

Scribblings in the margins of church affect how readers read the main text of church and some of the scribblings even become incorporated in future editions of the main text.

CHAPTER FOUR

Community as Gathered and Sent

Reaching for Definition

INTRODUCTION

Matthew's Gospel is especially clear about the discipling process. Being disciples means being gatherers of people, using the metaphor of casting fishing nets (Mt. 4:18-22). They are to make sure that people's lives are savory ("salted" is the metaphor), and they are to do good works that cast great light and give glory to God (Mt. 5:13-16). True disciples are to be informed, not stupid like the one who built a house on sand (Mt. 7:27). The disciples are to take their stand against the powers of darkness and drive evil out (Mt. 10:1), and they must be ready for the consequences of taking public stands because they will be brought before church authorities (Sanhedrin and synagogue), governors, and kings (Mt. 10:17). Jesus picked out the twelve and sent them out on mission. Mark says that Jesus asked them to go out two by two, to take their stand against the powers of evil together, to ask people to live in new ways, and to heal suffering (Mk. 6:7-12). The disciples, in a word, imitate Jesus who was a great gatherer of people, all of whom would be missioned as well as gathered. The Spirit who led Jesus into his public life (Lk. 4:14) is the same Spirit who guides the disciples and tells them what to say when the going gets rough (Mt. 10:20). Matthew's final word is a sending into the whole world with the Good News (Mt. 28:16-20)—the great commission.

Paul develops Christ the gatherer into a christology in his First Letter to the Corinthians. It is the task of Jesus the Christ to gather all people into one body, and then bring that community of saints and himself as a gift to God (1 Cor. 15:20-28). The building up of community is so important to Paul precisely because it is a christological activity. Gathered and being gathered, sending and being sent, are at the core of our discipleship.

62

THE TWO BASIC DIMENSIONS OF
SMALL CHRISTIAN COMMUNITIES

At the center of our conceptual analysis of small faith communities is the recognition that they are what Evelyn and James Whitehead have called intermediate (or "hybrid") social forms (1992, 19-20). Small Christian communities are like what sociologists call "primary groups" (e.g., families) in that they are characterized by an emphasis on acceptance, loyalty, and close personal relationships. But they are also like what they call "task groups" (e.g., teams in the workplace) in that they have a work to perform. A proper concern for how they are gathered—for the capacity of their members to communicate mutually, seek consensus, and utilize conflict creatively—is one of the hallmarks of authentic SCCs. The other is due regard for how they are sent—for the capacity of the community to join with others in seeking the well being of the larger social world to which they belong. In our view the motivating heart of SCCs is their commitment to sustain both an inner and a public conversation, to be like a family and like a task group simultaneously. The purpose of this chapter is to lay out the dimensions of that challenging, double-edged vocation.

The distinction between the primary ("gathered") and task ("sent") dimensions of SCCs is analogous to the difference between psychological and sociological understandings of community. We want to introduce each of these in turn.

In his classic work on community-based approaches to mental health, psychologist Seymour Sarason offers a magnificent description of the "psychological sense of community."

> Precisely because we all experience the presence or absence of a psychological sense of community, however restricted it may be in terms of the size of the referent group, some of its characteristics are not hard to state. The perception of similarity to others, an acknowledged interdependence with others, a willingness to maintain this interdependence by giving to or doing for others what one expects from them, the feeling that one is part of a larger dependable and stable structure—these are some of the ingredients of the psychological sense of community. You know when you have it and when you don't. It is not without conflict or changes in its strength. It is at its height when the existence of the referent group is challenged by external events; ... it is also at its height ... in times of celebration.... It is one of the major bases for self-definition and the judging of external events. The psychological sense of community is not a mystery to the person who experiences it. It is a mystery to those who do not experience it but hunger for it (Sarason 1974, 157).

Here we view the phenomenon of community from the inside out, as it were. Sarason's description emphasizes what community feels like and entails subjectively. Small communities must gather in mutuality. This is the "primary group" aspect of small faith communities. It corresponds to what we shall call their "inner" (gathered) life, which is the focus of chapter 5.

The other side of a small community's life is its engagement in the larger social world of which it is a part. The understanding that the church does not exist in isolation for itself alone but rather in and for the world is deeply embedded in the historic Jewish and Christian traditions. The classic expression of this aspect of biblical faith is to be found in the voices of the Jewish prophets. In *The Prophetic Imagination* Walter Brueggemann offers the following account of the public vocation of people of faith.

> Surely history consists primarily in speaking and being answered, in crying and being heard. If that is true it means that there can be no history in the empire because the cries are never heard and the speaking is never answered. And if the task of prophecy is to empower people to engage in history, then it means evoking cries that expect answers, learning to address them where they will be taken seriously, and ceasing to look to the numbed and dull empire that never intended to answer in the first place (Brueggemann 1978, 22).

Here the faith community is looked at from the outside, so to speak, from the perspective of its mission to engage in history, to make its presence felt in the current empire of economics and politics. Small communities must be sent prophetically. This is the "task group" aspect of small faith communities. It corresponds to what we shall call their "public" (sent) life, which is the focus of chapter 6.

The use of sociological categories helps us interpret many of the challenges of Christian discipleship. We are more than "a hybrid group with primary and secondary characteristics," but neither are we ever less than that. Grace has many names.

We want to declare our firm conviction that both of these dimensions are integral to the biblical character of small faith communities. A "small community of faith" with a strong inner life but no viable public presence is in actuality a support group; a "small Christian community" with notable public impact but little development of its inner life is in truth a social action group. We will argue both on biblical grounds and in light of our own experience and research that to claim the title "community of faith" authentically means to accept the challenge of developing and integrating an inner and a public dimension. To participate in an SCC is a complex and challenging process largely because it demands of its members high levels of *both* relationship and task orientations if it is to work. A faithful, vibrant small community will provide a strong psychological sense of belonging for its members, even as it will learn how to address hard and timely questions regarding justice and mercy to the powers that be. And it will discover that, far from operating at each other's expense, the inner and public dimensions, when held in creative tension, deepen and enrich each other. In fact we suggest that balancing and rebalancing these two concerns in the real world in which a community finds itself and with the guidance of a biblical vision *is* the life of a small community of faith. Small faith communities are gathered and sent.

SMALL CHRISTIAN COMMUNITIES AS INTENTIONAL

The communities which we described in the previous chapters are made up of Christians who have deliberately chosen to cast their lots with other Christians. This deliberate choice makes them intentional communities rather than simply spontaneous or random gatherings. Despite our legendary cultural loneliness, it is not at all easy for us Western individualists to cast our lot significantly with anyone outside our primary groups. Intentional community is not natural for us.

"Intentional" means deliberate or consciously chosen. This word is our way of highlighting the fact that within the relatively affluent contemporary culture of the West, large numbers of persons will ordinarily not be drawn into small communities out of necessity, as has been the case in Latin America. The worldwide movement of small Christian communities can be authentically appropriated in and for Western culture only in a voluntary and democratic fashion. It is a way of life to which persons must be invited. The kind of community life which we are about to describe in detail cannot and should not be forced on anyone. It must be chosen intentionally.

We want to present a working model of small Christian communities. We call it a working model because it is intended as a practical tool for reflection and action. Let's begin with a definition. A small Christian community is a relatively small group of persons committed to ongoing conversation and shared action along four distinguishable but interrelated dimensions:

- They are consistently committed to a high degree of mutuality in the relationships among them.
- They pursue an informed critical awareness of and an active engagement within the cultural, political, and economic realities of their society.
- They cultivate and sustain a network of empowering connections with other persons, communities, and movements of similar purpose.
- They attend faithfully to the Christian character of their community's life.

We have just named the four core dimensions of an SCC in contemporary language. Terms like "mutuality" and "network" and "empowering" are drawn from our contemporary vocabulary. But such terms can also be translations, attempts to revitalize the ideals of our ancient Christian story in the everyday life of our time, to help us name and envision a form of Christian praxis in and for our today.

"Mutuality," for instance, is a way of naming the *koinonia,* the belonging and equality, the solidarity among persons characteristic of authentic Christian existence. As we saw in chapter 3, *koinonia* pertains to relationships *within* particular small communities as well as to relationships *among* various small communities. As we learn to participate in face-to-face relationships of mutuality, we are actually nurturing *koinonia* among us. As we learn to network effectively with others of common purpose, we are extending and deepening the web of *koinonia*—of belonging and equality—which our Christian story holds to be sacred.

"Pursuing an informed critical awareness of and an active engagement within the cultural, political, and economic realities of our lives" is simply a contemporary way of naming a form of the *diakonia,* the caring service, to which authentic Christian existence calls us. "Private Christianity" is a profound contradiction of our ancient tradition. Faith is never "just between me and God." Our Christian vocation is radically social or relational, including our relationship with God. When we learn to reflect together theologically in a constructively critical fashion and to engage actively with the world around us in the light of such reflection, we are extending our *diakonia*—our caring and serving presence—into the contemporary world. This extension is not elective; it is our biblical obligation.

Finally, "to attend faithfully to the Christian character of our community's life" is to keep the Christian *kerygma* with its dangerous memories and transformative hopes at the center of our collective consciousness (and unconsciousness), and to celebrate that memory and hope together in the sacramental moments of Christian *leitourgia.* In rituals of word and sacrament, members of SCCs keep their personal and collective moods and motivations attuned to the challenging and consoling contours of their sacred story. In doing so, they place the everyday acts of their interaction with one another and the surrounding world in the ultimate context of the sacred Christian narratives of justice and love.

Therefore, to say that SCCs are characterized by mutuality, social engagement, networking, and Christian remembrance is to say that these small groups are concretely involved together in the genuine praxis of *koinonia, diakonia, kerygma,* and *leitourgia.* It is to say that they are truly ecclesial units, truly church. Many human groups are characterized by one or several of these four attributes; an SCC is the social form that it is because it intends to strive toward the faithful embodiment of all of them simultaneously.

PRACTICAL THEOLOGY:
REFLECTION AND ACTION IN SMALL CHRISTIAN COMMUNITIES

A special form of conversation requiring action, reflection, and action—and wonderfully suited to SCCs—is often named "practical theology." This expression has a comfortable ring to the ears of most Americans, known as they are throughout the world for their no-nonsense, down-to-earth attitudes. But our usual associations of the word "practical"—that is, "useful" or "applicable" or "relevant to everyday concerns"—are misleading in this instance. In order to eliminate the confusion, the method could have been entitled "theology of praxis," but that would only have substituted one kind of ambiguity for another.

Practical theology names a cluster of methods for doing theology. What those varying methods have in common is the insistence that the point of theological interpretation is not simply to contemplate or comprehend the world as it is, but to contribute to the world's becoming what God intends that it should be, as that intention has been interpreted by the great theistic traditions. The view that theology has a concrete contribution to make to the actual world might seem like common sense now, but our Christian religious instincts have long been primarily formed by the perspective of classical theism, namely, that religious interpretation is about knowing or contemplating the essence of God, the beatific vision. The title "practical theology" signals the intention to stress faith's vocation to affect history.

The version of practical theology which we will outline here is our revision of the "revised correlational method" proposed by theologian David Tracy in *Blessed Rage for Order* (1979). Tracy's approach is a reworking of the correlational theological method developed by Paul Tillich. Such methods are called correlational because, as we will see, they work by holding two things in reciprocal relationship—our religious traditions and the state of the actual world in which we live. Our revision of Tracy's model for practical theology consists in our insistence that the critical conversation between faith and culture, which every Christian community must continuously undertake, always has concrete objectives in action: namely, the transformation of persons, societies, and cultures so that our treatment of each other and the earth brings peace. Our version of practical theology, in other words, involves not only our critical intelligence but also our capacity for committed and effective action. The version of practical theological method outlined below has been developed by the authors in collaboration with other members of the faculty of the Institute for Ministry of Loyola University, New Orleans.

Practical theology requires that members of SCCs intentionally interpret their social and cultural situation. This process begins by prayerfully considering the world as it is, then lifting up some aspect of it which particularly concerns us, and articulating the nature of our concern, including our "gut" reactions to it. We intend for the word "concern" here to carry the meaning that it has developed in the Quaker tradition, that is, of having one's attention called to some aspect of reality by God. The Quaker understanding of "concern" is very much like the meaning associated with the term "burden" in African American churches. When a black pastor says that "God has placed a burden on my heart for public housing residents," what he or she means is that God is directing him or her to pay special attention to the people who live in those circumstances.

Through their membership in a broad-based community organization (which we will discuss in chapter 6), small communities of faith in New Orleans first identified and are now pursuing their concerns for the well being of the larger community in the areas of public education, child care, affordable home ownership, and living-wage jobs. Which initiative a particular community commits itself to depends upon its discernment of its primary concerns and available resources.

Having identified a concern we must subject it to appropriate critical scrutiny, lest we become caught up in the "concern *du jour*" mentality so pervasive in our culture, in which pressing situations of need get their fifteen minutes of attention in the public eye and are then forgotten, with no serious long-term commitment to address them having been made.

Having submitted our concern to critical reflection, we must undertake a disciplined, practical investigation of what is causing the situation, with a view to understanding it well enough to affect it positively. In doing so we are not seeking the knowledge of the expert, but we are in search of something beyond what "everybody knows" about our concern. We call this range of knowing, which lies between expertise and common sense, practical wisdom or working knowledge. It is the kind of knowledge which makes one a good parent, principal, minister, or community leader: a knowledge which lets one make the best of concrete tasks facing real people in real situations. Practical wisdom leads not only to the accomplishment of necessary tasks, but also to the empowerment of those involved.

Through participation in their community organization's working group on public education, SCC members in New Orleans have begun to develop a working knowledge of the dilemmas facing public schools in a racially divided urban environment. They have discovered, for example, that the Louisiana state constitution provides that owners of homes assessed at less than $75,000 in value shall pay no real estate tax. So property taxes, a major source of financial support for public schools in most communities in the United States, are not available under Louisiana's current constitution. Those who seek to increase the level of financial support for the New Orleans public schools must either seek an amendment to the state constitution, or create some other source of public financial support for community schools.

When we have developed a practical understanding of some aspect of our situation which concerns us, we then prayerfully select some aspect of our faith tradition—scriptural text, theological classic, or church teaching—which seems relevant to it for an initial reading and response, including our "gut" reactions to what we have chosen. Then we undertake a historically informed exegesis of the material chosen from our tradition so as to come to a deeper understanding of its significance, one that takes us beyond initial impressions and responses toward a fuller appreciation of that which is being interpreted on its own grounds. Such disciplined interpretation requires that we attend to the historical circumstances which gave rise to our chosen text (the "world behind the text"), the form and content of the text as we have received it (the "world in the text"), and the possibilities for transformed living which the text provokes us to consider (the "world in front of the text").

In response to the vision of an African-American pastor, SCC members belonging to a broad-based community organization in New Orleans have reflected upon, studied, and taken to heart in a very special way the 29th chapter of the book of Jeremiah. That text is a letter which the prophet sent from Jerusalem to his people just exiled to Babylon at the end of the sixth century B.C.E. The seventh verse of that chapter takes the form of a remarkable admonition: "But seek the peace of the city where I have sent you into exile, and pray to the Lord on its behalf, for in its peace you will find your peace." The SCCs of metropolitan New Orleans have been repeatedly accosted by that text and are attempting to fashion a public life which is both feasible and faithful in light of it.

The standard of knowledge to which members of SCCs must hold themselves accountable in interpreting their faith tradition is like the one to which they are accountable in interpreting their situation. The expertise of the scripture scholar or academic theologian is not required, but neither is an uncritically received, taken-for-granted understanding of our tradition good enough. A practical knowledge of our faith tradition is one which lets us interpret accurately what it really had to say to a community of our ancestors in faith then and there as well as being aware of its distortions by the "-isms"—sexism, ethnocentrism, classism, or anthropocentrism. Only such a disciplined process of shared interpretation allows a community of faith to be properly appreciative and critical of what their tradition's classic symbols, texts, events, and persons have to say here and now.

Having interpreted both their situation and tradition with care, members of SCCs must then discern their contemporary obligations as people of faith in the world as it is and decide how to act accordingly. In doing so they must prayerfully consider what would constitute feasible and faithful responses to the situation which concerns them, in the light of the aspect of the tradition to which they have paid attention, and they must then make a choice from the available possibilities. A feasible response is one that is possible for this community in the world as it is; a faithful response is one which rings true to the religious tradition which they take as their guide. To paraphrase Edward Schillebeeckx: feasibility without faithfulness may become grim and barbaric, and faithfulness without feasibility becomes reduced to mere sentimentality.

Through a process of discernment beginning with the list of concerns of their broad-based organization outlined above, some of the New Orleans SCCs have joined the task force at work on public education while others have made access to affordable child care for persons of low to moderate income their focus for concerted action.

Having made a choice for a particular course of action, SCC members must then plan an adequately detailed intervention based on that choice, implement it carefully, and rigorously evaluate both what practical difference it made in addressing their concern, and its religious adequacy from the standpoint of their tradition. Then the community opens itself to its world anew, making itself receptive to what God will call its attention to next.

In collaboration with members of larger congregations in an effort which crosses lines of race, religion, and economic status, New Orleans SCCs are currently involved in careful ongoing analysis of the realities surrounding public education and child care in their metropolitan area. This analysis has led so far, to give one example, to the initial implementation of a strategy for rebuilding the base of adult support necessary for success in seven carefully selected public schools by reaching out to principals, teachers, staff, parents, and other concerned adults in the wider community.

So this is what we mean by "doing practical theology" in SCCs: we attend carefully with our heads and hearts to the world as it is and to the world as our faith traditions teach us it should be. We ask, "What must we do?" in the light of that attention, we do it, and then we evaluate what we have done. This disciplined rhythm of reflection-action-reflection by members of SCCs *is* practical theology. It is at the center of the vocation to which members of faith communities are called. In engaging the world and their tradition through practical theology, members of SCCs are continually challenged to recognize that a poorly understood world is as much a disaster as a poorly understood Word (Hanson 1986, 529).

At the risk of overstating a point, we want to emphasize once again what we mean by "reading" our faith tradition and our world. That these are indeed complex realities is indicated by the fact that scholars devote their entire lives to relatively small facets of them. For example, some scholars are experts on John's Gospel, others on the theology of Augustine, others on Catholic social teaching; other specialists focus on urban poverty, public transportation, or local government. This kind of specialized expertise cannot be required of Christian disciples or their leaders, nor would such a requirement be appropriate. The point is not that SCC members become urban sociologists or scripture scholars, but rather that our practical abilities to read our world and our tradition—and to empower others to do so— are enhanced by serious study of the work of experts. The goal is for our practical wisdom—our capacity to act faithfully and feasibly in the real world—to be deepened by what the experts know, not for us to strive for expert status in all the disciplines to which we turn for knowledge. Christian discipleship, ministry, and leadership must be informed by the work of experts, but should not be dominated by it. Our point might be put in this way: experts have their place in the work of practical theology, and must be kept in their place! Responsibility for theological reflection leading to committed action rests finally with members of local communities of faith.

It is our conviction that some method of practical theological reflection needs to become part of the habitual repertoire of SCCs. It is quite likely that some communities are already engaged in some or all of the steps outlined above. Practical theology is a flexible and forgiving method. It can be broken into parts which are engaged in successive meetings or worked through in one session. It allows SCC members to return to previous steps and rework them in the light of new information or changing circumstances. As SCCs experiment with a suitable form of practical theology, they must remember that the underlying purpose of practical theological reflection is to sustain a disciplined conversation between the faith community's vision of the world as it should be and the often harsh realities of the world as it is, a conversation that leads to faithful and feasible action.

THE SOCIAL ECOLOGY OF
INTENTIONAL CHRISTIAN COMMUNITIES

Small Christian communities exist as ecclesial units within a complex social web. "Ecology" is our contemporary name for the study of relationships between organisms and their environment. We are coming to realize that the ecology of all life is systemic in character, that what happens and fails to happen in our world for good and ill is a matter of relationships and their effects on everything and everyone concerned. We have begun to accept the fact that no aspect of life can be adequately understood apart from a profound awareness of its context. Human beings are slowly but surely arriving at an awareness of our natural and social ecological web; we are developing the capacity to live in a systems world. Christian communities can simply not afford to ignore their embeddedness within this web of systems.

Members of Christian communities begin to appreciate the relational character of our world when we recognize that anyone's individual becoming really refers to how she or he emerges from the particular contexts—planetary, familial, social, economic, political, and cultural—of life. We are always already situated within a particular world with a concrete history; the futures we might create will always bear the mark of our context and its history. One pertinent example of this insight for our purposes here is that, like dioceses and parishes, the contemporary movement of SCCs is situated within and emerging from the history of the larger church of which it is a part.

To live responsibly in a relational world is to have one's life profoundly shaped by the awareness that existence is an individual matter only to a limited extent. It is to realize that, like it or not, we are all in this together. To paraphrase Teilhard de Chardin, our past is not part of history possessed by us totally, but rather all of history possessed by us partially. By the same token our future is not an isolated piece of what might be which we own autonomously, as if it were our private property; it is part of the common possible future of our species nested within the universe's possible futures. Something analogous might obviously be said about the reality of SCCs today in relationship to the larger church. They are not the sole possessors of their own piece of church, but rather all of church history is reflected in their unique character. Their possible futures are of a piece with the church's possibilities.

It is illuminating for members of Christian communities to understand our world as a complex relational web. In fact we are convinced that the principal public commitments of such communities in our time—peace; the full inclusion of people of color, women, and other formerly "invisibles" within society; economic and social justice worldwide; and intercultural communication and respect—cannot be adequately understood and addressed apart from a practical and systematic analysis of human society and history. In order to foster that kind of understanding for members of Christian communities, we will present a brief overview of the web of relationships within which the everyday lives of persons in our culture are played out and then use that overview to situate the particular social form called community.

This model of the social web of our lives is conceptualized as structured in three levels: microsocial, macrosocial, and mediating structures. Like all models it is a simplification. In order to be useful it should be complex enough to capture something of the interrelatedness of the social world, which is the real context in which Christian communities must survive and thrive, and simple enough to support reflective action by community members.

Microsocial Structures

"Microsocial" structures are the small, immediate groups of our everyday lives. Families or other living groups, work teams, support groups, citizen boards, and certain voluntary associations are examples of microsocial groups. In contemporary Western society, most of our time is spent interacting in a complex variety of such settings, for example, families, workplaces, classrooms, and church groups. The quality of these relationships obviously has an enormous effect on people's sense of well being and quality of life. According to this definition small communities of faith are microsocial groups.

The structure and dynamics of any small face-to-face group constitute a kind of dance in which the participants have interlocking and reciprocal roles. The effects of this dance on individual participants are indeed profound; in fact, it is clear that we must carefully rethink what "individual becoming" means in light of our contemporary understanding of relationships as systems. For, as contemporary family-systems theories have made clear, no person in a group is an island, immune, or cut off from the system's effects. Interpersonal events in microsystems are in important ways a matter of internalizing and otherwise reacting to a system's repeating pattern of interpersonal events. We revisit this issue in depth in chapter 5.

The extent and lasting effects of our interdependence within important groups at the microsocial level is further revealed when we recognize that typical patterns of behavior and feelings are not only ways that people cope during the period they are members of a particular system. The pattern of

events in the lives of adult "graduates" of family systems attests to the ongoing effects of the systemic roles which we learned to play initially in order to
survive in a particular system. Those roles constitute the social and emotional foundations of our individual personalities. They provide our basic
training for personhood. Microsocial groups are not just places where
autonomous individuals hang around playing certain roles for a while; they
are the place where we experience the web of relationships face to face. And
that web is the source of the selves we are becoming.

Remaining at the microsocial level, it is important to be aware of the networks of microsocial groups in our lives. Thinking this way can help us to
remember that we are not just a family member and then later a participant
on a work team and still later a participant in a faith-sharing group; rather,
we belong to a set of microsystems simultaneously. The pattern of reciprocal
effects among our microsocial groups constitutes another aspect of the overall relational context within which Christian communities arise. What happens in our household has profound effects on our participation in the
workplace and vice versa. Indeed, one of the most common complaints of
contemporary people is that there is never enough time and energy for adequate participation in our network of microsocial groups—we are chronically
torn among our roles.

Like individual persons within a group, individual groups within microsocial networks affect and are affected by each other. Together they constitute
a system of their own, a complex and recurring pattern of mutually influential interaction within which our personal development is always unfolding.
Sociologically speaking, SCCs are part of that system. Our network of face-to-
face groups is like a smaller web within a larger one. This larger web we call
the "macrosocial" structures.

Macrosocial Structures

The term "macrosocial" refers to those large institutions and organizations
which, while not immediately present to us in everyday life, have profound
effects on our existence: for example, the I.R.S., the New York Stock
Exchange, and the Roman Catholic Church. The institutions and organizations of government, the economy, mass media, religion, and education have
profound and continuous effects on events at the microlevel. The smaller
systems can and do also affect macrosocial structures, though we typically
and understandably experience the influence as running primarily in the
other direction. In the next section of this chapter we will begin to consider
how microsystems like SCCs might affect macrosystems; we'll continue that
exploration in more depth and specificity in chapter 6 on the public life of
small communities. For now, let's concentrate on the influence of larger
structures on smaller ones.

The microsystems of U.S. society, including small Christian communities,
are situated today within the larger socio-economic context called an
"advanced industrial society." Such a society is one which has undergone

two important transformations in its basic economic structure. The first of these is a shift of the majority of workers from agriculture to various industries. The second, which continues rapidly in U.S. society today, is the movement of a significant number of workers from industrial to service occupations. Thus, an advanced industrial society is one in which a large proportion of the labor force is employed in retailing, health, education, information technologies, or government. Such a society requires an incredibly intricate network of production and distribution, transportation, communication, government, and legal systems. This interlocking network of large, influential institutions and organizations is one aspect of the macrosocial dimension of the web of relationships.

Advanced industrial societies did not appear in the world full blown; they evolved over the course of human history. As a result of macrosocial changes, the role of such microlevel groups as the family has undergone significant transformation. Let's take a moment to look at an example of such a transformation, one which by analogy will speak to us about the importance of macrosystem events for the life of small Christian communities.

Until quite recently the economic division of labor in advanced industrial society (a macrosocial reality) had tended to send males out into the world outside the home to provide the material resources necessary for their families' survival. It had likewise tended to keep females at work inside the home, providing the social and emotional resources required by their families. Most men and women in such a society didn't experience a clear moment of personal choice about whether to go out into the marketplace or work at home; it was a matter of fitting into the economic realities, the macrosocial norms of their time.

These norms fostered the economic dependency of women, who were expected to take up their economic roles within the home. This meant that many of the educational and on-the-job experiences which allowed men to pursue economic security outside the home were systematically denied to women. When a woman has been outside the employment mainstream for a significant period of time, it is difficult if not impossible for her to move outside the home and make a living adequate to support a family. For similar reasons, she probably has no version of a pension plan or other form of economic security, which her husband has been steadily accruing over the years by virtue of his employment outside the home. As a consequence, she typically faces bleak economic prospects on her own.

Sometimes the very bleakness of these prospects kept (and keep) women in marital relationships where they are victims of various kinds of abuse. We now know clearly that marital relationships characterized by such desperate dependency and abuse predispose all family members to dependent and abusive patterns of relationship, not just during their childhoods but in their adult lives as well. Clearly such a macro-economic situation is in no sense a result of the personal decisions of individuals; it is its own reality, with complex social and historical causes. This example illustrates the power of large systems over the course of individual lives and the functioning of groups at the microsocial level.

Macrosocial structures exert powerful formative effects on the functioning of all other levels of society and, therefore, on the development of all persons. Its functioning is likewise affected by them. Macrostructures do not unilaterally determine events elsewhere within the web of life, but their effects are felt always and everywhere. Small Christian communities are of course not exempt from these effects.

The other macrodimension refers not to particular persons, groups, organizations, or institutions, but rather to the culture that is always forming and being formed by them. Culture itself affects and is affected by the ways that the other social levels take shape. Culture is an inherited set of understandings and practices which organize a people's life. It is a world of shared meanings, which is carried and transmitted in symbols, especially language. As persons become acculturated, which always happens within the web of systems just described, they learn to experience and to understand their worlds in specific ways. They come to take for granted a particular assumptive world or map of reality.

Culture lends its shape to and is shaped by the structure and dynamics of our small, face-to-face groups and the large institutions and organizations just described. The pattern of events within the whole systemic web of our lives emerges from complex, multidirectional interactions between the micro- and macrolevels. No level dictates events at other levels, but only influences them, albeit sometimes so profoundly as to appear almost a determining force. In this view, members of intentional Christian communities will certainly be affected by realities in the web of macrosocial relations in which they live, such as the myriad ways in which pressures to achieve and consume are brought to bear on them and their children through advertising and peer pressure. SCCs may in turn affect those events as well. The capacity of small communities to exercise such transformative effects, to have a potent public life, depends on their ability to join with others in mediating structures.

Mediating Structures

As we have seen, the lives of persons, groups, organizations, and institutions function in a complex pattern of influences. While by no means always symmetrical or equal in their effects, these interactions are always reciprocal: every person, group, organization, and institution is affected for better and for worse by participation within the web of relationships, and each has its effects on that web. No vital, sustainable movement of SCCs is possible unless its relationship to the web of social systems at both micro- and macrolevels is carefully taken into account. Even then it won't be easy!

Small Christian communities are free, indeed required in many instances, to challenge how events are taking shape within the web of larger structures which constitutes their society. Sometimes that is the very reason for their coming into existence. And such communities are always interacting within the web of social systems, being affected by as well as affecting its character. If such communities have not fallen prey to the Robinson Crusoe fallacy, then they recognize that there is literally no place outside the web of society where they can live, move, and have their being.

Persons in our society routinely move back and forth between smaller, more personal microsocial groups and larger, impersonal macrosocial systems. Because these larger systems are so often alienating and depersonalizing in their effects, the citizens of complex advanced industrial societies often feel no choice but to seek meaning and participation within smaller, face-to-face groups. Because we so often feel relatively helpless about such things as racism, inflation, consumerism, and foreign policy, we understandably tend to leave them to others and turn to family, friendship groups, and community for acknowledgment and feelings of efficacy.

But there is a two-fold problem with this common and understandable strategy for coping with events in the contemporary world. First, it tends to alienate us further from the larger systems which have and will continue to have so much effect on possibilities for life in our country and on our planet. As a consequence our political and economic order—the bedrock of any social order—can lose legitimacy in the hearts and minds of more and more of its participants, heightening the temptation to abdicate our proper roles as bona fide participants in the institutions of government, economy, institutional church, and culture—to leave the guidance of all of that in "their" hands. In our absence these macrostructures go right on having massively important effects on everyone's lives. So genuinely democratic public order among us becomes more and more difficult to sustain.

Second, the capacity of microstructures like the family to carry the entire weight of meaning and involvement for us is actually quite limited. How can families, friendship groups, or small communities possibly counterbalance the massive alienating effects of society and culture on the large scale? Clearly, they cannot do so alone. In fact, as current debates on welfare and medical care in all Western societies illustrate, politics and the economy have major effects on what is likely to occur within microsocial groups. Events at the microlevel of society are so often at the mercy of events at the macrolevel that it often seems that the smaller and more personal systems of our lives can offer us a kind of "haven in a heartless world" at best. The increasing fragility and vulnerability of these havens is, however, more and more apparent.

If SCCs are to be more than islands of belonging and support for their members, to have more than an inner life, they must develop their capacity to connect with religious and civil groups and institutions around common concerns and interests. The power of cultural and religious groups and of local, politically attuned voluntary associations to affect the life chances of their members was nowhere more powerfully evidenced than in the civil rights movement in the United States. Black church leaders and leaders of other local associations of various kinds coalesced into a formidable collective agent of social transformation and liberation for their people. The improved life chances for some people of color resulting from the struggle for civil rights are directly attributable to the social bonds which gave meaning and purpose to those engaged in that struggle, and the black church was the primary locus of those empowering bonds.

The web of relationships within which we exist is constituted not only by economic layers and political institutions (macrosocial structures) and small, face-to-face settings (microsocial structures), but also by the cultural groups to which we belong, the congregations with which we are affiliated, the neighborhood organizations in which we participate, and a myriad of other forms of voluntary association. The pattern of these affiliations, which sociologists call "mediating structures," contributes to our location within a social world. To mediate is to be in the middle, linking two other things. Mediating structures have the power to give microsocial groups like families and small communities a voice and some power in the arena of macrosocial structures. As the example of the civil rights movement clearly indicates, a well-organized web of mediating structures—congregations, neighborhood organizations, civic associations—can indeed move macrosocial mountains. Chapter 6 of this book will show how understanding the logic of mediating structures allows intentional faith communities to be creatively and prophetically engaged with the larger social systems which shape our lives so profoundly.

CLOSING

Pressing, often overwhelming, sometimes demoralizing dilemmas face people in our time—issues, for example, of economic and social justice for African-Americans, women, and other marginalized groups. The hyper-individualism of Western culture makes solidarity with other persons a dilemma. Given the huge, intricate web of institutions and organizations confronting us in advanced industrial societies like our own, the possibility of participating in a group where a high quality of belonging is experienced through mutual relationships, where society and history are engaged and not retreated from, and where the centuries-old conversation called Christian tradition is faithfully and ritually celebrated in and for our time touches the deepest longings of many people.

This is indeed the claim and promise of small Christian communities. It is a claim not in the sense of ownership, but rather in the sense of a piece of earth to be worked painstakingly and with fidelity. And it is a promise not in the sense of a guarantee, but rather in the sense of a possibility which might unfold into concrete actuality. As we have seen in our discussion of mediating structures in this chapter, the social form we are calling small Christian community does indeed hold the potential not only for deeply creative interaction with other individuals (inner life) but also with the larger cultural, political, and economic structures of our world (public life). But this creativity will emerge in society and history in a sustainable way only if small Christian communities intentionally stake their claims and keep their promises in their specific social location and in fidelity to the sacred stories of their tradition.

At one level, an intentional commitment to Christian community is a promise to stay engaged over time with a particular group of persons in the four tasks described above. Such a promise gives the community a special right to our time, energy, and care. But at a deeper level, commitment makes our very *selves* available to specific others in a privileged way. Something of our cherished privacy and individuality is always given up in authentic commitment to community. This is in fact one of the major uphill struggles facing a movement of such communities in a country such as the United States, with its profoundly individualistic and autonomous world view and ethos. On the other hand, the distress that many Americans feel in our collective "pursuit of loneliness" is a powerful cultural incentive to a new form of belonging.

Beyond granting a particular group of persons privileged access to our selves, a commitment to community is an acknowledgment of the fact that being-related is central to human existence. It is a way not merely of coping with, but even of celebrating life as participation in a complex and diverse world of relationships. What we acknowledge in committing ourselves to intentional community is that our individual and collective identities do not exist prior to our relatings, but arise out of them. Our sense of identity—as individuals, Christians, or Americans—emerges from and is continually being transformed within our concrete web of connections to life.

Commitment to the shared life and work of an SCC is a recognition of the relational character of human life. Commitment to the shared life and work of a small Christian community is an acknowledgment of the sacred character of our relationships. Christians in small communities are attempting to allow the profoundly relational character of their sacred narrative to shape their existence profoundly. At the center of the dangerously liberating memory that is Christian tradition is a communitarian or relational vision of human life in the world. In such a vision my life is never just about me, it is always about us as well. We matter and we affect each other, all of us, living and dead.

We have said that commitment to a small Christian community entails a promise over time. There are many worthwhile experiences that can happen in an hour or a weekend or a month; intentional community is not one of them. There is an issue of continuity here, of the staying power of our claims and promises. When an intimate relationship is working well there is a strong tendency for persons to commit and recommit themselves to it. It is as if there is a natural strain toward permanence in creative, intimate relationships. In our experience an analogous point can be made as regards creative community dynamics—they naturally incline members toward commitment and recommitment.

The promise that is commitment to an SCC is generated and regenerated in the everyday acts of community life: in mutual conversation, collective engagement with the world, standing in common cause with others of similar purpose, and shared experiences of Christian memory and anticipation in word and sacrament; that is to say, in our shared praxis of *koinonia, diakonia, kerygma,* and *leitourgia.* In sustaining an inner and a public life in everyday acts over time, we come to feel the efficacy of intentionally belonging to an SCC flowing into and out of us. The disciplining, liberating conversation which is community is a relentless call to conversion.

CHAPTER FIVE

Conversation, Consensus, and Conflict

The Inner Life of Small Christian Communities

INTRODUCTION

The two passages of scripture that have most captured the Christian imagination are both from John. The first is that the Word was made flesh and pitched his tent among us. The second is that God is love. Each in its own way is as full of incredible requirement as it is of incredible consolation. Both passages force the worldly shape of God's presence and the worldly shape of God's love upon our sensibilities. One cannot take leave of the world, of historical experience, to find God. One cannot take leave of loving one's sisters and brothers to love God alone. Whoever claims to love God but meanwhile hates another person is a liar, says John. Whoever backs away from the difficult areas of human love backs away from the difficult areas of loving God. John didn't write those words, but he might have. In love we have to keep showing up whether we feel like it or not, and often we don't. Special moments in loving relationships are not random highs. They come as unplanned, uncontrived gifts, as sudden flowers—but only when the relational earth has been tilled and cared for. This chapter is about tilling relational earth in a garden called small Christian community, where our love for each other and our love for God are flowers on the same stem. The concrete demands of turning over relational earth—tilling it—are daunting. There's no flowering without it. That's why conversation and conversion are connected. We hope to place some of our contemporary interpretation of communication at the disposal of our understanding of the Body of Christ.

The glue that holds any web of relationships together is communication. In fact researchers have established the fact that human beings in each other's presence cannot *not* communicate! But when boundaries are not clear and people become overinvolved in each other's lives, relationship becomes fusion, and growth is stifled. It is equally true that when interaction remains politely superficial there is no real connection, and consequently no vitality, in interpersonal life. Creative relationship makes its appearance in the space between fusion and isolation.

Small communities of faith are not exempt from the principles which govern all interpersonal communication. In this chapter we explore the role of face-to-face interaction in SCCs, for the pulsing heart of a small community is its communicative interaction. The quality of communal existence can be no better than the quality of conversation which constitutes it. That is as true of our conversation with God as of our conversation with each other in community.

The concept of inner ("gathered") and public ("sent") dimensions discussed in the previous chapter is at the center of our analysis of small Christian communities. Before proceeding with our interpretation of the inner life of SCCs in this chapter, we must observe that the quality of both dimensions of a small community's life depends upon the adequacy and depth of communication among community members. There is no pre-existing blueprint for creating the two basic dimensions of the life of an SCC. Taking joint responsibility and holding one another accountable for that creative work is precisely what community membership entails. An inner and a public life emerge only through sustained, creative conversation within a community.

BIBLICAL PERSPECTIVES ON CONSENSUS AND CONFLICT

For members of small Christian communities, being with one another is never merely a pragmatic concern about good communication as a means to some other end. How we are together in the world with other persons is for Christians also a matter of religious significance. Members of SCCs are challenged by an authentic reading of their own sacred texts to take relationships in community life with ultimate seriousness.

The account of communication in SCCs which follows here is a modern-language version of the ancient awareness that relationships must embody certain qualities if they are to bear good fruit. Chief among these qualities is equal respect and care for one's own experience and that of others. To comport ourselves with such respect in our everyday communication is to engage in mutual conversation. It is one crucial expression of loving our neighbors as we love ourselves. For Jews and Christians such love is at the same time the primary symbol of our covenantal relationship with a God who loves us. The authentic religious heritage of Judaism and Christianity is primarily a communal and not an individualistic one. It shows how we are to be together in the world, not just how to be good individuals. It reminds us that "who is my neighbor?" is a very fundamental kind of question.

People must communicate with one another in certain ways, must engage in a certain quality of conversation, if the reality called community is to emerge among them in vital form—if, in the ancient Pauline language of our tradition, they are to become "one body in Christ and members of one another." When Paul offers directives about the truth that must characterize relationships, about handling anger and grudges, about the kind of language we ought to use in speaking to one another, about gentleness and patience, he is not speaking only of good community dynamics in a pragmatic sense, but of "the way you have learned from Christ," of "the one Body and one Spirit," of "the peace that binds you together." He is speaking of ultimate realities. We become the people of God as we become one Body.

That there is a crucial connection between the quality of interaction—of "one bodyness"—in Christian community and the ongoing, creative transformation of community members and their world is one of the central assumptions of the biblical tradition. This strong Jewish and early Christian emphasis on the social or relational character of being human has been dangerously eroded in modern Western culture. The contemporary American cultural ethic of individualism is a case in point. This erosion is also apparent in the widespread modern privatization of religion ("The only important question is: Have I accepted Jesus Christ as my personal savior?"). Within the dominant culture of individualism we have come to live as if we first exist and then form relationships in the pursuit of our interests.

The apostle who gave us the metaphor of the Body of Christ was not an academician who prepared treatises. He was a brilliant pastoral theologian responding to specific issues in community, and his theology welled up out of the encounter between his interpretation of the crucified and risen Christ and the specific issues of life in the communities he founded. Paul taught that if, as the Body of Christ, we are members of one another, then we are mutually implicated in one another's lives. The Greek word for "one another" is *allelon*, and it occurs 94 times in the New Testament, about a third of them in Paul's letters. He uses the word to describe what is best about community, when we honor one another, and what is worst in community, when we dishonor one another. We can pick up the flavor by seeing just a few of these as examples. The word *allelon* occurs in each of the following.

> I am longing to see you so ... that we may be strengthened together through our mutual faith, yours and mine (Rom. 1:12).

> In your brotherly and sisterly love let your feelings of deep affection for one another come to expression (Rom. 12:10).

> So then, my sisters and brothers, when you meet for the Meal, wait for one another [to eat] (1 Cor. 11:33).

> Greet one another with a holy kiss (2 Cor. 13:12).

When Paul hears of the self-centered behaviors of the Corinthian community at their gatherings for the Lord's Supper, he confronts them because they fail against *allelon*. He is not upset because they are being impolite, but because they fail to recognize that being the Body of Christ radically alters their relationships with one another. When Paul reprimands the community because they eat and drink "without discerning the body," he does not mean that they are failing to observe proper ritual rubrics, but rather that they have failed to recognize the Body which they are. They have failed to connect their behaviors outside of the Lord's Supper with the meanings that are lodged inside it.

Because of our connection with one another, Paul pleads for agreement between us, for all the consensus we can muster:

> So if in Christ there is anything that will move you, any incentive in love, any fellowship in the Holy Spirit, any warmth or sympathy, I appeal to you, make my joy complete by being of a single mind, one in love, one in heart, one in mind.... Make your own the mind of Christ Jesus (Phil. 2:1-2, 5).

For Paul the issue is almost ontological. One body can't have two minds! There has to be a singleness of spirit that animates us in our togetherness.

At the practical level of daily living, and especially in communities that have a tight enough texture to recognize and address the exigencies of common life, genuine mutuality is a necessity. Skills at building consensus are not simply desirable, they are requisite.

> May the God of encouragement help you to be like-minded toward one another (Rom. 15:5).

Paul is, of course, aware that community also has to face up to "tough love," to borrow a contemporary phrase. He knew that dealing with conflict stemming from differences was part and parcel of membership in the Body.

> My brothers and sisters, I am quite sure that you, in particular, are full of goodness, fully instructed, and capable of correcting each other (Rom. 15:14).

But it is to Matthew that we look for sustained attention to conflict resolution.

In Matthew 6 Jesus instructs his followers on the nature of prayer in words that have come to be known as "The Lord's Prayer." One of the petitions is, "forgive us our debts as we have forgiven those who are in debt to us." After the familiar prayer is completed, Matthew has Jesus underscore the reconciliation text:

> Yes, if you forgive others their failings, your heavenly Father will
> forgive you yours; but if you do not forgive others, God will not
> forgive you your failings either (Mt. 6:14-15).

This is an extraordinary teaching: our reconciliation with God depends utterly on our reconciliation with each other. It gives rise to the requirement that Christian community be a place of reconciliation. Understanding that, any community should certainly be pressed to develop effective ways of handling conflict, and Matthew's narrative even outlines a specific process for doing so.

> If your brother or sister does something wrong, go to them and
> have it out alone, between your two selves. If that does not work,
> take one or two others with you: whatever the failing, the evi-
> dence of two or three witnesses is necessary to sustain the
> charge. And if there is a refusal to listen, report it to the commu-
> nity. Finally, if that person does not listen even to the whole com-
> munity, it may become necessary to treat such a one as an
> outcast (Mt. 18:15-17).

Christian community cannot tolerate sustained failures of reconciliation.

As we noted in the introductory chapter, our word in this book for the kind of communication which makes one body of individual members is *conversation*. It serves as the inclusive framework for the material which has preceded in this book and that which follows. As Paul reminds us, Christian communities can create a vital shared life only by seeking *consensus* among their members. So we treat consensus in this chapter as the first of two critical moments of conversation within community life. As Matthew well understood, because people are different, authentic relationships inevitably entail some degree of *conflict*. Thus conflict is the second critical moment of conversation to be treated here. Conversation, consensus, and conflict as the heart of the inner life of SCCs, then, are the subject matter of this chapter.

CONVERSATION

> Conversation is a game with some hard rules: say only what you
> mean; say it as accurately as you can; listen to and respect what
> the other says, however different or other; be willing to correct or
> defend opinions if challenged by the conversation partner; be will-
> ing to argue if necessary, to confront if demanded, to endure nec-
> essary conflict, to change your mind if the evidence suggests it
> (Tracy 1987, 19).

> A precondition of friendly relationships was the systematic avoid-
> ance of any topic of conversation that might touch politics or reli-

gion and the concealment of everything that in fact divided them (Wright 1987, 152).

If the first quotation captures the ideal of face-to-face interaction, surely the second names what is all too often the reality. There is a way to move beyond fearful civility, while both maintaining the integrity of our own committed identities and doing respectful justice to the differing, even contradictory, views and values of others. The metaphor of "conversation" from contemporary hermeneutics offers a guiding image of this way.

In our lives together there are no uninterpreted facts. Dialogue between people is but one instance of the back-and-forth movement of questions and answers, agreements and disagreements, confusions and clarifications which characterizes all interpretation. The fact that we are typically unaware of this process of reciprocal interpretation, that so much of interpersonal and intergroup communication goes on seemingly automatically, makes it important that we come to an awareness of the ubiquitous process of reading and being read in everyday interaction. To be in dialogue is to interpret and be interpreted.

As we first listen to each other's positions, we will find ourselves agreeing, disagreeing, surprised, or confused in varying combinations and degrees of intensity. Initial interpretive reactions are an aspect of all face-to-face communication. They occur as your presentation of yourself interacts with my expectations, and mine with yours. These mutual expectations—what each of us takes for granted and values at the outset of our exchange—partially but importantly account for our initial responses to each other. First impressions are first interpretations. In order to transcend initial impressions, we must have the discipline to temporarily suspend concern with our own position in order to grasp the other's point. Attention to two levels of communication may help us to do so. Communications research has shown that all face-to-face messages are comprised of content and emotional dimensions. We will better understand each other's positions if we deliberately attend to what each of us is saying, and to the signs of its emotional significance. The former is typically conveyed in words, the latter, nonverbally in tone of voice, facial expression, and posture. It may also be the case that in order to grasp each other's points here and now, we may have to work at comprehending something of the history which has brought us to them. Once again, this requires that we temporarily suspend concern with the delivery of our own views.

The intentional, disciplined, temporary suspension of concern with one's own position which we are urging here is emphatically not to be equated with agreement with the other. In authentic dialogue the extent to which we finally agree and/or disagree must be allowed to emerge from our exchange. The more crucial the matters at stake, the less likely that things will be settled in initial efforts at mutual understanding. The purpose of these efforts at initial understanding is to build a bridge of trust and mutual respect for the subsequent negotiation of differences in interest and perspective.

When we have done the best we can to understand one another's positions, both initially and in whatever additional depth seems necessary and appropriate, the back-and-forth movement of authentic conversation may now more fruitfully unfold. This will include necessary moments of confrontation and argument, in which real differences are tested. Authentic conversation is a mutual search for truth and fairness. To enter into it, we must be prepared to subject all positions to a critical and creative suspicion, to expose and challenge systematic biases on both sides. Those seeking mutual conversation must be prepared, in the words of David Tracy, "to change our minds if the evidence suggests it."

Genuine communication is characterized as much by a willingness to modify one's own position in the light of convincing communication from another, as by the commitment to present one's own position and its warrants unapologetically. The capacity to be affected is as truly a sign of integrity as the capacity to have effects. Because of its thoroughly mutual character, participants in authentic interaction cannot know in advance what its outcomes will be. If we know how a prospective dialogue must (or must not) turn out, we have foreclosed the possibility of becoming caught up in the give-and-take of authentic conversation. All we can know in advance of any human interaction is that genuine receptivity to the other, including the painful possibility that the other's perspective may expose inadequacies in our own, is the necessary requirement for mutual conversion of heart and therefore for the reconciliation of differences.

As we jointly pursue the issue with which we are engaged in the back-and-forth movement named conversation, we are continually confirming, negating, confusing, or bringing each other up short. We are constantly making each other aware of similarities and differences between our respective positions. To allow what we habitually take for granted to be provoked, to risk provoking the other—and to sustain ongoing relationship when such mutual provocation occurs, these are the fundamental requirements of an authentic life with others. To behave otherwise is to seal ourselves off from the ongoing stream of revelation of which receptive and assertive mutual encounter is the wellspring. If we would say with Buber that in the realm of interpersonal relations as elsewhere, all real living is meeting, we must add in the same breath that all meeting is mutual interpretation. There is no such thing as uninterpreted meeting, in which we stand before each other as naked facts.

As we insisted in chapter 1, conversation requires a receptivity to otherness which always puts our world of meaning at risk. The source of that risk is clear: the other's communication has the power to affect our world view, that overarching interpretation of life itself through which we maintain coherent meaning. To have the meaning of one's very existence called into question is the ultimate risk for creatures of meaning. There may be no one with greater power to confirm or disconfirm our identities and values than those in the category of "enemy."

It is also the case that mutual interaction requires that we be prepared to indicate plainly where we stand on an issue and why. Mere receptivity is no basis for creative mutual conversation. The risk associated with disclosing, and where necessary defending, our views and values must be borne. Complete other-centeredness is not only illusory, but signals the abdication of one of the two primordial responsibilities of our relational lives. It is a failure of mutuality. The receptive and assertive solidarity that sometimes grows out of sustained mutual relationships requires exchanges in mutual vulnerability. Such exchanges lie beyond collusive civility, and inevitably put it at risk. It is perhaps not a coincidence that a poet born "between the mountain and the gantries" in the profoundly divided city of Belfast expressed so beautifully the subjective experience and ultimate significance of having one's world put under question.

> Yet each of us has known mutations in the mind
> When the world jumped and what had been a plan
> Dissolved and rivers gushed from what had seemed a pool.
> For every static world that you or I impose
> Upon the real one must crack at times and new
> Patterns from new disorders open like a rose
> And old assumptions yield to new sensation;
> The Stranger in the wings is waiting for his cue,
> The fuse is always laid to some annunciation (Macneice 1979, 195).

Receptivity to otherness even at the cost of extreme provocation to the world we take for granted, coupled with the willingness to risk the vulnerability associated with appropriate disclosure of one's own view: such is the double-edged discipline of authentic dialogue between persons and communities. As we meet in the reciprocally interpretive encounters of everyday life, the stranger in the wings is indeed waiting for a cue; the fuse is always laid to some annunciation. The ground of all such meeting is conversation.

While our particular focus here is upon the conversation of small Christian communities, we want to observe that the quality of conversation that constitutes the life of the larger institutional church benefits from the same attention to conversational dynamics. A church that for obvious reasons has been guided by a Eurocentric self-interpretation is now opening itself to become a world church. It will take new modes of conversation to allow the genius of the gospel to become incarnate in cultures in ways we never could have imagined. In order for Christianity to move out of Jewish confines, God worked through Peter's dreams to assure us that God plays no cultural favorites, and that means putting cultural presuppositions at risk, and with them, cultural appropriations of Christian discipleship. The Spirit is asking a lot these days.

The practical fruit of mutual meetings is the difference they make for the subsequent directions of our lives. Possible futures, ways that our lives might unfold, inevitably surface in authentic dialogue, in the form of invitation and confrontation. Those possibilities then await our response.

The genuinely mutual exchange that we have named conversation, which is difficult under any circumstances, becomes integrity-threatening under conditions of communal strife. The negotiation of fundamental interests of respect and inclusion is muted because a more primal interest—the community's survival—is put at risk in honestly dealing with such basic human interests. The civility which persons pragmatically and understandably adopt so as not to have everyday peace and security continually threatened by escalating cycles of animosity is finally a collusion in denial. Such collusion results when the world is not safe for the sacred game of conversation, with its admittedly hard rules and necessary vulnerabilities. Collusion and denial in the name of civility will never move persons with differing interests toward solutions responsive to the legitimate interests of all. Only the honest revelation and disciplined receptivity of real conversation can do that.

Receptivity to otherness in interpersonal conversation requires a willingness to have our interpretation of life put at risk. Others may be carrying a message which will force us into the painful realization that something else might, and perhaps should, be the case with our life. They may come bearing a radical affirmation of our existence. It may be that both things happen. Only the meeting will tell. Our name for such meeting, which we take to be integral to the vitality of any small community of faith, is conversation.

Levels of Mutuality in Conversation

In recent New Testament theology the expression "discipleship of equals" has gained currency, in large measure from the work of Elisabeth Schüssler Fiorenza. We mentioned earlier that God reminded Peter in a dream that God never plays favorites. Paul's expression of the discipleship of equals in Galatians 3:28 is unequivocal: for those baptized in Christ Jesus, privilege can neither be granted nor withheld because of gender, ethnicity, or social standing. The level ground of discipleship is, as it were, the ontological rationale for mutuality. There is no other way to honor who we are together. Jesus makes the point in Matthew 23, insisting that we are siblings because we all have the same Father [parent], a reality that requires us to avoid titles that belie mutuality. And, as Paul insisted, it is only the Spirit at work within us that makes us cry out "Abba," that makes us recognize that who we are together is because of who God is. The language of mutuality is the language of grace.

The basic relational option facing members of intentional community is either to enter conversation with one another or not. Conversation does not occur when we are unable to let others know about our point of view appropriately or when we let our frame of reference and agenda be the only, or at least the most important, one involved in communication with others. Conversation is made possible and limited by the capacity of persons to share their perceptions, feelings, wants, needs, beliefs, and knowledge appropriately with each other, and to understand accurately and to respect the differences that exist among them as these emerge in the community's conversation. In mutual conversation within SCCs, persons engage in direct and nonmanipulative interaction, with each attempting to understand and respect the frame of reference of others; controlling and being controlled are rejected as ways of being in relationship; consensus among respectful equals becomes the preferred mode of making communal decisions; and disagreement and conflict call for genuine negotiation.

In order for mutual conversation to characterize relationships among a community's members, those involved must be able and willing to tell their own stories, including the accompanying feelings; to understand accurately the events and feelings of other members' stories; to give constructive positive and negative feedback to members of the community at appropriate moments; and to receive feedback from others with a measure of openness. Disclosure, empathy, giving, and receiving feedback are thus the four basic moments of mutual conversation. Together they constitute the necessary everyday way of communicating together in SCCs. Please note the word "necessary" in the previous sentence. Without an adequate level of mutuality in its ongoing conversation, a group should not call itself a community. Note also that the other three core conversations of SCCs discussed in the previous chapter—with the social world as it is, with other groups and institutions in the web of mediating structures, and ongoing with the Christian tradition—are likewise necessary conditions. Considered alone, each of these four aspects is a necessary but not sufficient condition for authentic Christian community; taken together these four interrelated conversations constitute such a community.

The four moments of mutual conversation described above can be thought of as involving two basic levels. Disclosure and empathetic understanding constitute a primary level of conversation. At this level most of the time I will tell you where I am concerning the issue at hand appropriately and directly; you will understand my disclosure from my point of view and indicate your understanding to me. Most of the time you will say where you are, and I will receive your statement accurately. These reciprocal behaviors feed on each other. If you want to encourage me to tell you where I stand, one effective way is to give me access to your position and experience. If I want you to understand me from my perspective, I can try to walk in your shoes for a time. Engaging in these reciprocal behaviors consistently establishes a level of basic decency, trust, and care in human relationships. This is the basic or foundational level of mutual conversation.

Giving feedback and receiving feedback move conversation to a deeper level of mutuality, one in which, for the most part, I will convey my interpretation of your behavior or of events in our relationship appropriately and directly; and you will consider what I am saying with genuine openness prior to deciding whether you agree with my view. Most of the time you will be willing to give me similar feedback, and I will receive it as a gift for my consideration. Like self-disclosure and empathy, the giving and receiving of feedback also reinforce each other. If you want me to give you clear, direct, and specific feedback, it will help if you can offer such feedback to me. If I want you to take my feedback on board openly, I will try to do the same with your feedback to me. Engaging in these reciprocal behaviors consistently and well makes our relationship one of significant belonging and mutually creative transformation.

We describe the first level of mutual conversation as basic, because engaging in it is what makes it possible to move to the deeper level. If we want our community's inner life to grow to the deeper conversational level, we must consistently cultivate the primary one. For example, if you want me to take your feedback with openness, be sure that I have experienced your understanding. At the primary level of conversation we demonstrate basic respect and care for each other; at the secondary level we invite each other to ongoing creative transformation. Engaging consistently in primary level mutuality earns us the right to move to deeper levels of conversation.

The notion of four moments points out the building blocks of genuine conversation; the concept of two levels helps us to see conversation as a dynamic process at work between and among persons. Both aspects are crucial to a vital inner life in a SCC, and both are the product of an ongoing commitment.

As we noted in *Dangerous Memories,* if the members of an intentional Christian community are to move toward mutual conversation as the standard in their life together, five interrelated factors must come into play: self-esteem, working knowledge, skills, values, and norms (Lee and Cowan 1986, 127-133). The absence of any of these factors is sufficient to account for a lack of mutuality within the community's web of relationships; the presence to some degree of all of them is the bedrock of vital and creative conversation in SCCs.

Every human group is composed of persons with particular strengths and weaknesses as conversation partners. As we participate in various groups in our everyday lives, our communication skills may develop or diminish, but whatever happens in that regard is ordinarily haphazard. By contrast, the shared life of an SCC offers an ongoing experiential location wherein the capacity for conversation of every member, and therefore the overall depth and quality of mutual interaction within the entire community, can be deliberately and systematically enhanced. In the area of communication, among others, small communities function as learning communities.

Trust between and among members of an intentional Christian community is both a cause and an effect of mutuality. A kind of basic trust is required before we will risk disclosing ourselves to others; disclosing ourselves to others is one important factor in building trust among us. If the basis for trust inside us as individuals and among us as community members is quite limited, our capacity to let ourselves be known in community will be similarly limited. There is no more adequate way to build trust among us than to foster mutuality among us.

We close this discussion with a final word on conversation, intimacy, and mutuality. A perusal of the self-help section of any bookstore would reveal that some of the language and imagery just used—"disclosure," "empathy," "vulnerability"—is also invoked by the many authors writing today on the subject of intimacy. We, however, are not using "conversation" as a synonym for "intimacy," and believe that it is not helpful to do so. So what's the difference? We believe that the term "intimacy" is best reserved for the level of mutual exposure and vulnerability that we ordinarily associate only with the deepest relationships which can occur between two people. Intimacy, as we understand the term, is best reserved as a name for what happens between some spouses, family members, and friends, a level of self-revelation and response which would simply be inappropriate not only in the workplace, but also in SCC gatherings. We understand intimacy as two-person conversation at the deepest level; it is not and cannot be a group event. Such a depth of exposure and vulnerability is not a requirement for vital communication within an SCC, and to assume that it must be is to misunderstand what constitutes appropriate self-revelation in small community life. To speak quite plainly, someone who joins an SCC primarily in search of intimacy as we have just defined it is looking in the wrong place. We might summarize our view on this point in the following way: authentic intimacy always entails conversation, but authentic conversation need not be intimate. The mutuality necessary for any good conversation, not intimacy, is the appropriate standard for interaction in SCCs.

CONSENSUS

As we noted in introducing this chapter, there is no prefabricated plan for creating a community's inner and public life; these are matters about which community members must come to agreement. Within a community of mature adults, there is no one else to make those decisions. It is within the dynamic ebb and flow of conversation as defined above that community members seek to make mutually acceptable decisions regarding the shape of their inner and public commitments and the proper balance between them. The quality of our conversation sets the limit for the quality of our arriving at consensus. And because these matters cannot be settled once and for all in a dynamic community existing within an ever-changing world, the work of arriving at and revising consensus is ongoing.

By "consensus" we mean the process of arriving at shared decisions which are maximally respectful and inclusive of the differences in point of view, priorities, and values among members. Consensus, then, is a form of *shared* decision making. As such it may be contrasted with two other forms.

In *autonomous* decision making the designated leader of a group decides things by him- or herself. In *consultative* decision making the designated leader makes decisions, but only after conferring with other group members. In the form of joint decision making that we here call consensus, no one person or subgroup of people decides things for the community. Decisions are shared.

Group Conditions for Consensus

Paul often asks members of the various Christian communities to commit themselves to being of one mind, and that the one mind should be that of Jesus Christ. It would be a very naive reading to suppose that there must always be total agreement on all points. We know from the words that Paul uses—variations of the Greek verb *phronein*—that a better rendering might be something like this: *the meaning of the world and our life together in the world* should be a basic point of agreement, and Jesus Christ is the touchstone of meaning. That is the most fundamental call to consensus.

But Christians must engage in particular strategies that help build a particular world out of meanings they co-own. That particular world might be about what a family does, how two friends structure their friendship, the decisions a parish council makes for the life of the parish, or community organizing. So, functionally, we also have to reach consensus on many other issues than just the meanings out of which we live.

Researchers and experienced practitioners of consensus forms of decision making have identified a number of group conditions that foster high quality consensus: unity of purpose; equal access to power; autonomy from external, hierarchical structures; time; willingness to attend to process and attitudes; and willingness to learn and practice the skills required for consensus decision making (Avery, Auvine, Streibel, and Weiss 1981, 19-21). Each of these bears brief elaboration given the context and purposes of this book.

Without some *unity of purpose,* the attempt to seek group consensus is like having two people on either side of a boat row alternately—the boat ends up going in circles. In the context of an SCC we suggest that "unity of purpose" means some level of shared affirmation of the basic commitments to *koinonia, diakonia, kerygma,* and *leitourgia* as discussed in chapter 3. The specific ways in which each and all of those commitments are to be met by a particular community at this stage of its life is, of course, where the community must seek consensus. Like so many other dimensions of SCC life (for example, the relationship between trust and mutual conversation mentioned above) unity of purpose and shared decision making both require and strengthen each other. As our capacity to arrive at inclusive, respectful, creative consensus deepens, so does our unity of purpose; as our unity of purpose grows, so does our ability to seek and find good agreements.

Equal access to power is and ought to be one of the hallmarks of SCCs. Indeed, our experience has been that the wish for shared power as adult members of a community of faith is one of the great attractions which SCCs continue to hold for their members. This undoubtedly has much to do with an acutely felt exclusion from power in most persons' experience of both church and society. Equal access to decision-making power is particularly significant in addressing the pervasive sexism which women have routinely experienced in church membership, as well as the clericalism which has long denied lay people full participation in the Body of Christ. In faithfully and resolutely engaging in the practice of shared decision making, adult members of SCCs can reclaim a power which was always rightfully theirs, and learn to exercise it gracefully.

The issue of *freedom from external, hierarchical structures* flows directly from the previous point. As we noted in chapter 3, while all SCCs in the United States are outside the traditional mode of parish life, they have made their appearance in both more mainstream and more marginal forms. The choice of a form of relationship to the church's institutional structure characterizes an SCC as one or the other. The most mainstream SCCs are formed within and maintain strong connections to parish or congregational life. The most marginal communities take their stand outside parish or congregation, in a way which implies dissatisfaction with and critique of typical patterns of governance, worship, service, or fellowship. Both forms of SCC have emerged as a response to what is and is not occurring in institutional church practice. For that reason they will often and understandably be in varying states of tension with that structure. Tension is one source of growth in all healthy relationships.

Arriving at decisions via consensus ordinarily takes more *time* than autonomous or consultative decision making. It takes time for a group to clarify its understanding of an issue, as well as to share differing interpretations of the problem, its place within an overall set of priorities, and possible solutions. In any reasonably lively community, differences will be present in all these areas and more. A consensus decision requires weaving those differences together into a unique whole, one which could not have been arrived at by any individual group member precisely because it emerged from the members' conversation. Such a process can and does yield unpredictable and creative results, but only when a community is willing to put in the time to engage in it deeply, patiently, wisely, and respectfully.

A willingness to attend to process and attitudes as a condition supportive of consensus means that members of an SCC must be as concerned with the quality of their engagement with each other in consensus building as they are with its particular outcomes, and that they must note and respond appropriately to indicators of whether or not members are fully engaged with community decision making. Research in small group dynamics suggests that a satisfying process and constructive attitudes within a group are signs that the group is dealing adequately with four recurring issues of group life: inclusion, power, closeness, and collaboration. We will examine these issues later in this chapter.

Finally, *a willingness to learn and practice the relevant skills* is a crucial condition for building the capacity for reaching good agreements within an SCC. A skill is simply a behavior that we are able to engage in at will when it is appropriate. First and foremost the skills required for consensus are those of good conversation partners as discussed above: self-disclosure, empathy, giving constructive feedback, and receptivity to others' views. Beyond that there are particular skills which seeking consensus requires: brainstorming, selecting options, and collaborative planning. In SCCs the gift of these various skills will have been distributed differently by the Spirit throughout the membership. Given a consistent climate of mutual conversation and an ongoing commitment to decisions based on consensus, these gifts strengthen and multiply.

Steps in Building Consensus

There is, of course, no formula guaranteed to produce a good agreement among people. There are as many models for consensus available as there are for communication, leadership, or intimacy. The following series of steps, which is drawn from the literature on consensus and our own experience in SCCs and other small groups, offers one way of conceiving how an SCC might seek consensus on any issue which it faces. The subject of each of the following sentences is the community; a word will follow on the role of facilitators.

1. Specify the decision to be made clearly.
2. Provide all members with relevant background information at the outset of discussion and as necessary along the way.
3. Seek necessary clarifications regarding the decision and background information before proceeding to deliberate.
4. Converse together about what the community might do, given its resources and available background information.
5. Encourage all members to express their provisional views of the matter, including both possible solutions and value priorities.
6. Use a brainstorming process to generate a list of possible choices.
7. Identify the preferred choice(s) of the group at this juncture.
8. If there is more than one preferred choice at this juncture, explore each further, then test again for consensus.
9. Should consensus not be reached at this point, the community can decide to adopt a choice now because to do otherwise would have negative consequences, or to postpone a decision to allow for further prayer, reflection, and conversation on the matter.

Whoever is facilitating the community's conversation while consensus is being sought is responsible for keeping the conversation on the subject, clarifying statements by community members, encouraging participation, summarizing developing positions, and moving the conversation through the steps just outlined in a timely but flexible manner. That person must either take her- or himself out of the decision-making process except as facilitator or refrain from allowing her or his own views of the matter at hand to influence the process unduly. The reason that many experienced facilitators choose the former option is that the latter is often quite difficult, and sometimes impossible.

We have stressed that a willingness to attend to process and attitudes is a necessary condition for strong shared decision making. The following paraphrase of "Rules for Building United Judgment" from the Institute for Nonviolence Education, Research and Training is eloquently expressive of the spirit which must ground the behaviors just outlined if creative consensus building is to become a seasoned and integral dimension of the life of small Christian communities (cited in Avery, et al. 1981, 14).

1. The spirit of consensus is that of a calm, hospitable gathering of friends to determine truth, rather than a tense contest to see which side can prevail.
2. When the meeting becomes tense, or when people begin to repeat themselves, wait in silence.
3. If nothing new emerges, or if the atmosphere is becoming unfriendly and pressured, suspend judgment and agree to return to the matter again.
4. Take no action as a group until the matter has been satisfactorily resolved for all members of the group.
5. Be willing to repeat this process patiently as often and as long as it takes to find a mutually acceptable solution.

The above advice notwithstanding, we are not advocates of a pure (another word might be rigid) model of reaching consensus. That is, we do not believe that an SCC should in principle refrain from decisions until all members wholeheartedly agree. While that might be a desirable outcome, it is a rare one in the real world, and not necessary for vital group life. A "good enough" agreement is the standard we propose for SCCs seeking consensus. By that we simply mean that, while all members of the community may not fully agree with a particular course of action, they feel that their views have been respectfully considered, and they can live with the choice in good faith. A member not in full agreement with a particular choice may nevertheless opt to go along with it because he or she realizes that to do so is preferable to doing nothing. It is, of course, possible that situations may arise where a member may choose to leave the community rather than assent to a particular agreement. We have seen such choices made in an atmosphere of respect for the integrity of all involved. Our conviction that "good enough" consensus is good enough is partly based on the assumption noted above that in the life of a vital SCC the process of coming to agreements is as important as the agreements reached.

A final word on this important subject. Remember that consensus is a moment within a more fundamental process named conversation. When community members are seeking consensus, just as when they are sharing their faith or engaging in social analysis or supporting one another through difficult times, they are in conversation with each other. So the keys to reaching satisfying, creative, respectful agreements are appropriate disclosure, accurate empathy, and giving and receiving constructive feedback. Shared decisions characterized by wisdom, creativity, respect, and integrity arise among conversation partners who learn to speak the truth in love to one another.

CONFLICT

The earliest New Testament texts, the writings of Paul, frequently address divisions in the Christian community and outline fundamental attitudes that people need to adopt to address conflict. From Acts we learn that conflict was there in the beginning. There was even conflict between John, Mark and Paul that made Paul refuse to engage in missionary travel with him. An entire chapter in Matthew's Gospel is devoted to conflict and reconciliation. Matthew insists that being forgiven by God depends upon our own abilities to reconcile with each other. That is frightening, yet we commit ourselves. Community like friendship and love is never free of conflict.

Conflict has a bad reputation in polite company generally and in Christian company particularly. Did not many adult Christians grow up with a more or less clear sense that angry outbursts were sins? Unfortunately, too many people's experiences of conflict are laden with unresolved feelings of anxiety, sadness, anger, and shame. In fact, many adults unknowingly continue to have the limits of their understanding and ability to deal with conflict set by childhood experiences. As a consequence, some of us flee conflict as we would the ebola virus, others seek out every opportunity to re-engage in the unresolved battles of childhood in nonproductive ways, while perhaps most folks deal with conflict when they have to but would much prefer to have it leave us alone.

One of our colleagues, an expert in negotiation, entitles one of his seminars not "Conflict Resolution" or "Conflict Management" but "Conflict Utilization," because of his judgment that conflict situations are valuable, perishable moments in the life of groups and institutions. We want to explore his countercultural intuition a bit further as the prelude to this section. Rather than some kind of error or breakdown or sin, conflict is better understood as arising naturally because of differences in people's assumptions, perceptions, needs, feelings, thoughts, values, expectations, and goals. Where there are differences, there will be conflict. A group that is conflict-free has somehow suppressed its awareness of its differences beneath a facade of shared vision. It has also deprived itself of its primary source of growth. Recall for a moment our discussion of the crucial place of the "other" in the life of conversation. We find out far more about who we are, about our strengths as well as our limitations, in the presence of one who differs from us than we do in interacting with someone who shares much of what we already know and believe. The truth of this observation is best illustrated by the phenomenon of cults, in which uniqueness and therefore diversity must be surrendered at the gate as a condition of belonging. Once that surrender is made, there is no other to let us see ourselves. There is only more of the same.

Even if we were able to re-evaluate conflict so that it began to appear to us as a resource to be utilized for growth, we would still face the question of how to respond constructively. Our purpose in this section is to share with SCC members and leaders one well-tested and highly regarded model for dealing well with the opportunities that conflicts provide. In 1981 Roger Fisher and William Ury of the Harvard Negotiation Project published a book entitled *Getting to Yes: Negotiating Agreement without Giving In.* It has since become the most widely used and frequently cited practical resource for dealing with conflict in the English-speaking world. As fate, or more likely the tastes of popular culture would have it, another best-selling work on negotiation entitled *Looking Out for Number One* was published at the same time. A perceptive review in *Newsweek* magazine nailed the difference between the two books squarely on the head. The underlying philosophy of the latter work is clearly revealed in its provocative title—negotiation is about getting as much of what you want as you can. To negotiate is to look out for your own interests. We need not deny the partial truth of this view, even as we recognize its grievous inadequacy. The underlying assumption about negotiation in *Getting to Yes* is, however, quite different. The authors refer to the process taught in their book as "principled negotiation." The principle which underpins their method is that a good agreement must respond fairly to the legitimate interests of both parties, that it is in both parties' interest that any agreement meets the needs of all involved, especially when negotiation goes on in the context of a continuing relationship. It is a principle which we endorse in the context of SCCs, perhaps not least because it is so profoundly congruent with the biblical injunction to love the neighbor as the self. Indeed, it provides community members with a quite straightforward means of moving that injunction from notion to behavior.

The method of principled negotiation of conflict involves four steps, which we shall describe and illustrate. The first step is to *focus on issues, not on personalities.* When we find ourselves in the presence of difference become conflict, it seems quite natural to hone in on the other—their stubbornness, selfishness, short-sightedness, and need to control—as if that is where the problem lies. Then our challenge is to overcome or overwhelm these limitations in the other. The other, of course, is typically doing the same thing on her or his side of the problem: that is, seeing our personal shortcomings as the source of the conflict, and responding accordingly. That these are not propitious vantage points from which to resolve differences becomes even clearer when we recognize how quickly, indeed instantaneously, they spawn circular arguments. The wife who says to her husband, "I'd be much more willing to cut down on my drinking if you weren't nagging me about it all the time," is very likely to receive the following rejoinder: "If you would just cut down a little on the drinking, I wouldn't have to hassle you about it so much." From her perspective the source of the problem is his nagging, from his, it is her drinking. As long as they hold to their respective views and act accordingly, the outcome—an escalating vicious cycle of mutual misunderstanding, blame, and defensiveness—is highly predictable. Chronic conflicts between persons and groups very often involve this process of an escalating, circular focus on the other-as-problem.

The simple, but not easy, alternative to the trap of mutual blame is to shift the focus of conversation from personalities to the issues on which the parties differ. Fisher and Ury offer four communicative guidelines for accomplishing this.

1. "Listen actively and acknowledge what is being said." Nothing interrupts a process of unproductively focusing on and blaming the other more expeditiously than working to understand and convey to them our comprehension of their position. One person cannot actively listen to and acknowledge another and blame them at the same time. When either party caught up in a cycle of mutual blame stops, the entire process is interrupted. And as we insisted in our treatment of conversation, to understand another's view is not to agree with it, or to surrender one's own.

2. "Speak to be understood." The emotional pressures and intensities of conflictual situations too often lead us to speak aggressively or defensively to the other, rather than attempting to explain our position as simply and clearly as possible. Like listening actively, speaking to be understood often interrupts an unproductive focus on the other's shortcomings. To be understood is not to dominate or to win, but to represent one's position assertively and fairly.

3. "Speak about yourself, not about them." It is unfortunate that this insight has been trivialized in the self-help and personal growth literature into an unnuanced exhortation to make "I statements." Without some practical wisdom about when speaking in the first person singular makes sense and why, such advice carries little weight. In the context of negotiation the importance of speaking about your own experience is captured in the difference between accusing someone of selfishness and naming your disappointment or hurt or anger in response to some specific action of theirs. The latter is harder to dismiss than the former.

4. "Speak for a purpose." The anxiety provoked by situations of conflict often pushes people toward two extremes, running off at the mouth or withdrawal into muteness. In an emotion-laden situation, too much disclosure on your side makes it harder for me to negotiate with you, and too little makes it impossible. One requirement for being able to negotiate well is to have a reasonably clear awareness of what we are trying to accom-

plish in negotiating and the skill and assertiveness to name it at the right time, neither under- nor overstating our position.

These four behaviors give us valuable guidance on how to focus on issues rather than personalities. The best way to invite the other into this way of negotiating is simple: do it yourself. To do so is to take the first step in principled negotiation.

The second step in principled negotiation is to *focus on interests, not positions.* In teaching small community members and leaders to recognize and utilize this difference over the past ten years, we have come to the judgment that it is the most insightful point in this remarkably valuable model of constructive negotiation. People who understand the difference between interests and positions, and who can put their understanding into action, are well on their way to utilizing conflict creatively. Fisher and Ury teach this point most effectively by way of the following story.

> Two men [are] quarreling in a library. One wants the window open and the other wants it closed. They bicker back and forth about how much to leave it open; a crack, halfway, three quarters of the way. No solution satisfies them both.
>
> Enter the librarian. She asks one why he wants the window open; "To get some fresh air." She asks the other why he wants the window closed: "To avoid the draft." After thinking a minute, she opens wide a window in the next room, bringing in fresh air without a draft (Fisher and Ury 1981, 41).

Those who seek to utilize conflict as a source of growth through a process of principled negotiation will do well to remember and reflect on this parable. "I want the window open" is a position; "to get some fresh air" is an interest. "I want the window closed" is a position; "to avoid the draft" is an interest. A "position," then, may be defined as a proposed resolution to a problem or choice facing two or more people, while an "interest" may be defined as the agenda underlying a position. We want to stress the point that one key to dealing with conflict creatively is not letting your positions override your interests!

The authors of *Getting to Yes* make a persuasive argument that all too often what passes for negotiation is actually a process of compromising mechanically between positions. If I have a car to sell and am asking $2000 for it, and you offer me $1600, it would not be unusual for us to strike a bargain by splitting the difference, that is, compromising between our respective starting points by agreeing to a sale price of $1800. It just seems fair somehow to proceed in this fashion, does it not? But what if my initial position, or yours, was really a bargaining ploy having nothing to do with the market value of the car? As long as we simply shift positions in the effort to compromise, the merits of what is being negotiated need never arise. Perhaps such positional bargaining works reasonably well in one-time transactions like selling a used car to a stranger, but how do we split the difference between positions when we are in conflict about the division of labor and rewards in our workplace or an acceptable balance between career and family commitments in a marriage, or the tension between inner and public commitments in an SCC?

Simple positional compromise is typically not much help in such circumstances because it does not allow us to get to the interests underlying real-life conflicts. Fisher and Ury propose that a reliable way to move from positions to interests is to take any position and ask why it is being taken. Toward what ends are negotiators of a decision or conflict taking their respective positions? What are they trying to accomplish, that is, what are their interests? We have observed, for example, that in many contemporary SCCs an almost predictable tension can arise between women and men around a variety of inner and public issues. From the perspective of principled negotiation this suggests that a basic interest of some kind is in conflict beneath the surface of conflicting positions on specific matters. When small communities get to the interest underlying this tension, it will often prove to be some form of the question of equal recognition of the talents and rights of women to exercise leadership in all aspects of the life of the community. No amount of compromising on positions will make this fundamental issue go away. It must be addressed forthrightly as a fundamental question pervading all community decisions. Two thousand years of patriarchal disrespect and disempowerment of women within Christianity cannot be exorcised by polite compromise. A much more demanding conversation is required of those who would see that pattern brought to a halt. And one of the places where it is being halted today is among women and men in small communities of faith.

Because a good agreement is one which is responsive to the legitimate interests of all parties involved, to engage well in a process of principled negotiation entails being clear about our respective interests. (The word "legitimate" in this context simply indicates our conviction that dominating or disrespecting another is never a legitimate negotiating interest.) Community members must become adept at recognizing why they are advocating a particular decision during a consensus-building process, as well as developing their capacity to recognize other members' interests. In doing so they will do well to recall that parties in conflict always have not one but rather a range of interests. Some of these will be shared between them, some will be unrelated, and some will be in conflict. Good consensual decision making explores this range of interests, seeking possible agreements responsive to legitimate concerns of all parties.

A last word on the subject of interests: Fisher and Ury remind us that we usually have two kinds of interests as negotiators, resolving the issue at hand and sustaining our relationship with the other for the future. In SCCs, where *koinonia* is a fundamental commitment, the interest in sustaining relationships is present in a particularly strong form—indeed, as a sacred value—in all attempts to negotiate. The method of principled negotiation teaches that the best way to strengthen a relationship for the future is to negotiate mutually respectful agreements in the present.

The third step in principled negotiation is to *invent options for mutual gain.* In light of the preceding discussion of interests, it becomes apparent that "mutual gain" means "responsive to the interests of all parties." If the relevant interests have been well articulated and understood by both sides, the next step is to craft possible agreements that are responsive to those interests. This ordinarily requires generating a list of possibilities, prioritizing them in relationship to the relevant interests, and compromising as necessary so that all parties' interests are recognized in the final agreement. Compromise around interests is the real stuff of all negotiations: how do we fairly and wisely balance the differing, legitimate interests of all parties by creating an agreement with which we all can live? As we hope the foregoing explanation makes clear, attempting to compromise by adjusting positions actually keeps parties with differences from getting to an exploration of their real interests, and, therefore, precludes the possibility of seeking new options for mutual benefit.

The authors of *Getting to Yes* suggest that negotiators who have assumed the posture of inventing options for mutual gain have figuratively shifted from facing each other as the problem across the table to sitting side by side with the problem in front of them to be jointly resolved. As in the wonderful story of the library windows, there are often other positions than the ones which the parties to a conflict initially take which quite adequately meet the real interests of those involved. Once again the caution here is clear: do not let your positions defeat your interests.

The fourth and final step in the process of principled negotiation is to *agree on criteria for monitoring the agreement.* This simply means specifying who is responsible for doing what and by what time. Experienced negotiators and mediators are well aware of the fact that what is accomplished in the arduous work of the first three negotiating steps can be lost if the parties involved fail to agree concretely and unambiguously about what each will do and the time-line for doing it. The underlying interest here is mutual accountability. Agreements don't work just because they have been reached; they work when they are implemented. Specifying criteria for monitoring an agreement allows those involved to practice mutual accountability. These criteria reduce the possibility that at a later date one or the other party can say "I didn't realize that's what you expected me to do," or "We never agreed to a specific date." There is no genuine consent without agreement, and no effective agreement without specific commitments.

We ask you to remember that conflict, like consensus, is a moment within the ongoing process of conversation within a web of relationships, and that it is not a sign that something is wrong, but that there are differences present which must be addressed. An SCC's capacity to deal with conflict sets a limit on the depth and quality of its inner life. For any community (indeed, for any relationship) the question is not whether there is such a limit, but rather where it is. Like families and friendships, SCCs unravel when problems are not addressed forthrightly. Members of a community which has never experienced a significant conflict have simply not drawn close enough to each other to warrant being called a community. Engaging in the disciplined form of conversation called principled negotiation allows community members to test the limits which their differences have placed on their relationships.

A final, pointed suggestion: Get a copy of *Getting to Yes,* read it together, and put it in your SCC's library!

STAGES IN THE INNER LIFE OF A SMALL CHRISTIAN COMMUNITY

For better and for worse, communication goes on from the first instant of the first meeting of an SCC until the last moment of its final meeting. We have tried to show here that the foundational task in creating a vibrant inner life in a community is to make communication become conversation. We conclude this chapter by moving one step further. The literature on small groups and our own experience with small communities suggest that there is a certain predictability to what members of SCCs will find themselves conversing about.

In a splendid essay entitled "Leadership and Power," our colleague Evelyn Eaton Whitehead draws on contemporary social psychological studies of small group development to identify four recurring issues in the life of all groups: inclusion, power, closeness, and effectiveness. While all four issues are always present in the life of a group, they tend to come into focus at different times, and often in a somewhat predictable sequence. "The best image perhaps," she writes, "is one of shifting priorities: at different moments in our life together as a group, different questions come to 'center stage' and demand more of our time" (Whitehead 1987, 52). The life of SCCs will predictably involve cycling and recycling through times of primary concern with these four issues. Let's look briefly at each of the four basic tasks of group life.

Inclusion is the task of group life that involves members coming to be a part of a group's interaction, to feel as if they belong. In the absence of an adequate sense of being included on the part of at least most of its members, a group will not be able to muster the collective energy necessary to fulfill either side of its mission. In the formative stage of an SCC, hospitality, the personal welcoming of members to the newly forming group, is crucial. There is no more profound way of including people in the life of an intentional community than by inviting them to tell their stories and then acknowledging the contributions that are forthcoming. It is important that anyone functioning as a leader at this juncture share her or his own stories and hopes for the community's life, for in doing so they identify themselves as conversation partners in an incipient community of equals.

An important way to foster the telling of stories and sharing of gifts is by providing a simple structure to help a community get going. The literature on small group dynamics demonstrates clearly that such a structure can support and integrate a group while its own inner cohesion has the opportunity to develop. These beginning structures of inclusion must, of course, be in the service of the group building up its own identity and agenda, rather than promoting anyone's personal agenda. Potential community members will be quite sensitive to which of these approaches is actually operating.

While belonging is inevitably a focal issue in the beginning of an intentional Christian community, inclusion issues can and will arise from time to time throughout the life of any group. In that sense, as Whitehead's comment quoted above indicates, these issues never go away.

Power is the task of group life in which members learn to engage in mutual influence in a creative, reciprocal fashion. The issue here is how a group enables its members to exercise their different gifts appropriately and potently in the service of the group's mission. Groups always function as more or less than the sum of their individual members. A group's power or influence will similarly be more or less than the individual powers of its members, depending on the kind of leadership resources it mobilizes.

When an intentional Christian community is relatively comfortable as regards inclusion, it becomes highly likely that a kind of contest of influence will emerge in some form. When it does, whoever had been exercising a leadership role is likely to experience a challenge. These contests and challenges vary in their quality and intensity, from bitter and hostile attacks to assertive and respectful proposals of alternative courses of action for the community's life. Whitehead reminds us that, far from simply being negative events, this development signals a growth in group maturity. She also notes that leaders need not be passive victims of attacks during these inevitable attempts to balance power among us. She writes:

> The designated leader is usually in a position of some considerable power when the first questioning of leadership occurs. If the leader uses that power against the group member who questions, the rest of the group learns that new patterns of power will not be easily won. The message is given that the stakes are high in the process of change. If, however, the designated leader does not respond to this question as if it were a personal attack, a different tale is told. The message here is that power in the group need not be interpreted as a personal possession and jealously guarded from attack. Rather it is a resource of the group that needs to—

and can—be examined, accounted for, and even redistributed among us (Whitehead 1987, 59).

A creative inner life in small Christian communities means embracing and fostering the mutual, reciprocal practice of influence and initiative—the practice of relational power—among community members.

Closeness is the task of group life which involves negotiating an adequate and appropriate degree of personal revelation among members. Because an SCC has some of the characteristics of a family and some of a formal organization, it must find a level of personal sharing which is suitable to its goals and fits with the needs and preferences of its particular members.

Within some small Christian communities, the sharing of feelings and dreams and the willingness to work on relationships between and among members will tend in a deeply personal direction. Membership in such communities may be a primary source of emotional support and challenge, of companionship and closeness, in the lives of their members. Or cordial, supportive, but less personally involving relationships may prevail in a community, with members finding their primary connections elsewhere. As long as an adequate degree of mutual conversation is present within a community, either of these options, or any point between the two, offers a perfectly legitimate resolution of the issue of closeness. It is also not uncommon for communities to find that their norms and behaviors around closeness go through significant changes over time, changes that must be worked out in ongoing negotiation.

Dealing well with this issue of group life involves recognizing that differences are likely to exist in members' hopes and fears regarding closeness among them, and negotiating these differences directly, respectfully and with an appropriate measure of flexibility in the spirit of principled negotiation. At a deeper level, growth in this area calls for an awareness of how the unresolved wounds of past relationships can create barriers to closeness within an SCC, as well as a sense of when these barriers can be appropriately worked on within the community and when outside help is required for individual members or the entire community. Because of the intensely personal character of questions of closeness and the strong feelings they tend to generate in all of us, this issue will put the conversational skills and commitments of community members to the test in a unique way.

Effectiveness is the task of group life which involves movement from mission to goals to action to evaluation. In these moments of a group's life, Whitehead writes, "Its chief priorities now are clarity about its task and the effective use of its resources to meet this goal." If the basic tasks of SCCs are to develop an inner and a public life, then the effectiveness of such communities has to do precisely with the quality of their sustained efforts along those lines.

The pursuit of effectiveness is a matter of nurturing the community's sense of mission and vision, fostering community consensus about particular goals, coordinating and stewarding the resources of the community in pursuing its chosen agenda, assisting the community to evaluate its effectiveness realistically, and keeping the results of such evaluation in conversation with the community's mission and vision. Such conversation requires many of the kinds of working knowledge and skills that professional managers in our society use every day; what is different, of course, is the ultimate context within which members of SCCs locate their concern for community effectiveness. Authentic Christian communities are never concerned with effectiveness for its own sake or for the sake of profitability; they are always concerned with their effectiveness in inserting the dangerous memories and transformative hopes embedded in the Christian story into their history and society.

The presentation of each of these four issues in sequence may leave readers with the impression that all are of equal weight or require the same degree of effort from community members. This is not the case. While the experience of particular communities might be otherwise, our view, and that of others experienced with small group and community dynamics, is that a hierarchy of relative difficulty of the four issues would be as follows: power, closeness, effectiveness, and inclusion. Power is the relatively most difficult issue to deal with, and inclusion the relatively least difficult. Closeness and effectiveness fall somewhere in between. Please note that we are speaking here not of the relative importance of these issues, but of the relative difficulty of confronting them.

Gifts for community leadership in the areas of inclusion, power, closeness, and effectiveness do not automatically belong to those who may be currently designated as leaders, but are distributed within the community as a whole. Different moments of need in the ongoing conversation of the community will call forth these different gifts.

CLOSING

We are familiar with the situation in which good people are unable to accomplish certain tasks because they lack appropriate skills. That happens sometimes to each of us. The skills that facilitate consensus building and conflict utilization are not just pragmatically effective—they are redemptive of our life together in Christ Jesus. They may be our good work, but when they operate within our shared life because of our commitment to build up the Body of Christ, they are works of grace.

Seeking consensus and resolving conflict are critical moments within the ongoing conversation which constitutes a small Christian community. Commitments to working collaboratively to forge consensus that respects differences and to seeking reconciliation when difference becomes conflict are pledges to remain open to conversion. That is why Paul and Matthew placed such stress on being of one mind and dealing with conflict soundly in their respective communities. Conversation makes it possible to reject the narrow individualism of the dominant culture and seek the relational self-hood which appears in the biblical tradition's classic images: a world of just and merciful relationships; a world wherein the neighbor is loved as the self; a world where the widow, orphan, and alien are recognized as siblings; a world of peace. Conversation requires of SCC members an ongoing receptivity to conversion as they participate in forging their communities' inner and public lives.

CHAPTER SIX

Seeking the *Shalom* of the City

The Public Life of Small Christian Communities

INTRODUCTION: SCOPE AND LIMITATION

Something needs to be said at the outset of this chapter about the scope and limitation of mission—of being sent. First the scope. The Christ event is about God's intentions for our world, for our life together. The mission of community is incomprehensible in breadth and variety. Evangelization is a sending that tells the story where it has never been told before. There is the evangelization of culture, of my family life, of my work place, of my friendship, and—be it said—of the church itself. We are sent short distances as well as long, on small tasks as well as large. Our sending is always tailored to our gifts and energies. We are not sent at age seventy to do what we may have been sent to do at age twenty. We are sent on works of charity. We are sent on works of justice. We are sent on spiritual works of mercy and corporal works of mercy.

Our emphasis in this chapter, however, is a limited one. We want to focus upon justice issues in political and economic systems. We want to focus upon the potential of small Christian communities to make a real contribution to the *shalom* of the city. This is not the only work of God in human history, but it is an integral one.

Choosing this focus reflects two priorities. The first is that in this century we have come to a far better understanding of the impact of systems upon individual lives. That is why the church has become increasingly articulate about social justice in its teaching voice. As a church, we have a long history of commitment to works of charity. These are certainly not being abandoned. But if we meet immediate need and do not address the systemic causes of immediate need, we risk inadvertently extending the life of unjust systems by picking up the pieces they leave scattered.

The second priority comes from our conviction that within U.S. culture we are much more likely to focus upon a community's inner life. Our propensity to form support groups is well documented. In our judgment, a critical challenge to small Christian communities is to develop their faith's effective public life. Therefore, we are paying extended attention to this factor.

A further limitation to the scope of this chapter is that we have frequently chosen to reflect upon faith's public life from the perspective of very specific experience, that of broad-based community organizing. We speak from this experience because it is our experience, and it works—not perfectly, perhaps, but well. Our experience is not the only way of working for the *shalom* of the city. It is one way that, for us, has become compelling.

FAITH'S PUBLIC LIFE

The purpose of this chapter is to develop the theme of the public life of small Christian communities which we introduced in chapter 4. We want to provide a framework for thinking socially and religiously about the larger public life of our society, and then describe an example of such thinking in action. As we proceed we will retrieve the previously introduced concept of mediating structures and show how such structures hold the key to small communities of faith forging an authentic public life. We will end by describing an effort underway by SCCs to forge a strong public presence within their surrounding community through the medium of a broad-based community organization.

Two caveats are important at the doorway to this chapter. First, we have learned that the concept of organizing for power has a way of making white Christians nervous. Western culture's understanding of power as unilateral, and the regular exercise of that form of power in ways that do great harm to people and the earth, would give any thoughtful person pause. Our focus in this chapter is on organizing for power to be exercised relationally for the common good of a larger community. Second, the principles and practices of organizing to confront failures of justice and mercy in the organizations and institutions of public life are applicable not only to secular public life but to the public life of the church as well. We are convinced that one of the reasons why the institutional church changes so slowly is that its adult members have not yet learned how to exercise their proper authority in shaping church life by discovering how to organize themselves effectively to address prejudiced or capricious institutional decisions. Abuses of power and authority within the institutional church can be effectively confronted only by people who have learned to organize themselves well by observing how such organizing works in confronting secular power-brokers.

As we insisted in chapter 4, the public life of SCCs is about "evoking cries that expect answers," and "learning to address them where they will be taken seriously" (Brueggemann 1978, 22). It is in forging powerful public partnerships with others seeking the common good of the larger community and society that SCCs develop their prophetic imaginations and join their voices with others in a prophetic chorus.

We want to begin exploring how SCCs develop their public side by calling attention to our typical associations to two words. What does the term "public person" mean to you? For most of us what probably comes to mind is one of two kinds of people: celebrities from the arenas of entertainment, sports, or business; or politicians. Bruce Springsteen, Michael Jordan, Lee Iacocca, and President Clinton are public people. The concept of public personhood in our time is fed from two streams. The first is notoriety or name recognition, the second is involvement in electoral politics. Sometimes these streams come together in the careers of individuals whose fame in some area of life combines with subsequent involvement in electoral politics. Thus the ultimate "public person" would be the celebrity who becomes a politician— Dwight Eisenhower, for example, or Ronald Reagan. Understood in this way, and this is the dominant cultural understanding of publicness in Western democracies today, you or I or anyone else who is not famous or involved in electoral politics or both is not a public person.

There is, however, another more ancient and powerful way of understanding public life as essential to the character of our personhood. It begins today, as it must always begin, with the recognition that decisions are made daily which lead to outcomes affecting our whole social body. Let us give one concrete example of such a decision and its consequences. There is a large, metropolitan county in the center of the United States which is divided into twenty-three public school districts. In one of those more than $8,700 was spent per pupil during a recent school year; in another just over $3,100 was spent per pupil. This pattern repeats itself around the country today wherever great economic differences between urban and suburban living conditions are found, unless decisions have been taken at the state level to equalize spending per pupil. (Remember that this example deals with public education, that is, education supported by taxpayers.)

In this book we are defining public life as the arena within our society wherein decisions like the one we have just cited—decisions affecting the common good, decisions about matters such as job creation, employment, education, health care, housing, and pollution—are made. Public life is the place where citizens and people of faith exercise or fail to exercise our responsibilities for seeking the common good. It is the place where decisions are taken which mean:

- that each child of a wealthy suburban school district will typically have significantly more money spent on his or her education than each child of an inner-city district,
- that the viability of public education is increasingly subject to question and challenge especially in the great cities of this nation,

- that one in five children in the United States grows up in poverty,
- that in the United States, a nation that is 12 percent black and 84 percent white, there are proportionally more black prison inmates and welfare recipients than white,
- that if our planet were a village of one thousand people, seven hundred of us would be illiterate, five hundred of us would be hungry, and sixty of us would control half our total income.

Public life happens outside the boundaries of family and friendship, or it is supposed to at any rate! Public life is the social space where democratic citizens and those who hunger and thirst for justice must learn to register our claims competently and persistently. It includes but is not limited to what we call electoral politics. The right to vote and even the act of voting are in actuality minimal expressions of an authentic public life. The major crisis in the collective life of citizens of this country, namely the unraveling and discrediting of genuinely democratic governance, is a crisis of what we are calling public life.

Let's pause for a moment while you consider your personal response to a word which surfaces almost immediately when conversation turns toward public matters. The word is "politics." What are the adjectives which you most strongly attach to politics as it is carried out in our society today? How about "crooked," "corrupt," "untrustworthy," "wasteful," and "ineffective"? The frequency of such associations gives us a crude but real measure of how we feel democratic governance is working today. Low voter turnout for elections is another such measure. These are indicators of the degradation which our experience of public life has undergone. For the most part public life in our time has become equated with a corrupted and partisan politics, and if we attend to it at all we typically do so as disapproving but ineffectual spectators and complainers.

It is, however, important that we temporarily suspend our contemporary contempt for politics so as to be able to reflect critically on the political dimension of human existence in two particular ways. The first is philosophical and, at the limit, theological. Politics is about power, and power names the capacity to have effects (which we associate readily with power) and to receive effects (which we tend to associate not with power but with its opposite). To exist is to have effects and to be affected. To exist, therefore, is to be involved with power. If power has come to be equated with domination in Western culture, it is because our communal understanding and shared practice of power as a unilateral rather than a relational reality is distorted and distorting. To affect public life is to exercise power, to have a real influence on decisions that affect the common good. As we noted in our discussion of relational power in chapter 2, to be powerful is not simply to act unilaterally with only one's own group's interests in mind. The conception of power as one-directional has distorted our understanding not only of humanity but also of divinity. A unilateral vision of power yields a world view populated by rugged individualists who need nothing from other persons and owe them nothing, and an immutable and impassive God who cannot change or be affected by others.

Our second gloss on politics is historical, requiring that we retrieve an important bit of our Western cultural heritage. Politics is about how we behave together in the *polis*, in the city, or more inclusively, within whatever real world community we exist. Politics in the Greek tradition was the name for the process whereby adult citizens worked out among themselves ways to provide for the common good. Building on Aristotle in this as in so much else, Aquinas characterized politics as a practice of moral virtue. In our time, care for the common good—the shared exercise of a truly public life—has been given over to politicians, people and institutions of great wealth and influence, and experts. As adults most of us have little or no real participation in the political choices which create the public life we experience. The common good today is whatever "they" make it. We may grumble about politics or tune in more seriously from time to time when particularly disgraceful events occur, but in truth we feel little potency to transform the way democracy works in our "advanced" society.

The state of politics in the contemporary United States is powerfully presented and explained in an important book entitled *Who Will Tell the People: The Betrayal of American Democracy* by William Greider (1992). It is a book which anyone who is concerned about our common, public life should read. It is sobering because the citizens whose reflection we see in the mirror of Greider's text—ourselves—are so typically ineffectual in the face of the wealth and power of those who move the public agenda, not in the service of the common good, but rather in pursuit of special economic and political interests. One of Greider's metaphors in fact is that our political system is like a two-way mirror between officeholders and those who elect them, a mirror which "reflects the warts and virtues back and forth between them" (1992, 16). In other words our elected officials are a reflection of us, as we are of them. Think about it. For many of us it is not a comforting thought. In Greider's words, if electoral politics "is infested by fools and knaves, where did they come from and who sent them?" (1992, 17).

Greider relentlessly details the breakdown in democratic structures in this nation, describing the dynamics by which citizen voices in government have been limited if not silenced by wealthy and powerful forces. And he does so with a clear sense of what is really at stake in the vitality of our common political life. In his words:

> Politics is not a game. It exists to resolve the largest questions of the society—the agreed-upon terms by which everyone can live peaceably with one another. At its best politics creates and sustains social relationships—the human conversation and engagement that draw people together and allow them to discover their mutuality (1992, 13-14).

Politics—now understood as participation in public life as defined here—is, for better and for worse, the place where citizens and people of faith who do not have access to great wealth and power *must* find our collective voices if we wish to affect the shape of our public life rather than simply be the passive recipients of the effects of others. Most members of small faith communities, like most adult citizens of Western democracies, are not authentically engaged in public life as we have defined it here. That is, we are not exercising significant ongoing influence on the kinds of decisions just illustrated. Most small community members, like most citizens and people of faith, are in collusion with the degradation of public life in our nation by opinion polls, unrelenting partisanship, and periodic ballot-casting.

PUBLIC LIFE: AN EXAMPLE FROM BIBLICAL TIMES

It may help to grasp the state of our own public life by examining the same issue from another historical vantage point, one which is both strange and familiar to us. Once upon a time in a faraway place our religious ancestors faced a time of crisis in their public life. The time was approximately six hundred years before the birth of Jesus. The place was called Judah, the southern kingdom of Israel. A prophet stood up in the most sacred of his community's public places, the Temple in Jerusalem, to accost his people with the social devastation surrounding them. This is what he said:

> Thus says the Lord of hosts:
> Consider, and call for the mourning women to come;
> send for the skilled women to come;
> let them quickly raise a dirge over us,
> so that our eyes may run down with tears,
> and our eyelids flow with water.
> For a sound of wailing is heard from Zion. . . .
> Hear, O women, the word of the Lord,
> and let your ears receive the word of his mouth;
> teach to your daughters a dirge,
> and each to her neighbor a lament.
> "Death has come up into our windows,
> it has entered our palaces,
> to cut off the children from the streets
> and the young men from the squares" (Jer. 9:17-21).

Those of us who inhabit America's cities today can readily identify with Jeremiah's social analysis. One of the growth industries in urban America is home security—alarms, private guards, and bars for our doors and windows, lest death come up into them. How many parents today would even dream of letting their children go play in the city as they did as children? And the squares, the public gathering places of our cities, have indeed become killing grounds for young men, especially young black men, whose chance of being murdered before age 25 in the United States today is 1 in 5.

Please notice Jeremiah's prescription for beginning the healing of the sickness in Judah's body: that those women of the community who are skilled in dirges and lamentations must step forward to lead the people in collective grieving over the dying and fear which has arisen in their public life. Alas, Jeremiah's community not only failed to listen to the message, but chastised the messenger. Utter defeat and captivity in Babylon were close at hand.

Public acknowledgment of the great pain in our collective body, of our impotent complicity in it, and of our anxieties about our own well being and that of all our children is required of us as a part of learning to bear the public choices central to the vocation named adulthood. Perhaps we are required to grieve before we can begin to address the real issues of public life in our cities, states, and nations. Perhaps the hearts and eyes and voices of women must lead us through this necessary collective grief, thus opening the way to work for peace in our public life. But, having grieved, how do we create a base of influence through which we might increase the peace? For a plausible and hopeful response to this painfully pointed question, we return to the concept of mediating structures introduced in chapter 4.

MEDIATING STRUCTURES AND PUBLIC LIFE

A sense of skeptical estrangement and helpless insecurity regarding our public life grows alarmingly, even in democratic nations with highly developed economies. In *Democracy's Discontent* political theorist Michael Sandel describes the core issues which he believes underlie the pervasive estrangement from political structures which so many citizens feel.

> The political parties ... are unable to make sense of our condition. The main topics of national debate—the proper scope of the welfare state, the extent of rights and entitlements, the proper degree of government regulation—take their shape from the arguments of an earlier day. These are not unimportant topics; but they do not reach the two concerns that lie at the heart of our discontent. One is the fear that, individually and collectively, we are losing control of the forces that govern our lives. The other is the sense that, from family to neighborhood to nation, the moral fabric of community is unraveling around us. These two fears define the anxiety of the age (Sandel 1996, 3).

To address this anxiety, then, would mean establishing a measure of effectiveness in our ability to influence the political and economic forces swirling around us and reweaving the ethic of common concern that binds us together. In the words of Sheldon Wolin we must nurture "our capacity for developing into beings who know and value what it means to participate in and be responsible for the care and improvement of our common and collective life" (1989, 139). Wolin refers to this capacity for seeking the common good in collaboration with others our "politicalness."

Where might citizens and people of faith stand in order to build the relationships and learn the skills necessary to develop our politicalness—our ability to address political and economic decision makers respectfully, forcefully, and effectively? One answer to that timely but difficult question calls our attention once more to the myriad of voluntary associations, including but not limited to churches, unions, community betterment groups, and neighborhood organizations—the mediating structures discussed in chapter 4. Such associations constitute a "third sector," a zone within the overall web of relationships not controlled by government or business. Within the mediating structures of our lives, which the philosopher Hegel first named "civil society," values and identities are sustained and transmitted. If the concern of government is order, and the concern of business is profit, the concern of civil society is with the ultimate meanings and values—the humaneness and holiness—underlying political order and financial dealings. Some orders and profits are just; others are not. In addition to the crucial moral learning that goes on in our families, we also learn to recognize the difference between good and bad political order and economic profit through active engagement in civil society.

Taking mediating structures seriously will require that we call into question an image that Westerners tend to take at least vaguely for granted in interpreting our social world. Do we not share a tendency to think of our society as organized along lines very much like geological strata? When we use language like "upper class," "middle class," "lower class," and now "underclass," are we not employing a background image of stratification? It is crucial that we recognize two things about this stratigraphic image of society: It suggests first that the basic structure of our society is a uniform and pervasive layering of socioeconomic status or classes, and second that a person's occupation, how he or she makes a living, is perhaps *the* crucial indicator of her or his prestige and life chances. It is precisely this assumption which contemporary sociological analysis calls into question.

While there can be little doubt that the options which come with one's occupational status have a significant bearing on one's life chances, there is another dimension to be considered. What we are likely to accomplish in our lives is never solely a function of our personal options, even those associated with our occupational earning power; the wealth or dearth of meaningful relationships which characterizes our lives also profoundly affects our life chances.

Contemporary sociological research on the United States and other Western democracies makes it clear that two large-scale social trends have increased the complexity of society so greatly that the concept of social class in the sense of stratified occupational layers systematically associated with increasing or decreasing life chances needs revision. These two realities, which reflect not merely *economic* forces but also national *political* decision making within our society, are our military institutions and involvements and our public welfare system. Both of these have altered the life chances of millions of citizens of our society so fundamentally that socioeconomic stratification in the classic sense (the "upper-middle-lower" geological strata model) no longer adequately describes our social structure. Our position in society is more complex than the familiar class-stratification model can account for by itself.

And there is another problem with the economic stratification model for society. It does not take into account the whole set of nonoccupational relationships which loom so large in our lives. These include the complex pattern of ethnic and racial ties; religious affiliations; and a variety of local, regional, national, and international voluntary associations. These are the mediating structures introduced in chapter 4. Because these bonds often cut across lines of economic class, they also help to invalidate the picture of our social structure as a rigid stratification of occupational layers defining life chances.

The web of mediating structures into which people are born and which they further construct and modify is—along with their macrosocial status and options, and microsocial bonds—a crucial determinant of their life chances. But how do mediating structures become a vehicle for renewed participation in public life?

MEDIATING STRUCTURES AND SOCIAL CONTROL

For almost every reader of this text the term "social control" will initially have restrictive if not coercive connotations. Some will perhaps think of the roles of government, church, or the educational system in socializing people to take up and maintain constructive roles in society. For others the capacity of persons and groups to keep their behaviors within acceptable social limits may come to mind. For most of us social control has overtones of coercive pressure exercised externally.

You may be surprised to discover, however, that in the classical American sociological tradition, social control referred to "the capacity of a social group to regulate itself according to desired principles and values" (Janowitz 1975, 82). The concept was in fact propounded and developed by a group of social thinkers who insisted that an image of society as a collection of atomistic individuals pursuing their separate economic interests could not account adequately for society's actual functioning, and, furthermore, gave no acceptable basis for considering values or ethics in society. In their view, a social order based primarily on coercive external control rather than shared values was precisely the one which lacked adequate social control. How meanings change!

At the center of the classic understanding of social control is the assertion that legitimate differences of interest within a society are to be resolved by "persuasion, discussion, debate, education, negotiation, parliamentary procedure, diplomacy, bargaining, adjudication, contractual relations, and compromise" (Wirth, cited in Janowitz 1975, 88). What all of these modes of resolving differences have in common is their reliance on mutual communication—on conversation. Properly understood and practiced, each of these forms of communication disavows the use of domination or coercion to resolve disagreements. They are exercises in relational power.

Social control in the classical sociological tradition was a way of speaking about what we mean in this book by having a public life. When sociologists first spoke of social control they were not naming coercive or manipulative forces but rather the capacity of people to realize their values in the public arena, to have an effective public life. We reintroduce the classical approach to social control in this book because it is crucial for Christian communities of faith to be able to order our lives according to the fundamental convictions which give shape to our identity, and in doing so to witness on behalf of those convictions to other persons and groups in society. That is, we must be capable of social control in the sense in which we have introduced it here. Put differently, communities of faith must have an effective presence in public life.

As we noted in chapter 2, the classic Christian texts having to do with power teach us that we are not permitted to lord it over others, but are called to exercise our influence with others "as one who serves." In other words, Christian witness in society must be persuasive rather than coercive, relational rather than unilateral. We must order our communal life and challenge others to collaborate with us to shape our public life according to the biblical values of justice and mercy, and we must do so in noncoercive ways, through conversation, confrontation, and compromise. The historical Christian community understands very well what the classic social theorists were saying about social control. In fact, the classic notion of social control springs partially from the Christian vision of the dignity of persons and how power ought to operate among us. Exercising social control in the classical sense—being a formidable public presence in the name of justice, mercy, and love—is a hallmark of authentic Christian communities.

Social control as defined here occurs only when individuals, groups, and larger collectives can order their actual behavior in the world consensually according to the standards they hold. Social control requires not only that congruence exists between what we profess as values and what we actually stand for in the world, but also that we arrive at our public stance and address others from it by means of mutual persuasion. Social control is one of the great challenges and possible achievements of social life. It reflects the ideals of historic democratic, Jewish, and Christian traditions. It can be arrived at and maintained only by persons working consensually and collaboratively, patiently and tenaciously, in the public arena. It is particularly challenging amidst the extraordinary cultural pluralism of contemporary Western societies.

Human beings attempting to pursue personal choices in isolation from the relational bonds of family, community, church, and the other associations which make those options viable and meaningful, imperil themselves and others. Good and meaningful choices require good and meaningful relationships. Nor can we regulate our lives according to our values apart from effective, mutual relations both within the groups to which we belong and between those and other groups. Personal and group integrity depend upon our capacity to maintain noncoercive mutual accountability within the web of our relationships. This is true at the microlevel of face-to-face interaction (the inner life of small faith communities) and at the macrolevel of political life (the public life of small communities).

THE PUBLIC LIFE OF FAITH

The Christian community is committed to the well being of all the children of God. We stand under the extraordinary and challenging mandate to love our neighbor as ourself, that is, to value and work for the life chances of all our sisters and brothers as we value and work for our own well being. Human well being entails not only personal opportunities but relational bonds. To promote justice, mercy, and love within society and history is not only to stand for decent opportunities for every person, but also to defend and strengthen the mediating structures—the families, congregations, neighborhoods, schools—which make such opportunities meaningful.

The Christian community is called by its scripture and later traditions to link persons together into one body, into networks of mutual concern and involvement. We are to nurture a world of *shalom,* of right relationship, within human history. The Christian community is one of many forms of mediating structures. While our faith does indeed have a *personal* dimension, it is never a private matter, something just between us and God. Neighborliness is for us not merely a perfunctory or secondary obligation but a sacred one. Christian existence is fundamentally communitarian—or social—in nature. Whatever affects social relationships is relevant to the Body of Christ in history, which as Paul reminds us, we are and of which we are members.

Finally, the Christian community is under biblical obligation to order our internal and our public life on behalf of the reign of God in history. We are to contribute to the exercise of democratic social control by participating effectively in public life on behalf of God's intentions for history as mediated through our tradition. Biblically speaking these intentions finally may be reduced to two: God desires a social world characterized by justice and mercy. We must stand for these values by conducting our internal ecclesial affairs and our relations with the rest of the world in noncoercive fashion. It is our community's vocation to be a credible and powerful presence in the real world on behalf of justice and mercy, to be a community animated by love, and to embody those qualities by conducting our relationships in such a way that we exercise our influence without lording it over others.

Our concern for the realization of these goods is not subject to cultural or socio-economic boundaries. The inclusivity of the social vocation of the Christian community of faith forbids any form of dominance of one group of siblings over another. Coercive power is not to be our way of exercising influence, inside the community of faith or outside it. To speak plainly, the presence of racism or sexism within the community of faith is an especially egregious violation of the biblical vision to which we are accountable. Communities of faith cannot be credible witnesses or effective agents against such systemic evils, unless we have an unambiguous commitment to uproot them from our own ecclesial life. Such realities always have political implications, especially when we recall that politics simply names the realities of power in communal decision making. But this does not allow us to dismiss such matters as merely political rather than religious. It is precisely our inherited religious understanding of right relationships as just and merciful—as loving—that requires us to strive to free our ecclesial and civic politics of racism and sexism.

For those who live on society's margins, the exodus from slavery to peoplehood is a root metaphor for the kind of history they can make when they respond to Yahweh's promise. The Exodus event has been paradigmatic for the poor and marginalized in Latin America, for the African-American and other cultural communities in exile in North America, indeed for many of those dispossessed by the abuse of power. Middle-class people, however, have a different experience and face a different challenge if we are to stand in common cause with our sisters and brothers on the margins of the dominant society in making history today. Communities of faith that are socially located in the middle class inevitably read both their newspaper and Bible from the perspective of that location. Lest their faith become captive to their culture and society, middle-class communities must be prepared to put their received versions of faith and culture under creative suspicion, to test them in conversation with the social realities of marginalized others and the true otherness of biblical, especially prophetic, texts. Unless people of faith in the middle class are feeling unsettled by both of these, we are missing the point of both.

Walter Brueggemann popularized the expression "prophetic imagination" to remind us that the prophets imagine reality differently than most others; they have different images for interpreting life. They know that God has intentions for the world that would redeem human experience in ways we can barely imagine. They feel deeply that something else might be the case. They do not, of course, speak the language of practical theology as we have articulated it here, but they do their own version. They feel the contrast between what is the case (cultural and social analysis) and what should be the case (faith analysis). And their essential passion is that what could be the case should be the case. Why? Because that is the word their God has communicated to them. Abraham Joshua Heschel insists that while the prophets are moved by their own indignation at injustice in their cities and their nation, their real power comes from elsewhere. Their relationship to Yahweh is so profoundly personal that they feel the world with Yahweh's own feelings. At that point the mystical and political are of a piece. Then the prophet arises to warn us, in Heschel's words, that "a people may be dying without being aware of it; a people may be able to survive yet refuse to make use of their ability" (Heschel 1962, xii). Such is the burden of the prophets of Israel. As we have already noted, of the many christological titles given to Jesus (son of David, son of man, son of God, and even the title of Christ), perhaps only two belong to the historical life of Jesus, prophet and teacher. Both of these have been so eclipsed by later titles that they often do not shape our collective sense of who the Christ is and what it means to follow on the Way. Jesus called the something else that might be the case "the Kingdom of God" and urgently pressed for its realization with his life.

In the mutually critical conversation between culture and faith called "practical theology," which we outlined in chapter 4, small Christian communities open ourselves to the searing and inspiring words of Jesus and his prophetic predecessors and successors. In doing so, we find these surprising, challenging, consoling words addressed to us about the world as it is here and now. Through faithful and informed conversation with scripture and world, communities of faith not only retrieve those words but find our communal imaginations challenged and revitalized in the recovery. We are called to transformative action in the name of justice and mercy in our time and then to reflect upon both the effectiveness and the religious significance of that action. Can anything be said about specific biblical challenges to today's communities of faith? We want to approach that question first by way of an additional text from the prophet Jeremiah, and then by considering Catholic social teaching on the "preferential option for the poor."

As we noted above, Jeremiah's people did not heed his cry for public mourning and renewal, and near the end of the sixth century B.C.E., God's chosen people saw their political kingdom broken into pieces. The leaders and most of the people were sent into exile; the Babylonian captivity was upon them. In this time of painful banishment, the word of God came to this community from Jeremiah once again, this time in the form of a letter to the exiles. Yahweh Sabaoth, the God of Israel, says to all of the exiles deported from Jerusalem to Babylon:

> Build houses and live in them;
> plant gardens and eat what they produce;
> take spouses and have sons and daughters;
> help your children marry that they in turn may also have
>   daughters and sons. Increase there and not decrease.

But seek the well being of the city where I have sent you into
    exile,
and pray to the Lord on its behalf,
for in its well being you will find your well being (Jer. 29:4-7).

Biblical scholars note Jeremiah's realism. This may be a less than ideal situation, but the people should be practical enough to make the best of it.
They are not to rail against and resist the captors. They are to make a fruitful
and constructive existence in the city of Babylon, where they have come
against their will. Surely this is the voice of prudence. But Jeremiah does not
stop with prudent advice for survival in a strange land. He proceeds to make
the astounding claim that the well being of those in exile against their will
and the well being of those who dominate them are one: "in its well being
you will find your well being." Not only must we seek the well being of those
who devastated and now dominate us, but we must pray to God for their
well being. The word of God sees one world where partisan eyes can only
discern divisions. The word of God sees a world without tribal hatreds, a
world without strangers. Imagine the surprise of a vanquished, grieving,
angry community on hearing that they must seek a world of justice and
mercy on behalf of the very ones who have inflicted such disruption and tor-
ment upon them, that upon the peace of "their" city, hangs the peace of
God's vanquished people.

To speak plainly, many members of small communities of faith find ourselves today like our sisters and brothers in captivity in Babylon so long ago,
exiled within a public life which affronts our deepest religious instincts and
seems impervious to our influence. To make a decent living and raise a
healthy family in safety is no small concern today. Contemporary urban life is
particularly dangerous territory. We are well aware of individuals and communities suffering from burnout and compassion fatigue after courageously
attempting to address these stark and sobering social realities. As urban
exiles, many people of faith are challenged and inspired by Jeremiah's letter
to other despairing exiles like ourselves. He voices—as perhaps only prophets, who are not prognosticators but poets can—a repeatedly experienced
truth about the social and religious vocation named community: Without a
commitment to public life, the inner life of small communities of faith cannot
thrive. We have no choice but to seek the well being of our city and to pray to
God on its behalf, for like Jeremiah's people in Babylonian exile the urban
dwellers of today have no individual well being in isolation from the well
being of our cities. The same religious reality of course also holds in differing
social circumstances for nonurban residents.

The Hebrew word in Jeremiah's letter which we translate as "well being" is
shalom. To seek the *shalom* of our communities has a quite specific meaning
biblically. *Shalom* is the peace which emerges when human beings are in right
relationship with themselves, their neighbors, the earth and all its creatures,
and God. As we noted in chapter 3, in the Jewish world view (which was of

course the world view of Jesus, whom Christians call "the Christ"), right relationship has two characteristics: justice and mercy. Right relationship means the proper balance of justice and mercy called for by the real social circumstances within which we find ourselves in our time and place. What right relationship requires of us at any given moment is a judgment call which God has left to us. In making it we must exercise both religious discernment and practical wisdom. The fundamental challenge to adult citizens and people of faith is to exercise our influence and allow ourselves to be influenced by others as we seek right relationship (that is, *shalom*) in the give-and-take of public life. True *shalom* emerges only from the practice of relational power.

In sociological categories the well being of a people has to do with the life chances which they inherit as a result of their social location—their opportunities for health, education, safety, decent housing, nutrition, and so forth. Jeremiah's exhortation reminds us that one group's life chances cannot be divorced from those of others. To collaborate in the improvement of the opportunities of others for a decent, peaceful life, is to improve our own chances for such a life. Can middle-class people of faith exiled in the cities and suburbs of the United States and other Western nations today, witnessing daily to events which break our hearts and demoralize us, open our lives to the words of Jeremiah and risk crossing racial, denominational, and class boundaries in order to seek the *shalom* of the troubled and gifted places in which we find ourselves?

Let's examine a related perspective. Beginning in the South American context, contemporary theology has developed the concept of the "preferential option for the poor" to frame the deeper instincts of God's justice and mercy in both testaments. The last judgment scene in Matthew's Gospel is perhaps its quintessential expression. What we do for the hungry, the sick, the despondent, and the imprisoned expresses our relationship with Jesus Christ. For the sake of our collective salvation, then, we must be mindful of painful social facts regarding the life chances of all members of our society, for example, that the United States has a higher percentage of its people incarcerated than any nation in the world.

A preferential option for the poor does not mean that they are loved more than everyone who is not poor. Parents of a sick child do not love that child more than their healthy children when they give major attention, energy, and care to that child's recovery. But they want the sick child to be healed. That can be translated to something like this at the macrosocial level: There is an acceptable level of human resources and self-determination below which no one should be forced to live. Those below that level have first call on our energies and resources until as far as possible they are sisters and brothers with us in decent levels of human living.

There is a remarkable power for transformation—for seeking the well being of the city and especially those marginalized by poverty—in the middle class if we can learn to speak as citizens and people of faith in a collective voice that transcends race, class, and religion. If the middle class wants a better world for our children, there are serious reasons for binding coalitions with the poor and with others of good faith who have already made such coalitions. In solidarity with the poor and with those marginalized for other reasons (gender, race, sexual orientation), we are far more likely in our ongoing critical conversation to imagine vigorously that something else might be the case, that some different city might hold a finer world for tomorrow's children, that in the well being of the city we shall find our own well being. That is so largely because in real and sustained relationship with others whose world views and interests differ from our own, we inevitably find that new possibilities for life, for the *shalom* of our common world, emerge for consideration. When the time is ripe those possibilities become the basis for collective action.

SCCs who find themselves turned toward political and economic injustice because scripture has accosted them are no less subject to paralysis than an individual facing those challenges. If anything they may be in more jeopardy because their ongoing conversation with scripture inexorably calls their attention to the actual life circumstances of people in the social world we share. The usual individual processes of numbness and denial regarding racism, sexism, and other systemic injustices will inevitably be subverted by an ongoing shared reading of scripture. Reading the Bible and the world well with sisters and brothers in community, but without adequate channels for collective action, is like periodically re-opening a wound. That wound is our complicity with an unjust social order and the effects it has on the life chances of others as well as ourselves and our children. We repeatedly feel a kind of learned helplessness in the face of a public life gone wrong.

Today, seeking the well being of the city—our cultural and social world— is not primarily a private matter of being better individuals, although that is of course our responsibility as well. Nor is it simply a matter of gathering with others to share our faith in conversation and worship and to support one another personally, although no authentic community is imaginable without such fellowship. Genuine Christian community also requires that we look together as persons of faith into the true state of our social body—our public world.

When small Christian communities seek the well being of the city, they will inevitably be led into the arena which we have here called public life, that is, into the places where racism, sexism, and political and economic injustice are perpetrated and must be confronted. As noted above, the prophets of Israel were no strangers to this arena. Jesus and those who followed him had to deal with the sociopolitical arrangements of their time and place. The life of Jesus was in fact taken by the demonic use of unilateral power by Roman public officials. A Christian community which does not find itself in this public arena has lost its way. And the dominant culture of individualism and consumerism offers endless inducements for us to lose our way in the addictive pursuit of material possessions and endless self-actualization.

It is precisely in the public world that communities of disciples of Jesus Christ must be prepared to lose our lives in order to find them, as we seek the well being of all God's people. Christians on the margins of all societies (the "people of the base") understand this readily and find great hope in it. It is they, in fact, who gave birth to the movement of small Christian communities around the world, a movement which is now struggling to construct an authentic form in North America and elsewhere. It is a terribly hard saying, however, for communities of faith that find themselves in the middle-class sector of a highly individualistic, materialistic, and relatively prosperous culture such as ours.

Past experience has convinced us that continuing to read biblical texts in an isolated fashion is a prescription either for a retreat into a private, "spiritualized" ("me and God") reading of scripture, or for guilt-driven, nonsustainable plunges into charity. If we read the scriptural texts alone—whether as individuals or isolated communities—they will simply break our hearts. A larger solidarity is required of us if we are to be accosted but not demoralized by their powerful word. Individuals and isolated communities of faith cannot face events in the public arena alone with any measure of hope. Even communities which face these events in solidarity with others must expect moments of desolation. But our historical community of faith emerged and continues to exist out of the remarkable conviction that captivity in a strange land is not the last word; that there is a new form of life available only to those who are prepared to lose their lives by going on the Way; that in seeking the well being of the city, we will find our own well being. That seeking and finding will require that small communities of faith become part of a larger mediating structure, one whose overriding agenda is the common good of the larger community.

BROAD-BASED COMMUNITY ORGANIZATIONS:
SEEKING THE *SHALOM* OF PUBLIC LIFE

Near the end of his book on the state of political participation in the United States today, William Greider describes what in his judgment is the most promising effort now underway in the United States to reclaim true citizen involvement in the decisions of public life. He introduces his readers to the community organizations which together make up the Industrial Areas Foundation (I.A.F.) network. For the past thirty years throughout the United States as well as in the United Kingdom and South Africa, citizens and people of faith based in their congregations, civic associations, and labor unions have been rebuilding public life by patiently reconstructing and revitalizing democratic discourse and action in their communities across the barriers of race, class, and religion. In San Antonio, a city where people of one culture formerly functioned as menial laborers for those of another, a vibrant, bicultural civil society has emerged. In Baltimore, the largest scholarship and jobs incentive program in the nation has been created for public school students. In East London, civic participation has begun to function within a mix of cultures and religions that those who founded the mother of parliaments could never have imagined on English soil. In New York, communities of homeowners, including many former public housing residents, exist where politicians and experts said they never would. In California, a public battle has been fought and won over the issue of wages for society's most vulnerable workers. In New Orleans, the specter of racism is being addressed directly in open, public discourse between blacks and whites. In Johannesburg and Soweto, democratic institutions are being painstakingly created to fill the civic vacuum left in the wake of apartheid. In the city and suburbs of Chicago, the urban heart of the United States, the foundation is being intentionally laid for a metropolitan-wide, multicultural citizens' organization on a scale never before attempted.

Broad-based organizations are founded on local congregations of all sizes, economic classes, races, cultures, and religions, as well as other community groups and associations. By coming together in a larger form of solidarity— one which crosses racial, denominational, and class barriers—they learn to seek the well being of their social worlds in committed and effective ways. These organizations, which are large mediating structures composed of many institutions, create a new and sustainable base of power for change in which citizens and people of faith may involve themselves. As the preceding examples indicate, they have a remarkable track record in affecting the public life of their communities, and doing so in concrete and creative ways. They have made the views of their member institutions known and have affected public decisions in matters ranging from public education reform to affordable housing, from community policing to economic development and the creation of living-wage employment, from public health and sanitation to minimum wage levels.

The overarching goal of broad-based organizations is to empower citizen leaders to develop a common agenda for reconstructing the crumbling physical and social infrastructure of their communities, while strengthening their integrity and diversity. Their commitment is to social change at the most profound level: how citizens make those collective, public decisions regarding economic development, education and training, or housing that will determine the future well being of communities. One respected I.A.F. leader, the Reverend Johnny Ray Youngblood of St. Paul's Community Baptist Church in East Brooklyn, captures the vision and power of broad-based organizing in these words:

> There are some mandates loose out there. Thou shalt run. Thou shalt move. Thou shalt buy more alarms. Thou shalt put wrought-iron gates over thy windows. Thou shalt buy a gun. Thou shalt change schools. Thou shalt change cities. But we come from our own Mount Sinai and have another mandate before us. The mandate is East Brooklyn Congregations. The mandate is I.A.F. The

mandate is, thou shalt organize. Thou shalt organize, disorganize, and reorganize. Contrary to popular opinion, we are not a "grass-roots" organization. Grass roots grow in smooth soil. Grass roots are shallow roots. Grass roots are tender roots. Grass roots are fragile roots. Our roots are deep roots. Our roots are tough roots. Our roots are determined roots. East Brooklyn Congregations has fought for its member institutions' existence in the shattered glass of East New York, in the blasted brick and rubble of Brownsville, in the devastation of central Bushwick. Our roots are deep in this city (Freedman 1993, 322).

A defining characteristic of I.A.F. organizations is their plurality. Within these organizations African Americans, Hispanics, and Asian Americans collaborate as equal partners with Americans of European descent in the pursuit of justice for members of all faiths and cultures. Within these organizations Jews, Christians, and Moslems seek the well being of their cities. Within these organizations women and men share leadership, authority, and public roles. Within these organizations city dwellers and suburbanites come together to face issues which neither can address alone. Within these organizations citizens and people of faith from urban and rural communities collaborate on matters of mutual interest. Within these organizations conservatives, moderates, and activists seek common ground, refusing to allow ideological differences to become political divisions.

In the collective experience and shared vision of the citizen leaders and professional organizers who have willed the remarkable network of I.A.F. organizations around the world into being, and who have sustained and renewed them in the face of the divisive economic pressures and cultural tensions of our time, there resides a precious storehouse of practical, political, public wisdom. These women and men comprehend something that only those who have ventured beyond the confines of private concerns into the arena of public life can know. They understand what it means in practice to make common cause with people of other races, religions, and classes in seeking the well being of the larger civic communities to which all belong. They have celebrated exhilarating victories and experienced the sacrament of defeat in public life, and they have done both in the company of former strangers now become fellow citizens.

These organizations exist to amplify the sorrowful voices of individuals so that they will be heard throughout the community. They become stages from which choruses of lamentation rise up from the devastated and demoralized public life of their communities. Through their faith, their relationships, and their ability to negotiate, they have come to understand what biblical scholar Walter Brueggemann means: only when grief moves from private pain to appropriate, disciplined, public expression does true empowerment begin and the dream of a revitalized public life arise anew. Within these painstakingly built and constantly developing organizations, people who, for the most part, have no access to great wealth or power are learning how to evoke the cries of individuals, to see that they are heard in the corridors of real power, and to look to themselves as responsible and effective agents in the reconstruction of public life in their communities. Broad-based community organizations seek the peace of their communities.

SMALL COMMUNITIES IN BROAD-BASED COMMUNITY ORGANIZATIONS: A WORK IN PROGRESS

In *Dangerous Memories,* we suggested that small communities of faith could be thought of as mediating structures between households and the larger institutions of our social world. Subsequent experience has led us to another view: a small community of faith is simply too small to play the role of mediating structure alone. We have become convinced that to play this crucial intermediate role in the lives of their members, small communities must create forms of solidarity with other groups and institutions which share their vision of a world of *shalom.*

We close this chapter by describing one such experiment, a work in progress as we write. Beginning in 1992, a number of small faith communities have involved themselves in the creation of a broad-based organization, like those described above, in metropolitan New Orleans. At the time of this writing the New Orleans organization, which is called The Jeremiah Group, has more than fifty member institutions, four of which are small faith communities. Like the other member institutions, the small communities pay dues to the organization (typically $1000 per year), send some of their members to local and national training to learn how to create and move a public agenda, engage in public actions which draw elected officials and other power brokers into the community, and contribute to the overall leadership of the organization through participation in the collective leadership of The Jeremiah Group.

We want to recall the emphasis on diversity in broad-based community organizations mentioned in the previous section. The small communities which belong to The Jeremiah Group are mainly composed of white, middle-class, well-educated Catholic professionals. Through their membership in a broad-based organization they now have the opportunity to forge strong public relationships with members of African-American churches, congregations of other predominantly white denominations, and the Jewish community of our city. In this mixed multitude they experience not only shared social analysis and action, but common worship woven from the diverse strands of our many cultural heritages. Thus the diversity of a broad-based organization gives participating congregations and communities a viable solution to a vexing and chronic problem. In such organizations white churches do not have to recruit black members or vice versa in order to be in real relationship with diverse others. Those relationships take place not primarily within congregations or communities but rather within the larger organization in which they participate together.

As we write this book, the small communities mentioned above are involved in campaigns to address a number of critical public-life issues in metropolitan New Orleans through their active participation in a broad-based community organization. These issues include a desperately under-supported public education system, a shortage of affordable housing for low- to moderate-income families, and the lack of living-wage jobs within an economy too closely tied to tourism. These are indeed *public* issues, and in working within a broad-based organization which is initiating constructive action in response to them, the SCCs of The Jeremiah Group are learning what it means to have a public life as a vital complement to their continuing inner life. Following one of the organization's first large public actions, the mayor of New Orleans was quoted in press coverage as follows: "I'm touched when I look out and see white and black, brown and yellow, Jew and Gentile, Protestant and Catholic, old and young, Uptown and Downtown, together in one place for one purpose." New Orleans SCC members were in that number when the mixed multitude of saints mentioned by the mayor came marching in to seek his commitment to become an ally of The Jeremiah Group in seeking the *shalom* of our city.

In addition to the public work of the organization, members of the New Orleans SCCs have also been part of an ongoing public conversation called "Calling the Question of Race," in which leaders of The Jeremiah Group have gathered over the past two years across racial lines for dialogue and study about how race and racism distort both the public and personal lives of citizens of Western cultures. Those participating in these ground-breaking (and anxiety-provoking) conversations thus far have commented on how rare it is for blacks and whites to address these matters head on and together in the context of ongoing relationships in an interracial collective. It is precisely such ongoing public relationships which participation in a broad-based organization makes possible for SCCs.

CLOSING

Old Testament scholars like Norman Gottwald and Walter Brueggemann, and New Testament scholars like Bruce Malina, Gerd Theissen, and Wayne Meeks, help us understand why anthropology and sociology illuminate the nature of the people of God. To become "a people" is to become a system, with cultural, economic, and political characteristics and peculiarities. We think it is fair to say that while the Body of Christ is many things and subject to interpretation under many rubrics, it is also and always a body politic that interacts with other political bodies. Not to acknowledge that is to miss a very critical feature of our life in Christ, as Ronald Krietmeyer suggests in the following passage.

> I want to be guided in developing a spirituality that is not just private and interpersonal, but also political, institutional and public ... I won't want my children to be prepared for receiving the

Eucharist without knowing that the Body of Christ is not only a sacred presence to be received at the altar on Sunday, but is also a social, political and economic reality that must be nurtured and constructed in the wider community (Krietemeyer 1991, 13).

Our corporateness does not absorb our personal relationship with God. Our public activity does not replace our personal prayer. All the rituals of the marketplace will never add up to the Table of Eucharist. The "I" that prays and organizes never stops being a unique "I" of incomparable worth even as it never stops being a personal "I" whose identity is forever emerging from relationships with God and with each other. Each of us is truly one and many, and we pray and act in both ways.

Communities of faith exist within particular historical circumstances and are called to transform them in accordance with the intentions of our Creator as these are mediated to us through our religious traditions. A biblical reading of those intentions is clear: God wants a world of *shalom*, of peace. But, as rabbinic Judaism has traditionally taught, God cannot bring such a world into being without human partners committed to the fulfillment of creation through the practice of *mitzvot,* actions on behalf of mercy and justice. The transformative action to which the descendants of Moses and Mohammed and Christ are called by their ongoing critical conversation with culture and society has both a practical and a public character. What we are learning from the wedding of Christian communities and broad-based community organizations holds promise for a creative explosion of the public life of SCCs in the United States. We are equally certain that, as a crucial dimension of the coming church, communities of faith have signal contributions to make to effective and sustainable community organizing in the name of justice and mercy. There no doubt are and will be other ways for small communities of faith to have a public life. We offer this example as one powerful instance of small communities committing to an intentional public presence.

SCCs can be true to their name only by venturing into the public arena to build relationships with diverse others in the pursuit of the common good of the larger community. If they fail to do so, they are actually religious support groups. Having risked engagement in public life, they must return to reflect, pray, and converse as people of faith about what they have experienced in exercising their politicalness. If they fail to do so, they are actually activist groups. Authentic SCCs must develop their inner and their public life. And so we have come full circle: seeking consensus and utilizing conflict in their inner life and an ongoing commitment to seek the *shalom* of the city in their public life are the two crucial moments in the one conversation which constitutes small Christian communities. The price for such conversation is the willingness to risk what we already have and what we already know. The possibility which inevitably attends that risk is conversion.

CHAPTER SEVEN

Precious Community

Some Closing Words

Precious words are often in danger of losing their power and their beauty through overuse and overexposure. "Community" is a word like that. In our Judeo-Christian tradition this great word is intimately connected with both synagogue and church. Other words and expressions like "covenant" and "people of God" are immediate family words to community. The whole family is precious.

The word "community" is invoked regularly to cover a multitude of social experiences. A parish of 1200 families uses it. The political leaders of a city, state, or nation reach for it. A group of friends or the members of a twelve-step group choose it to name their experience of being together. No one definition is possible or desirable for a symbol that names such a crucial value and stirs such deep longings in the human heart. In this regard "community" functions like some other powerful words in our vocabulary: "love," "belonging," "family." The definition of small Christian communities which we have offered here is not prescriptively intended; it makes no claim to negate other possible definitions. We do, however, stand by our position that a community without a recognizable public life is better understood as a support group, and that a community without a strong inner life is better understood as an action group. That is a judgment which we believe to be warranted by both a biblical interpretation of the world as it should be and by the best social psychological descriptions of the world as it is.

The church needs many kinds of groups within it for its pastoral vitality: prayer groups, Bible study groups, St. Vincent De Paul, Altar Society, Holy Name Society, support groups for divorced Catholics, support groups for gay and lesbian Catholics, youth groups, young adult groups, civic action groups, broad-based community organization groups, and so forth. Support groups and action groups are good things; we simply think it best not to confuse them with small Christian communities. There is a gospel completeness for groups that are gathered by the Word they have heard to love one another, and sent by the Word they have heard to offer It to the whole world. SCCs are gathered and sent.

Having said these things, and knowing how widely the word "community" is appropriated by both support groups and action groups, we do not want to use the word as a battleground. There is, in fact, middle ground. For example, no one can start up a small community. You can start a small group, and you can help provide the conditions that will give it its best chance to become a community, but it takes time for both bonding and effective action to grow up, time to accumulate shared memories and hopes. Such a group will usually be moved from the beginning by its desire for being gathered well and sent effectively. So what do you call a group that wants to become a community and is in its first stages of life? There's no exact moment when it moves from small group to small community.

No small community maintains a perfect balance between being gathered and being sent. There are rhythms to this. Sometimes we must attend very closely and with major energy to the demands of our inner life or we will not survive. Other times we must spend major time and energy focusing on a task, on an intervention in some social system, and we want to act wisely, with hope for success. That can be, for a time, a consuming focus of energy.

We acknowledge that a support group can have the intention of also becoming an action group when it feels its inner life has jelled, or that an action group can see its need to attend to its own inner dynamics and can choose to add that to its intentions. Experience, however, tells us that it is more difficult to add sending to gathering, or gathering to sending, if there is not some conscious intentionality in that direction in the early history of a small group. Not impossible, but more difficult.

We have tried to give full attention to the gathered life and the sent life in SCCs in the U.S. Catholic church. As Americans with religious commitment, our cultural context makes it easier for us to gather as support groups than as action groups. The recent research by Robert Wuthnow, cited in chapter 2, indicates that four out of every ten Americans belongs to some kind of small group, and nearly always the groups are support groups or special interest groups. We also sense the need for patience and nurture in regards to mission, as these communities spring up in the U.S. Catholic church. Socially expressed public concern for issues by religious groups is not a natural instinct in this culture. Though frequently misunderstood, "separation of church and state" is a potent phrase in American society. Tax exemption is removed from any religious group that publicly, as a community, takes political positions. One advantage of marginal SCCs is that they can speak and act without being structurally identified with the institution.

It is too early to guess what church historians will say a century from now about the global phenomenon of small Christian communities. While they have come into existence on all continents and in many sizes and shapes, they are still a minority of the total number of Catholics. We believe that they have the yeast-like quality that Jesus mentions, the ability to leaven a mass.

In sociological categories, the phenomenon of small Christian communities is not technically a movement, for there is no kind of central organization that directs it. But there are some similarities. The SCC phenomenon is neither a fully structured institution nor a totally free-form reality. It is a complex blend of the hunger for *communitas* and the need for *societas* which we discussed in chapter 3. The SCC movement has some observable patterns to it, while including many variations. We have suggested, for example, that compared to familiar church structures like parishes within dioceses, all SCCs fall outside the norm to some degree. Within the phenomenon of SCCs, some are clearly organized in a more mainstream and some in a more marginal form. Some SCCs fit comfortably within the rhythms of parish life as we now know it; others emerge largely as a critical response to strongly felt shortcomings of today's parishes.

It is important to remember that, like all social structures, the church arrangements we now take for granted were once creative social inventions designed by someone to make church available to people who needed it in some new circumstance. Consider, for example, the creation of suburban parishes in residential settings that had never existed before the 1950s, or the parish without a resident priest-pastor administered by a lay woman or man in the current decade. This kind of creativity always requires some stretching of ecclesial structures. It is helpful to remember that present structures needing to be replaced probably caused some stretch marks when they first came into play. Today's solution to unmet needs within the community of faith has a way of becoming tomorrow's problem, as *communitas* and *societas* continue their tense, creative dance. If SCCs become more and more integrated into the formal structures of church, then they are likely to become the foil for some as-yet-unimagined transformative movement of the Spirit in due season.

In the meantime, the work of those who care about the movement of small Christian communities is to nurture the conversation which we have endeavored to describe in these pages in both its inner and public forms. And participation in that conversation, as we have insisted from our opening pages, cannot be separated from the risk of conversion. For members of authentic small Christian communities, the fuse is indeed always laid to some annunciation.

CHAPTER EIGHT

Epilogue

Futuring

As an epilogue—a word after many other words—we invited people with much Christian community experience to speak about their *realistic dreams* for SCCs ten years from now, and to ponder what it would take for those hopes to happen. "Realistic dreams" may sound like an oxymoron, but all interesting new things are first incubated in dreams. We wanted to ask, "Grounded in your significant experience, what intuitions do you have about what really could happen, if everything went right? And what is the 'everything' that needs to go right?" We feel that these epilogists, with their collective wisdom, can help us imagine ourselves into some interesting futures.

ROBERT BANKS
Pasadena, California

In 1989, Robert (Rob) Banks and his wife, Julie, left Australia to begin teaching at Fuller Theological Seminary. This institution educates students from more than sixty countries not only for pastoral and other church-related work, but for various lay ministries as well. At the seminary he has helped develop courses, a concentration, and a new degree program in the Ministry of the Laity. He recently moved half-time into setting up and codirecting a Center for Leadership, attached to the seminary, that is oriented both to the marketplace and the church. Rob and Julie live with six students in a community house which has a mission of hospitality to visitors, other students, and the neighborhood. He also works closely with members of the film and television industry in Hollywood. Rob is the author of *Paul's Idea of Community: The Early House Churches in Their Historical Setting* (Grand

Rapids: Eerdmans, 1980); and Rob and Julie co-authored *The Church Comes Home: A New Base for Community and Mission* (Southerland, Australia: Albatross Books, 1986).

EXPERIENCE

By background an evangelical Episcopalian, my first church experience was in migrant, blue-collar, and then middle-class settings. After doctoral work in biblical ethics and post-doctoral research into the earliest Christian communities, I underwent much soul-searching about the validity of ordination and the institutional preoccupations of the church. In time this led to my resigning from the Anglican Church and rejoining the laity. Two years later my wife and I returned to Australia and joined a newly established house church in our national capital.

Over the years this group multiplied and eventually developed into two clusters of house churches, each meeting as a whole about once a month, and both meeting together for two or three major Christian festivals during the year. These groups gradually established links with house churches throughout Australia, and also assisted congregations from a range of denominations to develop similar groups themselves.

Since moving to the United States we have helped plant house churches around the seminary, networked with other groups across the country, and worked with others to generate annual consultations bringing house churches together. We were also instrumental in bringing Catholic and Protestant small ecclesial communities into contact with one another. I also teach courses relating to house churches.

HOPES

What are the prospects for house churches? Looking back over more than a quarter of a century's involvement in small ecclesial communities, what might the situation look like twenty-five years from now? There are so many factors to consider that it is difficult to predict but here are my realistic hopes.

1. Small ecclesial communities will continue to develop across an even broader range of Christian constituencies. Although the number of people belonging to religiously based small groups appears to be dropping, many of their members are looking for "something more" beyond their still too individualistic ethos, and beyond their focus on largely personal and relational issues, to wider social and vocational concerns. Among older baby boomers there is the desire for a less work-oriented, more people-focused way of life, while the emerging generation Xers prefer to spend quality as

well as quantity time with each other, especially over food and drink. This is the world of "Friends." Meanwhile recovery groups for all kinds and purposes continue to proliferate, demonstrating the power of ordinary people willing to share their weaknesses to help and support one another. This grassroots phenomenon is at least as important as the spread of megachurches, which in most places has now peaked and only maintains impetus and develops depth where it contains a vigorous small-groups program. Biblical scholars' agreement that the earliest Christian churches were essentially small ecclesial communities will also give increasing validity to contemporary experiments of a similar kind. In some cases, the nurture of such groups within local churches will lead to a reshaping of their whole congregational life.

2. Many of these small ecclesial communities will increasingly begin to reflect the range of stances found in the wider Christian movement, though generally with some modifications. Some will exemplify more conservative attitudes to religion and society, others more liberal or radical views, though in most there will be a blurring or crossing of the boundaries between these. Some will be basically charismatic, others more oriented to instruction or action, though all will tend to include elements of all of these. Some will have a clearly defined leadership structure and network, others a more flexible and organic one, but on the whole they will lie somewhere between hierarchy and absolute egalitarianism. Some, because of their lack of a strong historical consciousness, will end up reprising earlier conflicts and divisions in the history of the church, others will have a strongly inclusive ethos that opens up a whole new chapter in "grassroots" ecumenism, gender partnership, and racial diversity. In my previous house church group, for example, there were people from three different racial backgrounds, four countries, and at least two types of subcultures, with women playing at least as significant a role as men within the group.

3. Though small ecclesial communities will continue to increase both inside and outside denominational structures, in Western democratic countries there is not likely to be any large-scale movement in this direction. While some speak of a new or second reformation, if any period is regarded as parallel to our own it is more probably the fifteenth than the sixteenth century. That was a time when new forms of church life were emerging on the margins of church and society. Often they lived a fragile existence, and their fortunes waxed and waned according to a variety of circumstances. We, too, live in a day of generally "small things." Although there are many signs of religious and moral decay—in both public and church life—we do not yet see a sufficiently powerful critique of the systemic roots of these problems, or a sufficiently widespread openness to change among churchgoers, to provide the basis for widespread reform. Given the increasingly pluralistic nature of our societies, we will also need more than two or three public advocates for such change to come. Even if, as with the fall of Communism, the primary impetus comes from below, there is still a need

for some higher profile figures to lend their assistance. I realize that this view of the future of small ecclesial communities may cut across the grain of those who believe that religious revival or cultural transformation is around the corner, but I believe they provide a more realistic reading of the medium-term future.

4. Nevertheless, small ecclesial communities will begin to affect aspects of the wider culture. Since they are essentially extended Christian families that offer hospitality to the stranger, needy, poor, and lonely, they will help others to see beyond the nuclear or single-parent family model that is everywhere under stress or breaking down. In some respects this may be their major social contribution, for until the family can be put together again and broadened, the foundations of individual personality and inter-mediate organizations in our society remain extremely fragile. Since house churches are also counterculture communities exhibiting a simpler, com-munal, service-oriented way of life, they will become an alternative model to the majority life style focused on self-fulfillment, individual achieve-ment, and career promotion. Since these groups develop a culture in which everyone counts, has a significant contribution to make, is material-ly and spiritually cared for, and makes joint decisions about the basic issues of their life, they will help others begin to catch a vision for a more inclusive, active, just, and participatory political order—much as earlier nonconformist forms of church life helped open up the possibility of a democratic society.

WHAT WILL IT TAKE?

I single out three requirements.

1. If small ecclesial communities are to have the influence I foresee, their members will need to build strong relationships with one another outside their meetings. This will enable them to develop a stronger communal cul-ture, one which includes the children as much as the adults. It will be diffi-cult to do this in a society where time is under such pressure and mobility is the order of the day. Radical life-style choices may sometimes be required to clear time for each other, including the decision to stay put when other considerations would suggest the advantage of moving on.

2. Members of these communities must commit themselves to assisting each person in the group, including children as they come of age, to discern their individual vocation and mission in life. Then they must commit to pray for and give support to one another, check in with and hear back from one another, and help one another to be accountable to whatever God is calling them to do. For most groups this will be more basic than developing a corporate mission involving much of the energy of all the members, though by no means does it preclude this having a secondary place.

3. It will also require a growing cadre of people who animate or plant small ecclesial communities among both churched and unchurched people. We cannot and should not rely only on the incremental multiplying of groups out of one another as individual groups grow too large. Some of these people should receive partial support by existing groups, supplementing this by working part-time for a living.

PEG BISGROVE
Bonita Springs, Florida

Peg Bisgrove says that small Christian communities in parish life and beyond formed her as a person of God, and changed the way she relates to the world. One of eight children, she grew up with "Leave it to Beaver," *Camelot,* front porches, dial phones, hula hoops, beehive hairdos, white gloves, patent leather shoes, confession, fear, and High Mass. Obedience, she says, was a high value in family, church, work, and school. Compliance was the rule. Vatican II changed her image of God from harsh to loving.

As an adult in a large New Jersey parish for eighteen years, Marriage Encounter, Cursillo, Retreats, and Renew were early small-group experiences. Writing and leadership entered her life at the same time. While parish coordinator of small Christian communities, and national coordinator of Buena Vista, Peg edited newsletters, created resources for small groups, and wrote articles for *Renew* and *Today's Parish* magazine. Her own small Christian community formed in 1986 as a core team, in response to the needs of parishioners for a place to belong, be heard, and connect faith and life. One of her two twentysomething daughters belongs to her small Christian community for the same reasons. Peg says that while her points of reference for small Christian community are U.S. parish and grassroots life, international meetings of SCC members hosted at the University of Notre Dame have broadened her understanding of people, oppression, and the need for SCC as a form of church.

STRETCHING THE BOUNDARIES OF IMAGINATION

Experiences woven concurrently through all of these settings have helped me recognize *metanoia* as an any-day possibility. People become more loving, open, and accepting of the other. They learn from one another that there are alternative pasts and alternative futures. It is a subtle process of turning the prism of possibility, and daring to leave the familiar in favor of a more developed Christ-like attitude or behavior. Really listening to another's story is an act of reverence. It changes both the listener and the storyteller. A common denominator among community members, living as church, is a growing penchant for risk. It is easier to risk when you know you are loved. SCCs can build complacency or courage. Complacent communities will not last. But a SCC rooted in Christ is a learning church. I believe that church without SCC is incomplete.

My belief in small Christian community as an ecclesial unit rests on the practice of essentials of church as articulated by authors Lee and Cowan in *Dangerous Memories*. The early Christians gathered in house churches and practiced those four characteristics of church in microcosm: *koinonia*/community; *leitourgia*/prayer and ritual; *kerygma*/gospel; and *diakonia*/outreach in service. That was the place where Christian leaders received their formation. The earliest Christian theology came directly from reflection on the Christian life experience of the community.

Today, we are called not only back to our roots, but to the challenge of future formation in the faith. Faith cannot be separated from life. And reality is mediated by both culture and church. For many adults under thirty-five, church doctrine is not an issue. It's simply irrelevant.

Pace of life and rate of change have accelerated. And when cultures get too busy, the first thing that goes is their rituals. Family dinners were the norm. Now, it's a challenge for a family to sit down together for dinner; it takes a conscious decision. Children used to play in the neighborhood. Safety prevents this many times, and now children play by appointment between lessons. TV networks are re-evaluating daytime news. Fewer are home to watch it. Accountability is demanded for use of one's energy, emotions, time, and money. America is mobile. People's desire to connect is heightened, yet often they do not know their neighbors beyond a nodding acquaintance, if at all.

The privatization and individualism of which Robert Bellah speaks of in *Habits of the Heart* creates loneliness. It is ironic that the faster we connect through modern communication, the more disconnected we feel from ourselves and others. "Touch 1 for customer service" is a joke to many, but we acquiesce, because America's automation leaves few options. Or so it seems. The sheer desire for meaningful human contact continues to grow.

Social behavior is being shaped more by the culture than the church. Manners are being rescripted. Cellular phones are used at restaurant tables during dinner. The method of social discourse on many talk shows is for all the guests to yell at once. The loudest gets to continue. Insults and disrespect are demeaning to humanity, and America has mistaken this behavior for an acceptable norm. Males rarely remove their hats when entering a building. That particular etiquette is returning—not as a social grace—but because banks require it so that security cameras can record, uncompromised, every potential robber. It is a nation of violence and fear. Children are killing children.

Each of us is impacted by an incredible barrage of information daily. The need to process, select, and learn has also accelerated. People are overwhelmed with life. Young adults' lives are strapped to a laptop computer. In some corporations, the definition of a sick day must include "in bed." If not, you are well enough to work at home and are expected to do so.

HOPES FOR THE FUTURE

1. SCC is a place where people can slow down, make sense of life, and determine what is morally right in the use of time, money, power, sharing of resources, and protection of human life. My hope is that more attention will be given to what it means to respect, honor, and preserve human dignity.
2. Parish will look different in ten years. Laity will be ministering increasingly to and with one another. I hope that small Christian communities will be a norm in every parish. I hope, too, that parishes will make a deliberate effort to include the essentials of church at every meeting taking place in the parish.
3. I hope that small Christian communities will be intentionally identified as the microcosm of church that it is, and not considered a program, fad, movement, or compartmentalized as a special ministry. In the next ten years, I hope that communities and parishes will address more deeply the images and behaviors associated with what it means to be church as neighbor, family, and servant. All require relational power, not just the ability to have effects, but the capacity to receive effects. The implication is that response to a person's needs comes from having received the story of those in need. The servant leader is there for the community. The community is not there for the leader. Mutually enriching relationship as a process requires partnership.
4. I hope that partnerships between parishes, corporations, communities, and cultures will increase dramatically. It is not only a Gospel value, but an imperative that resources of all types be shared. I hope that people in small communities will gain strength from each other, and grow through networking and prayer to imagine a different life than the impending global poverty. The middle class in America is under attack by the distribution of wealth and the way we do business. I hope that laity will continue to become better informed Catholics and committed Christians. The strategies I suggest for consideration might work best with groups who already know each other, or have become a small Christian community in infancy at least.

WHAT WILL IT TAKE FOR HOPES TO BECOME REALITY?

Strategies need to be named, reviewed, and revised regularly as real life intervenes. Good leaders will continue to encourage the people of God to trust themselves. I see the parish church of the future not only as a gathering place, but as more of a resource center. All aspects of formation including

prayer styles, ritual, scripture, teachings of the church, traditions, and methods—including conflict resolution—should be made available.

No small group becomes a small Christian community without conflict.
Treated with healthy communication processes, it empowers. For relational
power to be lived out through partnerships, we need more help with this
aspect of human/community development. I suggest that reconciliation be
incorporated increasingly as a regular spiritual process, not as crisis management. True spiritual leaders can help us to practice peacemaking skills individually and corporately. As part of a response to the fast-changing pace of
life, I hope that more seek out spiritual direction and are encouraged to consider meditation and contemplation. As prayer styles, they help balance the
noise of life, and invite God to in-spirit our imaginations toward peace, and
peacemaking.

"Risk Reflections," developed as resources to enable transcendence from
passivity to action over time, would be a real service in mission to the larger
world. Meeting processes could include naming of personal fears, prejudices,
and what it will cost to let go through intentional transcendence mediated by
grace. An SCC in Colorado stretched its imagination over time by processing
(not smoothly and not without conflict) what it means to have a homosexual
in their community. The person disclosed this after having been an accepted
member for some time. Scripture confronted reality and helped move the
people from ideological discussion to human relationship—from head to
heart. Transcendence occurred slowly but came to fruition when they invited a small community of gays and lesbians to share a retreat experience with
them. Celebration followed. They are better neighbors, and better human
beings.

In the same way, I hope that people will risk being more inclusive of all
kinds of people and cultures, but especially of small Christian communities
that are not parish-based. I do not mean inclusion with a goal to convert people to our way of thinking or our way of practicing the faith. I just mean simple invitation to co-exist within a church that has sometimes drawn black
and white lines. Invitation as a norm, not an exception, is the model that
Jesus fostered.

There are many excellent resources already. But we need help to be better
neighbors in a global village that is not on the horizon; it's here. Using simple
observations in storytelling of everyday life is the beginning, not the conclusion. Americans tend to go as far as the current resource takes them until the
next meeting. Often, people do not prepare because life is on the run. Staying
with one gospel theme for several months would allow a conversation to gain
depth, direction, and decisive action. A beginning would be to deal with the
new language of our culture, naming its oppressive effects on us as individuals, co-workers, parents, spouses, and the society around us and then naming how our culture is affecting other nations.

Faith formation with a goal of generativity can strengthen families as
church in SCCs. A parish in Maryland is fostering Intergenerational Christian
Formation, as opposed to Religious Education. I hope more families and

parishes will consider it. At a parish-sponsored night of inquiry for parents to learn what is offered, the families experience small-group process from the beginning. Cost is intentionally set lower than the traditional model of religious education to attract parents. The ongoing process includes planning by both adults and children, evenings once a month where all meet in both peer groups and large group for creative learning through shared fun, and family modeling. Children "do" the lessons at home with their parents the other three weeks of the month. Service is a norm, not an event. It makes the children feel part of a larger world family, and cared for in a style of church as family.

Faith formation beginning with immersion of an RCIA candidate in a small community before, during, and after the program helps both the catechumen and the community. Faith is experienced, refreshed, and motivated. I hope that bridge becomes a familiar path. Perhaps nothing could make the spirit of Fr. Jim Dunning happier than communion with the Trinity in our midst.

The last ten years of small community evolution has been more rapid than I expected in my lifetime. It has made me a person of radical hope. The strategies I have named are not the answers to every situation, but rather stretches of imagination deserving hopeful consideration.

MARGARET CAVANAUGH
Washington, D.C.

Margaret A. Cavanaugh has been a member of Marianist lay communities for more than thirty years, including communities in Dayton, Ohio, South Bend, Indiana, and currently in metropolitan Washington, D.C. Her interests include environmental policy, history of the Marianist tradition, and spirituality. Since 1993, she has been a member of the Marianist Lay Network of North America's Leadership Team. She represents North America, Australia, and a number of Asian and East African countries on the four-member Council of the International Organization of Marianist Lay Communities. Dr. Cavanaugh is a program director in the Chemistry Division, National Science Foundation, and previously chaired the Chemistry Department, Saint Mary's College, Notre Dame, Indiana. She is active in the American Chemical Society and is a member of the board of trustees of the University of Dayton.

IN QUEST OF UNITY IN DIVERSITY

Hope is not solitary, says poet Pablo Neruda. This rings true either way he may have meant it: not only is hope shared, but hopes are shared. Neither is hope unaccompanied by allies—allies like courage and humility and song.

But where did Alex's (remember the *Big Chill?*)—and all our—hope go? Fallen victim to isolation, perhaps, noisy hope replaced by quiet desperation? Perhaps hope has been shut out by frantic lives that leave no time for recollection. Or maybe it is yet another casualty of the good life's boredom, cynicism, and lack of imagination that can find no human struggle to engage.

Being involved in a community creates a structure in my life that jars me from isolation, forces me to take time for recollection, and confronts me with unmet human needs and aspirations. Thus it is that community nourishes hope. This experience is why I think that in the postmodern world, small Christian communities are called to be communities of hope and why I continue to be involved with Marianist lay communities (MLCs).

My commitment to MLCs began in student sodalities, as they were called then. The groups I was involved in were, gratefully, blessed by committed insightful leaders and influenced by the convergence of the post-Vatican II church, the civil rights movement, the war on poverty, and various intellectual movements in psychology, sociology, and science. As a result, the communities that developed assumed ownership of all aspects of community life: liturgy and proclamation, organization and direction setting, social justice and outreach, and mutual support. Some of these groups survived the transition from student to adult groups, gathering new members and forming SCCs in various parts of the continent. There were many other origins for MLCs because they were fostered by Marianist religious in different places. However, all emphasized similar themes, consistent with the Marianist tradition:

1. Marian spirituality, viewing Mary as a model for human development and spiritual growth;
2. a commitment to building communities as a method for social change and revitalization of the church;
3. a commitment to respond to the "signs of the times" and to work from within the world to help the world realize its full potential;
4. a desire to assist the least powerful members of society—the young, old, and poor;
5. and, an emphasis on changing social structures as opposed to offering direct assistance.

An important aspect of Marianist lay communities is that their connection to the institutional church is through a spiritual tradition—a charism—rather than through a diocese, parish, or other hierarchical structure. Their histories and lives are intertwined with those of the Society of Mary (SM) and the Daughters of Mary Immaculate (FMI), with an egalitarian cast characteristic of those foundations. The branches of the Marianist family share a common history that is especially compelling for those who wish to respond to current issues in society and in the church. In an attempt to rebuild the church in the upheaval following the French Revolution, a group of men religious, women religious, and committed lay people founded lay sodalities in Bordeaux. Out of these successful communities emerged the Marianist religious foundations, with commitment to resourcing lay communities as a primary focus.

Although submerged for decades, the concept of a Marianist family consisting of the SM, FMI, MLCs, and the Secular Institute has resurfaced, perhaps more clearly than ever. In 1996, the World Council of the Marianist Family, with representation from all four groups, was formed. Although the establishment of this body is a sign of the desired cooperative, equal, and interdependent relationship among the branches, much needs to be done to make it real and life-giving in Marianist locales around the world. Even in this nascent stage, however, formation of the World Council witnesses to the fact that collaboration is possible and that diversity can enrich the achievement of common goals.

In order for MLCs to be able to participate in the World Council, they had to form organizations that linked local communities. Until the mid-1980s, MLCs were little aware of each other's existence outside of those in the same city or in nearby states. Informal connections among religious and lay facilitated individual contacts among some lay members from various regions, as did various workshops and conferences, but no large meetings among adult lay members had taken place. MLCs were and are autonomous, forming their own agendas, and seeking their own resources and relationships.

The birthday of the Marianist Lay Network of North America (MLNNA) is arguably January 1986. It was then that a meeting of lay Marianists (promoted and supported by religious Marianists) from across the continent took place in a "back room in Chicago." Surrounded by the ambivalence of Chicago's pulsing urban life—a decision made, a strategy formed, a new thing done. Well, it was just an ordinary hotel meeting room and it wasn't smoke-filled, but I like the allusion when telling the story because it holds the promise that by insertion into the very midst of modern life, MLCs will have an impact on the human face of the world. Also, it is an image that reminds me to keep going despite MLNNA's shaky start and beyond my daily experience of it as a frail vehicle, source of personal frustration, and inspiration for numerous prayers of petition.

It was agreed at that meeting (I have heard this second-hand from a number of primary sources) that a convention of lay Marianists from across North America would be held in 1988. An organizing committee was charged to call the first North American Continental Assembly. At that time, none of the infrastructure was in place to arrange such a meeting—no address lists, no finances, no site, no speakers.

The first Continental Assembly did happen; about two hundred people gathered for three days in St. Louis for a program of speakers, workshops, and numerous discussions of the many aspects and challenges of community life. The theme was "Seed for Tomorrow's Church"—a conscious expression of the founding hope. Continental assemblies have been held triennially, with the fourth one to take place in Baltimore in 1997. Along the way, however, a transition took place as the assembly organizing committee became the Leadership Team for the MLNNA. In 1991, those assembled charged the organizing committee to propose a continuing structure that would not only plan assemblies, but offer other services to the approximately one thousand members of MLCs in North America. The goals, structure, and responsibilities for the Leadership Team were approved at the 1994 Assembly and the first official elections took place.

Although the birth of the MLNNA as an organization was a happy moment that marked resolution of many issues, it was also a challenging new beginning of a process that is not immune from the experiences of the North American church. Banners celebrating the church as "people of God" still cast shadows of self-doubt. Can the laity move from dependency to maturity? Can we prepare ourselves to serve as resources for communities ourselves— for their spiritual and personal growth, for their expansion, for their understanding of group process and conflict resolution, for their entry into social, political, and cultural issues? Given the state of the priesthood and religious orders, can we develop skills and means in time? Can we find the time and money to do so?

Because of its intertwining branches, the Marianist family is well positioned to take an alternate approach and form strong alliances to meet these challenges. There are many examples already of joint efforts by religious and lay members to provide educational and social services, develop resources for community development, and to build MLCs. Interaction in the overlap areas of common goals, such as vocations and volunteer work, continues to grow. While the branches have their own organizations, independence, and life styles, this does not preclude an ease of informal human interaction characterized by hospitality, friendship, and mutual respect.

Even so, formal structures for shared direction setting by the Marianist family in North America are in early stages of development. Leaders from the SM, FMI, and MLC agreed in 1996 to form a North American Marianist Family Council with representatives from each group; at this writing, the council is planning its first meeting. Analogous regional councils or teams have formed in various parts of the country, but are generally less than three years old. Implicit in the formation of these councils is that some things that were previously done separately will be done together. This raises the specter of loss of some prerogatives, the forfeiture of which could become a source of intra- or intergroup conflict.

Similar developments are also taking place on other continents. The International Organization of Marianist Lay Communities was founded in 1993 at a meeting of representatives from various countries held in Santiago, Chile. A leadership team was elected, and an international convocation will be held in 1997 in Valencia, Spain. The formation of the MLNNA was probably hastened by the need to develop a representative body for North America in this worldwide context.

The growth of associations of MLCs and of the various branches of the Marianist family in just five years was a surprise. While many have dreamed of the day when members of the Marianist movement worldwide would be a unified community in mission, few would have thought that it could happen in their lifetimes. No, the dream is not yet fulfilled, but it is clearly not an idealistic wish. It is a tangible hope.

I hope that men and women religious and men and women laity, vowed and unvowed, will understand themselves as members of a single global family dedicated to bringing the world to fullness in Christ. In them, there will be "no male or female, no slave or free." State of life or particular responsibilities will not be divisive. Rather, together they will witness to the church and to the world that it is possible for a diverse group to share leadership and to work together for common cause. Within the church, it is prophetic for women and men, priests and laity, to form a mutually respectful and well-ordered organization. Outside church circles, it witnesses that those from different cultures can cooperate gracefully and effectively.

I hope that the genuine friendships formed between those from the United States and Argentina, those from Korea and Japan, those from Poland and Germany, for example, will show that it is possible to transcend national boundaries to seek those things that are most truly human.

While I think that communities will continue and should continue to be local—in the sense of actions of personal support, prayer, responding to social justice concerns—I hope that a way will be found for this global community to offer a global response to global problems. Is there some way that we can impact issues of universal concern, such as economic or environmental problems?

In addition, I hope that the Marianist family in North America becomes more diverse, including more members who are from minority groups or who are not middle class. Finally, I hope that a new spirituality will break forth, deeper, broader, and more responsive to our times. We are already on our way to this vision. We have a common heritage, a fledgling organizational framework, and many dedicated, talented, and generous members. Our main challenge is to keep going and going in a way that will sustain long-term growth. We are challenged to find a path of organic growth and to nurture new patterns of authority. Great demands will be placed on our ability to learn and let go, to discern and change, and to balance holiness, humility, and spiritual growth with the inherent busy-ness of involvement in modern life, service, and building an organization. But now we are coming together.

Marianist communities, lay and religious, know that Pablo Neruda is right: Hope is not solitary.

BARBARA HOWARD
Arvada, Colorado

Barbara Howard, a Roman Catholic laywoman, has been actively involved in the public life of the church for several years. She has served on several boards and committees in the Archdiocese of Denver and was a member of the board of directors of the American Catholic Lay Network. She was a delegate to the Synod Conference on the Laity in Rome in 1987 where exposure to the international face of the church greatly challenged and broadened her understanding of the Spirit's powerful activity in the world today. Barb is a national speaker and has written for *Today's Parish* magazine. Her fields of interest include lay spirituality, women in the church, and the development of the early church. Her greatest passion, however, is the development of small Christian community where faith and life meet in an intimate and ongoing conversation. Recently she co-authored a sharing booklet for small Christian communities titled *Ubi Caritas (where there is charity and love there is God.)*

Barb is Coordinator of small church communities at Spirit of Christ Catholic Community, a 3400 household parish in Arvada, Colorado. She also chairs the National Joint Task Force for Small Christian Community. Barb participated in both the National and International Consultations on Small Christian Community at Notre Dame University and was the founding national coordinator of Buena Vista, a national network of people committed to the development and support of small Christian communities. Barb is married and the mother of three young adults. She and her husband, Mike, have been members of a small Christian community for twenty-five years.

WORKING THE PARISH MODEL

My involvement with small Christian community (SCC) began twenty-five years ago with an invitation from Claretian Father John Martens to "meet some other Catholics in my neighborhood." When my husband, Mike, and I accepted that invitation, it set us on a path that has profoundly influenced our lives. Our small Christian community (known to us as Mini-Parish) has formed the basis of a life style which has supported and nurtured us while challenging us to ministry and evangelization. As my husband and I began to see small community as something vital and integral to our lives, I was led to a part-time position in my parish, Spirit of Christ Catholic Community, working with the development of small Christian communities.

Mike and I designed a process called Journey, which created the environment for twenty small Christian communities to form in our parish between the years 1982 and 1984. In 1984 our diocese entered the Renew process, which I coordinated for our parish. During the Renew process, our parish staff struggled with the concept of SCCs. Were they solely Christian support groups, or was there a deeper significance in their gathering? To broaden the input into our discussion, Spirit of Christ, with the assistance of Fr. Philip Murnion and the staff of the National Pastoral Life Center, sponsored a gathering in April of 1986 to which representatives of ten large parishes throughout the United States were invited. The main topic of discussion for this week-long gathering was to be SCCs; however, the discussion greatly broadened, as discussions will, to include various concerns of large parishes, SCCs being just one of them. As a result of that meeting, the National Pastoral Life Center published a booklet *Big or Small, Parish Is Still Possible.*

Still struggling with issues surrounding the life of SCCs, our parish initiated another national gathering in January of 1987 inviting representatives of parishes and national organizations which were giving lots of energy to the development of SCCs. Some of the folks who attended were representatives from the national Renew office including Fr. Tom Dowd and Sr. Cathy Nerney, Fr. Art Baronowski of Troy, Michigan, along with some thirty other folks. That gathering, intended as a one-time discussion of SCCs, was the genesis of the national SCC network called Buena Vista. I served as the founding national coordinator for the network from 1987 through 1990. The Buena Vista network was tiny and distribution of its newsletter limited. The ever-present experiment in those early years of the network was whether SCCs would continue and expand as an emerging style of church in the United States or would they be only a short-lived phenomenon. The results of the experiment were and still are totally dependent on God's gracious Spirit.

Buena Vista linked with Fr. Bob Pelton of Notre Dame University, which enabled participation of grassroots people along with theologians and clergy in two gatherings at Notre Dame: a national and an international consultation on SCCs in 1990 and 1991, respectively. I was privileged to be part of both consultations and learned first-hand about the enormous energy of God's Spirit working in SCCs throughout the world. Since that time, I have been very pleased to participate in many national conferences on the topic of SCCs and have published articles and materials for SCCs. It was my pleasure to coordinate planning of a joint national convocation of SCCs in the summer of 1993 in Minneapolis and I am acting in that same capacity for a second joint SCC gathering planned for the summer of 1997 in New Orleans. I have also had many graced opportunities to speak about SCCs throughout the country.

While staying in touch with the national and international growth of SCCs and the attendant developing ecclesiology, I continue to work at the parish level in the ministry of SCC development and support. I find this ministry tremendously life-giving and at the same time tremendously frustrating. How to convince folks that small community is important is the frustration. Hearing the marvelous stories of support, friendship, and empowerment for mission in the name of God's reign is life-giving. I feel blessed to have been part of the unfolding story of small Christian community in our day and age.

FOUR HOPES AND ONE HOPE-NOT

My reflections on the future of SCCs come from the perspective of parish life, since that is the milieu in which I function on a day-to-day basis.

1. For a number of reasons, I believe that small Christian communities will continue to develop in parishes throughout the United States. I think that the strongest impetus will come from ordinary folks who have experienced SCCs as life-giving and want to share that experience. Given the high degree of mobility in our society, people who have experienced SCC in one area of the country will desire that experience in the new locale and the new parish. Those people will create an impetus for forming small communities if a vehicle is not already in place within the parish.

   Grassroots-up development of SCCs reflects the desire of people to connect in communal structures with intimate relationships that may have been lost with long- or short-distance moves. Recovery of relationships similar to those experienced in extended families and lost through corporate or individual relocation will continue to offer an impetus for people to join in smaller communities. The parish offers an immediate and convenient starting place for people to seek those relationships. Simply offering involvement in parish ministry or conventional programming to these seekers of an intimate, relational church will not be enough. Parishes which do not foster small communities in the future will find themselves greatly diminished in size and energy.

   More parishes are viewing SCCs as a pastoral response to the growing numbers of Catholics and the dwindling numbers of ordained clergy. As we know, small Christian communities offer an intimate environment where people can come to know and care for one another in such a way that issues or life experiences which may typically become a pastoral need addressed to the pastor or parish staff can be ministered to on the level of the SCC itself. Parish pastoral staffs will more and more trust SCCs as a faith community able to minister to one another in times of grief, marital and familial stress, sacramental preparation, etc.

   Parish staffs will take seriously the commitment of SCC members to a style of church which is collaborative, participatory, gospel-centered, missionary, and evangelical. SCC members' input will be sought in a consultative process as parishes define organizational structures and develop long-term planning. SCCs will be particularly important in "priestless parishes." They will be called on to create prayerful liturgical experiences of the Word for the entire parish community as well as to design and assist at liturgies at which a visiting priest will preside at Eucharist.

In two recent documents, *Communion and Mission* and *Called and Gifted for the Third Millennium,* the bishops of the United States have addressed the life of SCCs in a very positive light. The bishops' words will help the development of SCCs within the next ten years to become a normative part of parish life. Small Christian communities will be linked in a systemic way with RCIA and RCIC, a dream of Fr. Jim Dunning. Parishes will realize that what begins as an initial conversion to the Catholic tradition in Christian Initiation is lived in an ongoing conversion within the small Christian community. Also in parish sacramental preparation programs, the development of small communities will be encouraged as a way of living a sacramental life for families and individuals. No longer will enlightened parishes simply provide a filling-station for sacramental life, but will call people to community, not theoretically as so often presented in the theology of baptism, but to real flesh and blood community with brothers and sisters.

2. Small Christian community members will more deeply explore the connections between faith and life in civic and political issues based on a pursuit of the common good. This is perhaps one of the most difficult areas for SCCs to tackle but is one which will transform individual thinking into communal thinking. Small communities will more and more reflect on the Gospel and the social teaching of the Catholic church as a basis for reflection and action in behalf of God's reign. This activity will provide a consciousness-raising for the SCCs which will help them to effect change in personal life style as well as to critique and attempt to change those parts of culture which denigrate human life and human dignity. Small community members will more and more understand that pursuing the common good is constitutive of Catholic faith and tradition. For some communities this understanding will translate into community organizing efforts around particular issues. For others, engagement in the political process, beyond that of voting, will help create a civic climate cognizant of the common good. Some small communities will go as a group on immersion experiences that allow them to experience what it is like to live on the underside of society in big cities or in southern border towns such as Ciudad Juarez. This experience will help form consciences prepared for action on behalf of the poor and alienated of our world society.

3. Small Christian communities will assemble in larger gatherings both within and outside of the parish. These gatherings will challenge and inspire SCC members to be church in ways previously unimagined. They will realize that membership in their small Church community calls forth their gifts of ministry and their gifts of leadership. SCCs will model for the

rest of the church that discipleship is not dependent on gender, education, or socio-economic class but is a call given by God for the good of the whole body. SCCs will help people discover their call to ministry for the sake of God's reign. The larger church will see within SCCs a model of vocation and leadership that is not limited by gender or marital status. Reminiscent of the experience of the earliest centuries of the church, the small Christian community will offer a variety of styles of gathering, a variety of styles of prayer, a variety of ministries, yet all united by the Spirit of God.

4. Small Christian communities will move the ecumenical dialogue forward in a manner that honors people's lived experience. SCCs will allow people from different faith traditions (and no faith tradition) to gather and listen to one another in a way that allows conflicting viewpoints to exist without fracturing relationships. These conversations will not be an acquiescence to a relativism of truth, rather they will proceed based on an honest confession of humanity's inability to contain the vastness of God's ongoing saving presence solely within dogma and tradition. As members in ecumenical small communities listen to one another respectfully they will learn to appreciate differences in understanding God and God's Word. This appreciation will extend to the broader communities in which SCC members exist and will act as yeast in society for new levels of conversation and respect for differences.

What I hope does not happen in the next ten years would be that those who take on the role of leadership or facilitator in the small Christian communities would develop into a new hierarchy. If this new/ancient SCC style of church is to flourish and reach its God-given potential, it cannot be hamstrung early on in its development by folks who *think* they know the proper parameters, interpretation, methodology, or direction. God's Spirit can never be contained, but it can be squelched. The challenge to SCCs and to those who work with SCC development and support is to commit to a prayerful and reflective journey which will lead us to a new style of church. This future church will be one in which the proclamation of God's reign in both word and action is the *right* and the *responsibility* of every baptized Christian. The map is not yet clear but the destination is most worthy of the journey!

WHAT NEEDS TO HAPPEN

As I reflect on what needs to happen for my hopes for small Christian communities to be realized, I find myself somewhere between humming Frank Sinatra's song "High Hopes" in which the ant believes it can move the rubber tree plant, and Albert Camus's telling of the myth of Sisyphus, whose eternal struggle is to push the rock up the unconquerable hill. Some of the hopes that I have are quite achievable and will happen simply because of the social/cultural setting of our country today. More small groups will develop based on people's need to belong to and with other human beings while trying to survive in a sterile, individualistic, technical society which values the bottom line over people.

Other hopes should find little resistance in parishes which are really trying to be attentive to the "signs of the times." Offering structures that develop community among people is a vitally important effort, and anyone who is paying attention knows that. Those parishes will create strong links between programming and community building. They will know that sacramental preparation, adult education, religious formation, and youth ministry all need to lead to a style of life which is communal in nature and which has Jesus as its center and the reign of God as its goal. Parishes that do not have the foresight or energy to pursue community building will continue to be spiritual filling stations or will become irrelevant to the reality of people's real lives.

My hopes for SCCs to really enter into understanding a preferential option for the poor are a bit more tenuous. Their realization can only take place if SCCs are willing to be exposed to and touched by those experiences of our brothers and sister in the two-thirds world (including the underside of our own society) that challenge the socio-economic lifestyle of the dominant U.S. culture of which many of us are part. The enormous question is whether SCCs can become a countercultural force which does not totally subscribe to the goals of our consumer-driven culture. If the communal energy focused in small groups can also turn outward for the betterment of the larger world, then my hopes will be realized in a phenomenal way.

As SCCs continue to form they are contributing to the development of an ecclesiology particular to their experience. This has already been the case in the work of some Latin American theologians and is in the beginning phases of exploration in the church of the United States. If an ecclesiology is developed that validates the experience of small Christian communities, then a model of church which is inclusive, participatory, and nonhierarchical can emerge to give life to a universal church, one which finds itself using a model of church that is slowly dying. In a sense, this hope feels like Sisyphus's task, but our God is a God of surprises!

For a true ecumenical dialogue to occur in small communities, members have to first be willing to invite others of different or no faith tradition into their communities. SCC members have to be willing to listen to the stories and the understanding of others who do not share their world views. We have had good practice with this and know that even those of our own faith tradition within our SCCs come with a variety of understandings and outlooks. Hopefully, we have learned to listen to them with open hearts and minds. If SCCs open the circle to expand the dialogue to others who are even more different, then the potential for tolerance and acceptance grows enormously. If this can happen, hope for ever-expanding circles of conversation and understanding can come to fruition.

THOMAS KLEISSLER
Newark, New Jersey

Thomas A. Kleissler, a priest of the Archdiocese of Newark, was ordained in 1957. The first half of his forty years of priesthood was spent as a parish priest in vastly different settings: a suburban/country parish and in an inner-city parish in Newark. This pastoral background led him to develop with Msgr. Thomas Ivory in the Archdiocese of Newark the Renew process. He has directed Renew International, which has served over 12,000 parishes in 240 dioceses in 15 countries, since its inception. He has authored a number of articles about small Christian communities and along with Mary McGuinness and Margo LeBert co-authored *Small Christian Communities: A Vision of Hope,* which won first place in the category of pastoral ministry from the Catholic Book Publishers Association.

SMALL CHRISTIAN COMMUNITIES FOR THE THIRD MILLENNIUM: TO LIVE WITH COURAGE OR TO DIE

My interest and involvement in small Christian communities has spanned over fifty years. The "conversion" experience occurred in 1946 as a sophomore at Seton Hall Prep, South Orange, New Jersey. Knowing since the fifth grade that I wanted to be a priest, I now came to know precisely what I wanted to do in my priesthood. It was to work with small Christian communities.

A pamphlet on the Young Christian Workers is what captivated my imagination. They were young people who came together to connect faith to issues of working conditions in the factories, dating practices, economic concerns, relationships with parents and family, and every conceivable issue of their lives. It was what I would come to know as a holistic spirituality, one that was not limited to Mass on Sunday or other overtly spiritual exercises. Religion was a seven-days-of-the-week experience nurtured by the reflections in these small communities and the specific social actions that flowed from their meetings.

This conviction was lived out by participation in Catholic Action groups in high school and college. In the seminary I organized one hundred seminarians in small groups and then immediately launched small communities in the parish after ordination.

The remarkable transformation that occurred in people's lives in these small communities, and the incredibly significant things they did in their family settings, in the communities in which they lived, and in their places of work, deepened the conviction and broadened the vision of what small

Christian communities could do in enabling the church to fulfill the mission of Jesus.

The opportunity to present the vision of a parish community made up of many small Christian communities was first presented in a meeting with Bishop Walter Curtis in Bridgeport, Connecticut, in 1967. This vision came from a deep conviction from my experience in Our Lady of Mercy parish in Park Ridge, New Jersey. The time had arrived in our parish where large numbers of people were now ready to engage in small community activity. Six hundred adults and two hundred teenagers active in small Christian communities profoundly impacted upon the parish, on the surrounding towns, and even on archdiocesan activity even though the parish was at the outer boundary of the diocese.

The next step on my journey took place upon becoming pastor of St. Ann's parish in inner-city Newark. It was the poorest parish in the diocese. Consideration was being made to close the parish. What a wonderful confirmation to see that in an entirely different cultural, economic, and social environment, small Christian communities were as effective and had perhaps even greater impact on people's lives and the social circumstances of the neighborhood.

The conviction coming from these very disparate parish experiences led to the concept of an experience across the archdiocese that would call people to spiritual renewal and would flourish largely through the medium of small Christian communities.

This original Renew experience proved to be very successful based largely on the impact of the tens of thousands of people engaged in small communities. Since then more than four million people have had the opportunity to participate in faith-sharing small communities throughout the country and the world through Renew.

The current project of Renew 2000 is a particularly exciting venture in my life because it enables these varying experiences to be built into a process involving thousands of parishes—not on a temporary experience of small Christian communities, but a long-term journey of integration of small Christian communities into parish life. The goal and hope of setting a diocesan climate in which parishes can develop into a community of many small Christian communities now seems more attainable than ever before through this latest venture of Renew 2000.

HOPES ARE LIMITLESS AND SO TO NAME A FEW

How can one succinctly express future hopes for small Christian communities when these hopes are limitless? Our rapidly changing world makes new pastoral approaches imperative. We have been far too slow to take on a more outward and assertive style of pastoring. People will no longer automatically become involved in church activity because of a faith heritage based on ethnicity or family or neighborhood roots. The time has passed for sitting in rectories and confidently waiting at churches for people to come. It never should have been that way in the first place.

What an attractive contrast and pleasant dream it would be to see the normative parish of the future as a community made up of many vibrant small Christian communities. Wouldn't it be wonderful if bishops and pastors across the land took strong leadership to move us in this direction? But rather than focus on "what if," I would like to focus on what small Christian communities can and must do themselves if there is hope for our dreams to come true. If small communities are all that they can be, their future will take care of itself.

My hope for the next decade is that small Christian community developments could at least parallel or even exceed the growth patterns we find in our secular world. Look at the many and diverse breakthroughs in human knowledge in our time—breakthroughs in genetics, astrophysics, medicine, education, and technology, to name a few. Breakthroughs in science and technology take us on an interior journey to the depths of the nature of matter while at the same time stretching us into outer realms of creation. Mind-boggling discoveries of inner and outer space explode our knowledge and expand our capacity to wonder beyond the wildest imagination.

Scientists tell us that the vastness of outer space is replicated in the boundless expanses within a single atom. With new scientific discoveries, what was once thought to be lifeless matter is now seen in a new light. Through quantum physics we learn that matter has an inner dynamic dimension, the nucleus of each atom showing forth these inner dynamics. Planet Earth itself is considered to be a living organism because it is self-governing, self-healing, and self-propagating.

The expansion of our knowledge of the universe has not only led us to recognize a whole new interior world, but it also has brought us into a new realization about outer space. We have learned that our ever-expanding universe contains at least 40 to 50 billion galaxies, each with 100 billion stars. New planets have been discovered. The possibility of life on Mars has generated unprecedented acclaim.

Our future spiritual journey should expand our horizons in a comparable way. Our quest to know and discover our God more intimately should bring us into the depths of interior life. Discoveries in contemplation and a deeper union with God are breakthroughs our restless modern spirits badly need. On the other hand a clearer understanding of the mission of Jesus and the movement of the Holy Spirit in our hearts should propel us beyond the bonds of cultural Christianity into exciting new levels of outreach and ministry in our lives. Growth, inwardly and outwardly, is the greatest challenge facing small Christian communities. It is imperative!

Looking at what has already been accomplished, small Christian communities have come a long way. Once considered peripheral to mainstream parish activity, they now involve substantial numbers in parishes throughout the country. The fact that they have met pastoral and spiritual needs is large-ly responsible for this increased acceptance.

The popularity of small Christian communities is also a response to a basic paradigm shift that has modified social structures in a much more horizontal image. Small communities meet the need for community and a sense of belonging that are so inherent to humanity. For Christians there is fulfillment of a basic need to strengthen and support one another in a world of divergent secular views and values. For many Catholics, discovering the scriptures through faith sharing has added a fresh and exciting dimension and vigor to their faith life.

Despite the growing popularity of small Christian communities, there is, however, a danger. In fact the progress made can become the greatest danger. We can easily be tempted to settle in comfortably to what we already have—with the feeling that the only need is to bring more people into this enjoyable experience. The support we receive and the spirit of communion with our friends could make us self-satisfied, cozy groups, turned in on ourselves. Small Christian communities will be in trouble if the impetus for internal and external growth is lost. There must be an ongoing spirit of discovery and exploration.

One of the greatest apostles of the past century was Father Joseph Cardijn. When, as a seminarian, he saw friends who as young workers were being lost to the church, he decided that his priestly ministry would break the bonds of the status quo and make the gospel live in the realities of everyday life. Conditions in the factory, the dating problems of young people, relationships with their parents, economic concerns, alcohol, and recreation were all seen as a part of the fabric of life that make up one's spirituality. His utilization of dynamic small communities with the Young Christian Workers and the many magnificent movements that flowed from that effort provided effective and concrete ways to make the reign of God something more than a spiritual cliché; it became a reality lived out in daily life. Spirituality moved beyond a Sunday morning experience to become a seven-days-a-week commitment.

It is critically important for small Christian communities today to have the same spirit of exploration and to be connected with every area of human endeavor. Catholics are now in leadership positions on every level in business, finance, education, civic life, and in the world of communication. The question we face is: how much does our faith impact on these daily endeavors? As the gap between rich and poor continues to increase in our country and throughout the world, one may suspect that the connection of faith to life might be more separated than ever before. Small Christian communities must courageously expand their horizons and endeavors to be about the mission of Christ. If small communities live for themselves, they will die. They will die of their own weight. It is as simple as that.

Conversely, what better format than small Christian communities is there to help people with interior discoveries of faith? In John's Gospel we hear

Jesus say: "You are in me and I am in you" (Jn. 14:20b). Our communities provide us with a taste of this kind of union and challenge us to deeper union with one another and with Christ. People today, young adults in particular, are hungering for a rich spiritual experience that is devoid of the internal division and squabbles that have characterized recent decades. Small Christian communities are an ideal place for young people and people of all ages to discover the rich spiritual tradition of centuries of saints and mystics who sounded out the depth of union with God. A world filled with the cacophony of many strident and conflicting voices cries out in need of the serenity and peace that comes from this union.

If small Christian communities are a launching pad for growth in the inner journey of contemplation and the outward thrust of apostolic mission endeavors, then there is great hope for the future. History will then record for centuries to come that small Christian communities in our time were a stabilizing force for creative change in our society and the means of renewal for individuals and our church.

WHAT IT TAKES TO GIVE BIRTH TO HOPES

If a spirit of discovery and exploration is to prevail in small Christian communities, then we cannot rely on cruise control or self-maintenance. Growth will require developing deeper personal relationships with Jesus and returning more fully to the values of Jesus, clear pastoral objectives, as well as solid and well-conceived materials and good pastoring.

Keeping our eyes focused on Jesus is the best way to bring small Christian communities to fruition. Returning to the values of Jesus—values of total surrender to God, love of others, love of ourselves, love for the poor, respect for all living things including planet Earth—this is our challenge. Small Christian communities will grow and develop as communities of faith to the extent that they keep their eyes focused on Jesus, whose message is universal and for all times.

While small Christian communities are a response to the needs of our times and will undoubtedly continue to develop, having clear pastoral objectives will assist their growth and fruitfulness. One of the gifts that we as Americans have been given is the gift of planning and strategizing in order to accomplish a pastoral direction or a vision of life. Small communities will more likely prosper in settings where leadership encourages their growth and where the communities themselves have clear goals and objectives.

The great issues of life that need to be addressed cannot be expected to arise in small communities by some sort of internal combustion. Surely the power is in the scriptures, but long experience has shown that we don't always courageously or creatively connect the power of the gospel to some of the more difficult issues of today. There is a strong tendency to stay in the comfort zone. After all, exploring economic realities, business practices, racial tensions, women's concerns, and a broad spectrum of respect for life issues could possibly cause tensions within ourselves and within the community. It would be so much easier to keep our meetings "spiritual" and leave the issues to "life out there." Fortunately there is great hope today in materials being developed in the areas of family, civic responsibilities, ecology, nonviolence, international harmony, work, morality, hunger, media, the homeless, immigrants, business ethics, mysticism, and vocations. Spirituality embraces all human concerns and activities.

Jesus took three years to develop the first pastors who went out forming communities which they in turn pastored. While they kept moving about developing these communities, the sense of being good pastors kept them in contact with the communities they had initiated and gave them assurance that each community had its own pastoring leadership and was being cared for. Spiritual growth has always called for good spiritual direction, encouragement, a challenge to expansion of mind and heart, the setting of new goals, the evaluation of progress, and a regrouping of efforts. All of these are the ingredients of good pastoring and are needed for small community development in the same manner as parishes and dioceses require zealous pastoring.

Those starting small Christian communities have a responsibility as did St. Paul to keep in contact with and in pastoral relationship with the communities they have launched. Groups started and left on their own without good pastoring and good materials will only lead to a certain amount of malaise or disillusionment. They will be one more thing that was tried and failed.

On the other hand, properly encouraged and cared for, small Christian communities offer the greatest promise of hope for the realization of the reign of God in the new millennium.

ROBERT MORIARTY
Hartford, Connecticut

Robert K. Moriarty, S.M., is a Marianist brother in the Society of Mary and director of the Hartford Archdiocese's Pastoral Department for Small Christian Communities. He is a scripture scholar and principal editor of *Quest,* a widely used lectionary-based guide for small Christian communities. He is also national coordinator of the North American Forum for Small Christian Communities, an association of diocesan personnel working with SCCs in parishes. Bob's voice on the SCC experience reflects both his extensive, concrete involvement with them as well as the Marianist charism that considers community to be the primary instrument of the apostolate. For him, SCCs are not themselves the vision of the future, as much as they are a vital dynamic in a vision of the parish of the future. He sees the potential for SCCs as catechumenal communities in the Rite of Christian Initiation for Adults.

SMALL CHURCH COMMUNITIES: A VISION FOR THE PARISH OF THE TWENTY-FIRST CENTURY

In the Archdiocese of Hartford small church communities have been developing for more than ten years now. Many trace their roots to a very successful Renew experience, conducted in the archdiocese from 1983 to 1986.

I never speak about small church communities without speaking about parish. And I cannot think about parish without thinking about small church communities. Small church communities are not ends in themselves. They are living cells of the larger Body of Christ in mission for the sake of the world, and because they are, our attention must be directed not simply to small communities singly, but also to their inter-relationship and to their role in the larger body of which they are a part.

As convinced as I am about the promise of small church communities, they are not my first concern. It is parish which is my over-riding interest. The priority I place on parish stems from the simple fact that parish is the ordinary experience of church for most American Catholics who are connected to church.

In addition, in the effort to move small church communities more and more deeply into mission, parish and diocesan structures offer precisely the kind of networking potential needed to enable small church communities, locally and regionally, to address systemic issues of justice and peace.

FORMATIVE FEATURES IN MY WORK WITH SCCS

My identity as a Marianist religious, my years of involvement in parish ministry, and my current role as the director of a diocesan office for small church communities are the critical factors which combine to shape these remarks about parish and small church communities. A few words about each are in order.

A mixed congregation of lay and priest religious, the Society of Mary (Marianists) was founded in France in 1817 by William Chaminade, a priest of the Archdiocese of Bordeaux. Small church communities were at the center of his vision for rebuilding the church in the wake of the secularization that flowed from the French Revolution. The vision which inspired Chaminade, the multiplication of communities of faith in mission, resonates quite closely with what is developing today in the emergence of small church communities.

In time, schools became the principal work of the Society of Mary. But in recent years, while still significantly invested in school work, Marianists have reconnected more and more consciously with the founder's earliest inspiration. The fundamental mission is clearly understood to be "the multiplication of communities of faith in mission."

Our Rule of Life proposes that "community is a primary instrument of the apostolate." Consequently, our preferred style is not that of individual Marianists engaged in parish ministry, but that of corporate Marianist involvement in a parish through the presence of a community of at least three, reflecting the mixed composition (i.e., lay and priest religious) of the congregation.

During the early years of my graduate work in religious studies, I worked in a number of parishes on a part-time basis in the always invigorating world of youth ministry. As my own province began its move to corporate Marianist involvement in parish ministry, I joined my confreres in service to Sacred Heart Parish in Vernon, Connecticut (Diocese of Norwich). Building the parish as a community of faith in mission was a major priority, and the cultivation of community was a hallmark of our contribution in those years.

After some years at the parish I returned to academia to complete my doctoral work in scripture. As I completed my dissertation, I anticipated a return to Marianist life and mission in Connecticut. When I was invited to serve as the coordinator of the Pastoral Department for Small Christian Communities for the Archdiocese of Hartford, I sensed instinctively that the development of parish-rooted small church communities was exactly what was needed to animate parish life and mission today. And I knew in my bones that this effort is the warrant for Marianist involvement in parish ministry.

THE HARTFORD EXPERIENCE

Before beginning the work, I heard a talk by Fr. Art Baranowski, a priest of the Archdiocese of Detroit, and later the founder of the National Alliance of Parishes Restructuring into Communities. Here was a practicing pastor of a real parish speaking about his concrete experience of building a parish in which small church communities served as basic building blocks for parish. The penny dropped immediately. His was a focused, clear, realizable way to develop the kind of parish structure we need for the twenty-first century.

The development of small Christian communities in the Archdiocese of Hartford traces its roots to the experience of Renew. The small group gathered around the scriptures was a central feature of the Renew experience. As Renew drew to a close, people were heard to say again and again, "If these small groups are such a good thing, why do they have to end?" Archbishop John F. Whealon took that feedback to heart and established the Pastoral Department for Small Christian Communities as the successor to Renew. Priscilla (Pat) Linehan, the coordinator for Renew, became the first coordinator for the department. I succeeded her in 1989. Archbishop Whealon died in 1990. The work of the department for small communities now continues under the leadership of Archbishop Daniel A. Cronin.

Our day-to-day efforts are something like working the two ends of an accordion. On one end, we provide direct support to hundreds of small communities in approximately half the parishes of the archdiocese. This includes, for example, the publication of lectionary-based resources for small community gatherings (*Quest, Summer Reflections*). From the other end of the accordion, I work closely with pastors/priests to explore basic issues of vision for parish and the role small church communities can play as basic building blocks in a long-range plan for parish development.

Our generally very good experience with small Christian communities, and the presence of hundreds of them across the archdiocese, offers a platform to speak to the issues of a larger vision for parish in which small communities can play a major role in strengthening the overall life and mission of the parish. Only by projecting this larger vision can we ensure the long-term survival of large numbers of these communities, as well as draw from them the potential they hold for building a parish for the next century.

These days there are all sorts of assessments circulating about the health of the parish as we know it. Some of these judgments suggest that the parish as we now have it is ineffective. Anyone who has invested him/herself in parish life and ministry for any length of time certainly knows that this is not the whole story. At the same time, there are more than enough red flags in my experience of it all to give me substantial pause for thought.

Studies of church attendance by American Catholics suggest a decline from about 70 percent weekly attendance in the early 1960s to about 28 percent today. And sociologist Pierre Hegy reports that among the Catholic population under 25 years of age, only 13.2 percent attend Mass weekly (Hegy 1993). In the face of these numbers one might ask the admittedly chilling question: Just how much of a parish will there be in the twenty-first century?

Vatican II recovered for us the image of the church as the people of God. And we have been working to maximize lay participation ever since. But, ask the average parishioner coming out of church on Sunday: "Who is responsible for this parish?" Surely most people would answer simply, "the pastor." Some thirty years after Vatican II, parish is still put on by the few for the many.

CHRISTIAN COMMUNITY AS GATHERED AND SENT

Certainly, some of what we are up against today is cultural in nature, e.g., consumerism and individualism. Culture has given us so much loneliness, alienation, isolation, emptiness, absence of meaning, so many fractured families, so many broken lives. The phenomenon of increasing youth suicide is not just telling us something about these young people and their families, it is telling us something about all of us, collectively.

Happily, however, there are signals in the culture itself that a one-sided individualism is not really satisfying. The phenomenon of support groups is perhaps one of the most striking indicators. Princeton sociologist of religion

Robert Wuthnow has studied the small group phenomenon in depth. In 1994, he reported that four out of ten Americans were currently members of a small group that meets regularly and gives them caring and support. In addition, another two out of ten indicated that they would like to be members of such a group, and about half of them indicated that it was fairly to very likely that they would join such a group in the coming year (Wuthnow 1994). At its root, the support group phenomenon is a profound cultural indicator that deep in our hearts we know we cannot and do not really want to have to make it alone.

The recovery of community is one of the most important challenges that faces us in this culture and in our church in this culture. Unfortunately, the typical program-centered, activity-dominated parish all too often mimics some of the worst of the culture. Too often, it unwittingly aids and abets the delicatessen approach to parish and the one-sided individualism and consumerism that underlies that pick-and-choose approach to parish.

We are specialists in American Catholic parish life today at responding to the demands of the immediate and the needs of individuals as individuals. And that will always be one essential pole of the care of souls. In our day and age, however, we especially need to cultivate the other pole. We need to make a substantial investment in cultivating the communal, the corporate experience of parish. There are different tasks involved in meeting the needs of individuals as individuals and meeting the needs of the family as a family, of the parish as a parish. Community does not just happen, it has to be cultivated. Favorable conditions must be actively, consistently fostered.

We need a model for parish, centered not on activities targeted simply to the individual, but rather on bringing ordinary people together to help each other to connect life and faith, regularly. To realize this vision we need a mediating structure, a container that brings people together in face-to-face relationships and holds them together long enough for people to begin to make a real difference in each others' lives and faith. The small church community is coming more and more to serve as such a container. Small church communities are not the vision. The small church community is a vehicle for the vision. The vision is the development of a parish where ordinary people help each other connect life and faith, regularly. To the extent that it is a concern about strengthening the inner life of the parish, and its institutional viability, it is precisely for the sake of empowering it more effectively for mission, for positioning it to more effectively impact the societal systems with which it interacts.

Big and small, the call to evangelizing mission is constitutive of the church's very being. And the mission is aimed not simply at the transformation of individual hearts in coming to know Jesus as Lord; it is likewise directed to engagement with the world so that God may be all in all in a transformed world.

As church, we are a people both gathered and sent. More accurately, perhaps, we are a people gathered for the sake of being sent. The gathering is conducted in light of the sending to come, but the gathering comes first. The quality of the gathering has some bearing on the effectiveness of the sending. How to balance the emphasis now on gathering and sending is a matter of substantial concern. The occupational hazard of SCCs is contentment with coziness. Attending to both poles is an ongoing task.

Some people say, "We live in such an individualistic culture. If we push people in small communities to mission too hard, too fast, we run the risk of just driving them away from the small community experience." And others say, "We have such a penchant for meeting individual needs in this culture, that unless small communities confront the call to mission from their very foundation, they seriously run the risk of never getting to it." These voices constitute a tension which is not easily resolved. We need to attend to both voices.

My experience with small Christian communities in the Archdiocese of Hartford suggests that there is no lack of a disposition to service or absence of outreach. Small community members are among the most invested parishioners in the life and mission of the parish. They pour themselves out in service both within and beyond the parish. [Their stories are told in *Belonging, Believing and Serving: The Stories of Small Christian Communities*, ed. Robert Moriarty, available from the Pastoral Department for Small Christian Communities, Archdiocese of Hartford, 467 Bloomfield Ave., Bloomfield, CT 06002; 1 (860) 243-9642.]

SOCIAL TRANSFORMATION AND THE NETWORKING OF SMALL CHRISTIAN COMMUNITIES

Moving small church communities to engagement with systemic issues entails consciousness raising and the skills of social analysis. But the challenge is even more basic: generating a base, a critical mass of small church communities open to the kind of local and regional networking necessary to have a systemic impact.

Individual SCCs cannot have any more impact for systemic change than single individuals. We need interconnected networks of small church communities that cross urban and suburban lines. A parish- and diocesan-based approach to small church communities offers just the structural networking possibilities needed to empower small church communities for the systemic work of justice and peace. Congregation-based organizing efforts have long since realized the potential that Catholic structural arrangements hold for the promotion of social change. Rooted in the parish, interconnected networks of small church communities can offer substantial muscle in this effort to promote the common good.

The bottom line, at this point in time, however, is simply that small church communities are but a fledgling phenomenon. The major challenge we face at this point is the foundational task of drawing people together, of working to generate small church communities. And this begins with the very humble work of wooing, coaxing, cajoling people to slow down, to become more reflective about their lives, to ask about the things that count, to rediscover the ties that bind, to begin to discover how God might be present in the midst of it all even though they may not have even noticed. If we are to lead people to a sense of solidarity with humanity, an appreciation of its broken-ness, and need for healing, to the extent that it will move people to action for the sake of the common good, we need first to cultivate the fundamental experience of "we." We need to be about the foundational work of conversion to community.

THE CATECHUMENAL POSSIBILITIES FOR THE SCC

No reflection on small church communities and parish would be complete without some consideration of the enormous mutual benefit to be gained from drawing small communities and the adult catechumenate (RCIA) into intimate collaboration.

In the years just before his untimely death, Fr. James Dunning, founder of the North American Forum on the Catechumenate, had been heard to observe increasingly that the catechumenate sometimes seems like a revolv-ing door. Too many people, he noted, are being initiated into a church that is not really there. Having been introduced to a certain experience of church in an intensely communal catechumenal experience, the newly baptized/received are too frequently tossed like goldfish into the all too often relative-ly anonymous waters of larger parish life when initiation is complete. When the ongoing experience of parish life does not reflect the experience of church encountered in the catechumenate, these new Catholics often floun-der and do not survive.

Deeply concerned about this situation, Dunning came to see the potential that small church communities could play in developing more secure initia-tion. In the opening words of his keynote address at the 1994 meeting of the North American Forum for Small Christian Communities, he declared, "I see little long term hope for the catechumenate unless there is a connection between small church communities and the catechumenate before, during and after initiation."

The time of mystagogia, that period of special reflection on the saving mysteries which follows full initiation, is often held up as offering an oppor-tunity to introduce the newly baptized/received to small church communi-ties. This approach has been quite successful in some circumstances. But it also runs the risk of appearing to tack on unanticipated expectations, one more hoop through which the newly baptized/received is asked to jump.

From the point of view of the catechumenate, introducing small church communities only at this point fails to take full advantage of the support small communities can be to the whole of the initiation process. Doing the whole of adult initiation in the context of small church communities will much more organically lead to continued membership in a small community after initiation.

The catechumenate and small church communities have a great deal in common. Both are structured around the same four basic ecclesial elements: word, community, worship, and witness. Both are shaped by a baptismal and eucharistic spirituality: becoming the Body of Christ in mission for the sake of the world.

Not every small church community will be ready and able to double as a catechumenal community. A testing of preparedness is called for in each instance. Readiness depends on the discernment of fully cultivated engagement with the four elements of word, community, worship, and witness.

Developing connections between the catechumenate and small church communities will not only be good for the catechumenate, it will offer a great deal to small communities as well. It will challenge small communities to an ever-deeper engagement with all the dimensions of church (word, community, worship, witness). A marriage of effort by small church communities and the catechumenate will call for adaptation, indeed for dying and rising, on both their parts.

In 1995, just a few months after Dunning's death, his friend and colleague, Fr. Thomas Caroluzza, spoke to the North American Forum for Small Christian Communities about his own pastoral practice in bringing the catechumenate and small church communities together. His tribute to Jim, to his breadth of vision and openness to what needs to come, bears repeating:

> It was indeed generous of Jim Dunning to say that the only hope for the catechumenate in the future is that it be done in small church communities. Remember, that comes from someone who gave his whole life for the catechumenate. We're not talking about turf, but about a challenge from one of the great visionaries of our church. It's time for the wedding.

Now, while the needs of the catechumenate are acute enough that we can ill afford to put off the wedding, it takes two to tango. As with the imperative of moving small church communities to engagement with issues of justice and peace, the basic condition of possibility for integrating the catechumenate and small church communities is the presence of critical masses of well-cultivated small church communities in our parishes, communities which are ready, willing, and able to double as catechumenal communities.

The task before us is one of promoting a vision for parish that is centered on people engaged actively and regularly in helping each other to connect life and faith in every aspect of parish life. The task is one of developing small church communities as basic units of parish in a long-range plan for parish development. The investment of pastors is critical in realizing this vision for the parish. My diocesan experience suggests that pastors are more and more appreciative of the potential this vision has, not only for strengthening the life and mission of parish, but also for deepening their own sense of satisfaction and effectiveness in ministry.

HOPE FOR THE PARISH

As a Marianist religious, sometime parish minister, and current director of a diocesan office for small Christian communities, I imagine the future with a great deal of anticipation.

My deeper hope is for us to move closer and closer to embracing small church communities, not just as another nice program but as a major pastoral direction. My deepest hope is that ten years from now, fully 10 percent of the parishes of the archdiocese (i.e., pastors and people together) will be deliberately developing small communities as basic building blocks in a long-range plan for parish development. As critical masses of cultivated small church communities emerge in these parishes, I anticipate progressive efforts to integrate small church communities and the adult catechumenate.

As the number of parishes living this vision for parish increases, I look for them to collaborate together in mutual support. I anticipate that by ten years from now, these parishes will be networked with one another in a common effort which contributes to building up the life and mission of diocesan church as a whole. I hope for the emergence of an interconnected network of small church communities in a network of parishes linked across urban and suburban lines. And I earnestly look for the day when this networking begins to impact the larger region of southern New England on systemic issues of the common good.

Come, reign of God, come!

ROBERT PELTON
Notre Dame, Indiana

The Reverend Robert S. Pelton is a member of the Congregation of the Holy Cross at the University of Notre Dame. His interests in the Latin American experience of small communities reflect his own pastoral experience on that continent. He is currently the Representative for Latin American/North American Church Concerns at the Kellogg Institute for International Studies at the University of Notre Dame, where he is also editor and publisher of the quarterly *International Papers in Pastoral Ministry.* Bob has been the prime mover in two International Consultations on Small Christian Communities (1991, 1996), and is currently preparing a book manuscript on the October 1996 consultation at the University of Notre Dame. He is the author of the recent book, *From Power to Communion: Toward a New Way of Being Church*

Based on the Latin American Experience (Notre Dame: University of Notre Dame Press, 1994). Bob has also been an active convener of people and organizations who are committed to the development and nurture of small Christian communities in the U.S. Catholic church.

SMALL CHRISTIAN COMMUNITIES: AN EMERGING VOICE IN A FUTURE CHURCH

Small Christian communities are assuming greater importance in the Americas. This flows from their ecclesiology, or way of understanding church, which reflects a stronger commitment from the base. Although these communities began in Brazil (Barra do Pirai Diocese) in 1956 as "Sunday service without priests," they were quickly introduced into the Chilean church. On April 17, 1988, the President of the Chilean Episcopal Conference said:

"We are celebrating the twentieth anniversary of Small Christian Communities. In 1968 in spiritual communion with the entire Church of Latin America, the Chilean Episcopal Conference decided to promote these communities without negating the value of the parish." (In this way the Chilean bishops encouraged more intimate forms of participation which are closer to the lives of Christians.) They went on to say: "The years have passed. We thank God and all of those who have assisted this important work which has transformed in a significant way the face of our Church and our pastoral life" ("Caminos nuevos para anunciar a Jesucristo," *Documentos del Episcopado Chileno* 1988-1991).

In the last ten years there has been a gradual growth of similar communities in the United States and Canada. These communities, while being influenced by the Latin American experience, have assumed their own methodology and characteristics. The communities of the North began to institutionalize themselves in networks to support and complement each other. This was especially evident during the National Consultation on Small Christian Communities at the University of Notre Dame from 30 September to 3 October 1990.

Building on the momentum of this national gathering, an international consultation took place at the University of Notre Dame in December 1991. Even though the small Christian communities are a worldwide phenomenon, the United States and Canada continue to be influenced by their origins and growth in Latin America.

Some students of the Latin American church have observed an apparent weakening of the influence of the small communities there. They see this as caused by the tendency of some lay community leaders to separate from the hierarchy and become autonomous. Other community leaders have opted for secular political pursuits. Early on in Brazil many SCCs invented religious forms which they called "grassroots," but these were not recognized as such by the majority of the faithful. As a result of these developments, the theme which has been chosen for the next interecclesial SCC national assembly in Brazil 1997 will be "The SCCs and the 'grass roots.'" These communities continue to have life and influence, but in ways different from earlier years. In looking to the future of the church, we see both threats and hopes for these communities.

THREATS TO THE BASE COMMUNITY PHENOMENON

A number of Latin American theologians (e.g., Chileans Ronaldo Muñoz and Jaime Aldunate) believe that the greatest threat to the communities is the economic model of neoliberalism. This is putting pressure especially on youth throughout the Americas; the result is often drug addiction, loss of self-respect, and finally ennui. Even so, it is in the small communities that young people still experience solidarity.

Another danger exists in the tendency to institutionalize the communities and thus destroy the healthy balance between the prophetic dimension and institutional role. However, some perceive the role of the community in too spiritual a way. This leads to a movement away from reality rather than a prayerful discerning of that same reality. The Peruvian theologian Gustavo Gutiérrez believes that the response is to integrate the contemplative dimension with a deep social commitment. These cannot be separated.

THE FUTURE OF SMALL CHRISTIAN COMMUNITIES AND
A CALL FOR DIALOGUE

What are threats to the small communities can also serve as occasions for maturation. During the seventeen years of the Chilean military dictatorship, the communities provided the poor with opportunities to reflect together and to find ways to help each other, often dramatically. The Chilean Vicariate for Solidarity became well known internationally because of pressure and support from below; that is, from the small communities. They have much potential for further and strong influence.

Intentional Christian communities (i.e., those without a formal commitment to the institutional Church but with an allegiance to the tradition) can challenge the more main-line communities to become more daring and creative. In turn, lively interaction will evoke the latent generosity of youth and help them to make a more mature commitment to the church.

In the inter-American context the future of the SCCs will depend much upon a dialogue which reflects the spirit of the call of Joseph Cardinal Bernardin of Chicago. Such dialogue implies a deep desire for communion, such as exists in the SCCs of Bolivia, and a true listening stance on the part of official leadership of the Church. The Bolivians, due to the grassroots involvement of the miners in small communities, have always asserted themselves effectively. The official church leaders of Bolivia, many of whom are indigenous, listen carefully to their lay ministers. Can this be duplicated in the other churches of America? The vitality of the future church depends upon the answer.

TERRY VELING
Sydney, Australia

> Terry A. Veling is a member of the faculty at the Catholic Theological Union in Sydney, Australia. Terry, his wife, Mary, and their sons, Joel, Rueben, and Asher have been active in small Christian communities in the United States and Australia. Terry has been especially interested in the role of marginal communities in the life of the Catholic church, and the important ways in which prophetic SCCs "scribble" in the margins of a text called "church." Marginal words influence how the main text gets read. They are subversive and revisionary. Terry is the author of the recently published (and acclaimed) book, *Living in the Margins: Intentional Communities and the Art of Interpretation* (New York: Crossroad/Herder, 1996).

WHAT IF COMMUNITY WERE POSSIBLE?

There are times I am fearful of the word "community," of the way it is often read (or misread). For some it means commitment and constraint, something that impinges on my freedom, another demand on my time and space. Others see it as inward-looking and elitist, a gathering of the like-minded. Some are suspicious that community is simply the working out of who is in and who is out, so that community perpetuates excommunicative practices. Or there are those for whom all talk of community is simply a naive or utopian dream, or a fix for society caught in its own addictive self-gratifications. But what if community were not any of these things? What if the word "community" signaled this alertness? So that as soon as we speak of community, we are asking: what if community were possible?

What if—the possible? What if—the first revolutionary question, the question the dying forces don't know how to ask (Rich 1993, 241-242).

When I think of small Christian communities, I am thinking of the resurgence of this question: is community possible? And I am thinking of the alertness this question generates: Community won't be possible if we think just of ourselves; it won't be possible if we think only of "my place in the sun" (Levinas 1989, p. 82). It won't be possible if we move only in inner circles. It won't be possible unless we gather for purposes larger than ourselves. It won't be possible unless we assume responsibility for the faces of those around us: the faces of strangers, friends, victims, neighbors. It won't be possible unless we realize that community has little to do with itself, but everything to do with hearing the call and claim of the other.

The dying forces of Western culture have produced a society of empty, disengaged, alienated selves. Our culture proclaims the autonomous individual—the "I" who declares independence and the self's own certainty, an "I" in control, neither dependent nor receptive. A self such as this "is not connected to any particular ends, has no particular history, is a member of no communities, has no body" (Young 1987, 60). Where in our society do we find people gathering to say, "Here I am"—not as an assertion, not as a declaration of my existence—but as a response? Where, how, in what manner, is this "I am" spoken as an "I am" here for you, with you, bound to you, responsible for you?

This seems like an impossible message for our society to hear: that we are chosen to be responsible for each other. Emmanuel Levinas has helped me understand the centrality of the experience of "other" to community. This is a message of mystical-prophetic proportions in which the other gazes at me and concerns me as someone for whom I am answerable—a summons that the Galilean Jew labored under, whose whole life was an irreplaceable expression of answerability, of saying: "Here I am." In a society like ours—one that does not take easily to words like "responsibility," "obligation," and to the weightiness of commitment, one that proclaims the self rather than listens to the other—in a society such as this, I find great hope and inspiration among small communities who gather in this cultural malaise to ask a revolutionary question: what if community were possible?

The reality of most of those with whom I live and work and share my life is not far removed from Rebecca Chopp's description:

> For many of us in a highly transient society, life transforms itself almost continually. Changing practices of work, of lifestyle, of cultural forms require us to be skilled with new beginnings. Stability, assured by traditional bonds of never changing or slowly changing practices of employment, of family, of community, now appears in our culture as a lost possibility. We must learn a new art, the art of composing our lives anew and finding in that ongoing act of creation new forms of bonds, community, and identity (Chopp 1955, 22-23).

When I think of the future of small Christian communities, I do not imagine anything too grand, in the sense that small communities are poised to "save the day." Gospel images of mustard seeds, yeast and leaven, the widow's mite, sprouting shoots, gatherings of two or three, praying in secret, treasures stored in the heart, all come to mind. The struggles of ordinary, concrete existence are never too far removed from the yearning for community and a sense of social interconnectedness, a yearning for *shalom* and "well being." Working, trying to pay bills, parenting children, making promises, and seeing people all around trying to survive, often on their own, makes me wonder what it might be like if community were possible.

It's like being sick all the time, I think, coming home from work, sick in that low-grade continuous way that makes you forget what it's like to be well. We have never in our lives known what it is to be well. What if I were coming home, I think, from doing work that I love and that was for us all, what if I looked at the houses and the air and the streets, knowing they were in accord, not set against us, what if we knew the powers of this country moved to provide for us and for all people—how would that be—how would we feel and think and what would we create? (Brodine in Rich 1993, 14).

To imagine what things might be like, to believe that something else might be the case than is the case, to envisage different futures, to name new possibilities—perhaps this is why prophets never tire of saying, "I have a dream . . ." or "The Kingdom of God is like . . ."—so that we might transform despair, indifference, anger, and isolation into the startling recognition: "What if . . . ?" What would we create then, what might the world look like, what might the revelation of *shalom* mean if it broke through and captured a people's hearts and imagination? The poetical renaming and re-imagining of the world seems so essential to the political task, investing every act as an act of hope against the constant threat of withering despair. As poetic interpreters, small Christian communities have a vital task to perform—reflecting, acting, imagining—interpreting the primary questions, issues, and concerns of their sociocultural situation in conversation with the primary symbols, narratives, and visions of their faith traditions.

We live in times of great social and ecclesial change. Our world is marked, as David Tracy suggests, with a radical plurality and ambiguity. These are turbulent times that affect us all as we witness the old breaking down and the new breaking through. This is not a time to foreclose experimentation, risk, alternative possibilities. Rather, we need to allow community to evoke a wide range of ecclesial expressions. I have a hope that the commitment, skill, and art required for people to create new beginnings and new communal bonds will release significant social energy and imagination.

Our age is also marked by domination and oppression, and too often we turn ourselves away from the faces of those who tell us we are responsible. It seems imperative that we reclaim the "dangerous memories" of what inclusive community, transformative hope, and healing love might be like. Evoking dangerous memories means evoking memories of noncommunity, of brokenness, exclusion, oppression, suffering. These memories are dangerous because they unsettle the powers that be, the ones who enjoy a well-fed presence, the ones whose "wagons are loaded with corn" (Blake 1958, 149) I have a hope that small Christian communities will be places that choose the narrow, singular way—a way that remembers "both the long patience of the oppressed and a revolutionary impatience, a way opened by humble religious daring . . . and a language that has managed to call upon the Nameless" (Levinas 1993, 131).

"Community" is not a safe, secure, or certain word, a word to be taken too lightly. Perhaps this is why I am attracted to marginal communities, to gatherings that never quite settle down, that live always "in the midst," in the constant to-and-fro of listening and responding, that never cease in their imagination or their commitment to ask: what if community were possible?

Bibliography

Arbuckle, G. *Refounding the Church: Dissent for Leadership.* Maryknoll: Orbis, 1993.

Avery, M., Auvine, B., Streibel, B., and Weiss, L. *Building United Judgment: A Handbook for Consensus Decision Making.* Madison: Center for Conflict Resolution, 1981.

Azevedo, M. *Basic Ecclesial Communities in Brazil: The Challenge of a New Way of Being Church.* Washington, D.C.: Georgetown University Press, 1987.

Banks, R. *Paul's Idea of Community: The Early House Churches in their Historical Setting.* Grand Rapids: Eerdmans, 1980.

Baranowski, A. *Creating Small Faith Communities: A Plan for Restructuring the Parish and Renewing Catholic Life.* Cincinnati: St. Anthony Messenger Press, 1988.

Barreiro, A. *Basic Ecclesial Communities: The Evangelization of the Poor.* Maryknoll: Orbis, 1982.

Barrett, L. *Building the House Church.* Scottsdale, PA: Herald Press, 1986.

Branick, V. *The House Church in the Writings of Paul.* Wilmington: Glazier, 1989.

Bellah, R., Madsen, R., Sullivan, W., Swidler, A., and Tipton, S. *Habits of the Heart: Individualism and Commitment in American Life.* Berkeley: University of California, 1985.

Blake, W., and Bronowski, J., eds. *William Blake.* Middlesex: Penguin, 1958.

Boyt, H. *Commonwealth: A Return to Citizen Politics.* New York: Macmillan, 1989.

Briggs, K. *Holy Siege: The Year That Shook Catholic America.* New York: Harper Collins, 1992.

Brown, R. *Priest and Bishop: Biblical Reflections.* Paramus, NJ: Paulist, 1970.

Brueggemann, W. *The Prophetic Imagination.* Philadelphia: Fortress, 1978.

Buber, M. *The Legend of the Baal-Shem.* New York: Schocken, 1969.

171

Camille, M. *Image on the Edge: The Margins of Medieval Art.* Cambridge: Harvard, 1992.

Chopp, R. *Saving Work: Feminist Practices of Theological Education.* Louisville: Westminster John Knox Press, 1995.

Clark, E. *The Want Makers: Inside the World of Advertising.* New York: Penguin, 1988.

Cobb, J. *Christ in a Pluralistic Age.* Philadelphia: Westminster, 1975.

Crosby, M. *House of Disciples: Church, Economics, and Justice in Matthew.* Maryknoll: Orbis, 1988.

DeMott, B. *The Imperial Middle: Why Americans Can't Think Straight about Class.* New York: Morrow, 1990.

Dulles, A. *Models of the Church.* Garden City, NY: Doubleday 1974.

Emerson, R. *Essays and Lectures.* New York: Library of America, 1983.

Etzioni, A. *The Spirit of Community: Rights, Responsibilities and the Communitarian Agenda.* New York: Crown Publishers, 1993.

Fisher, R. and Ury, W. *Getting to Yes: Negotiating Agreements Without Giving In.* Boston: Houghton Mifflin, 1981.

Freedman, S. *Upon This Rock: The Miracles of a Black Church.* New York: Harper Collins, 1993.

Galbraith, J. K. *A Journey through Economic Time.* New York: Houghton Mifflin, 1994.

Geertz, C. *Local Knowledge: Further Essays in Interpretive Anthropology.* New York: Basic Books, 1983.

Greider, W. *Who Will Tell the People: The Betrayal of American Democracy.* New York: Simon and Schuster, 1992.

Hanson, P. *The People Called: The Growth of Community in the Bible.* San Francisco: Harper & Row, 1986.

Haughey, J. *The Holy Use of Money: Personal Finances in the Light of Christian Faith.* Garden City: Doubleday, 1986.

Hegy, Pierre. "The End of American Catholicism?—Another Look." In *America*, May 1, 1993.

Heschel, A. *The Prophets.* San Francisco: Harper & Row, 1962.

Holland, J. and Henriot, P. *Social Analysis: Linking Faith and Social Justice.* Maryknoll: Orbis, 1984.

Hollenbeck, D. *Claims in Conflict: Retrieving and Renewing the Catholic Human Rights Tradition.* New York: Paulist, 1979.

Janowitz, M. "Sociological Theory and Social Control." *American Journal of Sociology* 81 (1), 1975.

Kavanaugh, J. *Following Christ in a Consumer Society: The Spirituality of Cultural Resistance,* rev. ed. Maryknoll: Orbis, 1991.

King, P., Maynard, K., and Woodyard, D. *Risking Liberation: Middle Class Powerlessness and Social Heroism.* Atlanta: John Knox, 1988.

Kleissler, T., LeBret, M., and McGuinness, M. *Small Christian Communities: A Vision of Hope.* New York: Paulist, 1991.

Krietemeyer, R. "Policies and Priorities: The New Social Reconstruction." *Church,* Fall, 1991.

Lee, B. *The Future Church of 140 B.C.E.: A Hidden Revolution.* New York: Crossroad, 1995.

Lee, B. and Cowan, M. *Dangerous Memories: House Churches and Our American Story.* Kansas City: Sheed & Ward, 1986.

Lee, J. *Marginality: The Key to Multicultural Theology.* Minneapolis: Fortress, 1995.

Levinas, E., and Hand, S., eds. *The Levinas Reader.* Oxford: Blackwell, 1989.

Levinas, E. *Outside the Subject.* Stanford: Stanford University Press, 1993.

Levinas, E. "Ethics and Infinity." *CrossCurrents.* Summer 1984, pp. 191-203.

Lohfink, G. *Jesus and Community.* Philadelphia: Fortress, 1984.

Macneice, L. *Collected Poems.* London: Faber and Faber, 1979.

Malherbe, A. *The Social Aspects of Early Christianity.* Philadelphia: Fortress, 1983.

Malina, B. and Rohrbaugh, R. *Social-Science Commentary on the Synoptic Gospels.* Minneapolis: Fortress, 1993.

Meeks, W. *The First Urban Christians: The Social World of the Apostle Paul.* New Haven: Yale, 1983.

Meier, J. *A Marginal Jew: Rethinking the Historical Jesus.* New York: Doubleday, 1987.

Metz, J. *Faith in History and Society: Toward a Practical Fundamental Theology.* New York: Crossroad, 1980.

Moriarty, R., ed. *Belonging, Believing and Serving: The Stories of Small Christian Communities.* Hartford: The Pastoral Department for Small Christian Communities, 1994.

Myers, C. *Binding the Strong Man: A Political Reading of Mark's Story of Jesus.* Maryknoll: Orbis, 1988.

NCCB, *Called and Gifted for the Third Millenium.* Washington, D.C.: United States Catholic Conference, 1995.

Overman, J. A. *Church and Community in Crisis: The Gospel According to Matthew.* Valley Forge: Trinity Press International, 1996.

Owensby, W. *Economics for Prophets: A Primer on Concepts, Realities and Values in Our Economic Systems.* Grand Rapids: Eerdmans, 1988.

Pelton, R. *From Power to Communion: Toward a New Way of Being Church Based on the Latin American Experience.* Notre Dame: University of Notre Dame Press, 1994.

Phillips, K. *The Politics of Rich and Poor: Wealth and the American Electorate in the Reagan Aftermath.* New York: Random House, 1990.

Phillips, K. *Boiling Point: Democrats, Republicans, and the Decline of Middle-class Prosperity.* New York: Random House, 1993.

Quigley, W. "The Rich Get Richer: So What?" *America,* June 17, 1996.

Rahner, K. *The Future of Man and Christianity.* Chicago: Argus, 1969.

Reich, R. *The Work of the Nations: Preparing Ourselves for 21st Century Capitalism.* New York: Alfred Knopf, 1991a.

Reich, R. "The Secession of the Successful." *The New York Times Magazine,* Jan. 20, 1991b.

Rich, A. *What Is Found There: Notebooks on Poetry and Politics.* London: Virago Press, 1993.

Riesman, D. *The Lonely Crowd: A Study of the Changing American Character.* New Haven: Yale, 1950.

Rorty, R. *Philosophy and the Mirror of Nature.* Princeton: Princeton, 1979.

Sandel, M. *Democracy's Discontent: America in Search of a Public Philosophy.* Cambridge: Belknap, 1996.

Sarason, S. *The Psychological Sense of Community: Prospects for a Community Psychology.* San Francisco: Jossey-Bass, 1974.

Schillebeeckx, E. *Christ the Sacrament of the Encounter with God.* New York: Sheed & Ward, 1963.

Schreiter, R. *Constructing Local Theologies.* Maryknoll: Orbis, 1985.

Schüssler Fiorenza, E. *Discipleship of Equals: A Critical Feminist Ekklesia-logy of Liberation.* New York: Crossroad, 1993.

Schwartz, B. *The Battle for Human Nature: Science, Morality and Modern Life.* New York: Norton, 1986.

Scott, Sr. Macrina. *Picking the "Right" Bible Study Program: Reviews of 150 Recommended Programs with a Listing of the Top 15.* Chicago: ACTA Publications, 1994.

Sennett, R. *The Fall of Public Man.* New York: Vintage, 1970.

Simons, R. *Competing Gospels: Public Theology and Economic Theory.* Alexandria, Australia: E.J. Dwyer, 1995.

Slater, P. *The Pursuit of Loneliness: American Culture at the Breaking Point.* Boston: Beacon, 1970.

Theissen, G. *The Social Setting of Pauline Christianity: Essays on Corinth.* Philadelphia: Fortress, 1982.

Theissen, G. *Sociology of Early Palestinian Christianity.* Philadelphia: Fortress, 1978.

Tracy, D. *Blessed Rage for Order: The New Pluralism of Theology.* New York: Seabury, 1979.

Tracy, D. *The Analogical Imagination: Christian Theology and the Culture of Pluralism.* New York: Crossroad, 1981.

Tracy, D. *Plurality and Ambiguity: Hermeneutics, Religion, Hope.* San Francisco: Harper & Row, 1987.

Vandenakker, J. *Small Christian Communities and the Parish.* Kansas City: Sheed & Ward, 1994.

Veling, T. *Living in the Margins. Intentional Communities and the Art of Interpretation.* New York: Crossroad Herder, 1996.

Waetjen, H. *A Reordering of Power: A Socio-Political Reading of Mark's Gospel.* Minneapolis: Fortress, 1989.

Westley, D. *Good Things Happen: Experiencing Community in Small Groups.* Mystic, CT: Twenty-Third Publications, 1992.

Whitehead, E. "Leadership and Power." In Cowan, M., ed. *Leadership Ministry in Community.* Collegeville: Liturgical Press, 1987.

Whitehead, E. and Whitehead, J. *Community of Faith: Crafting Christian Communities Today.* Mystic, CT: Twenty-Third Press, 1992.

Wolin, S. *The Presence of the Past: Essays on the State and the Constitution.* Baltimore: Johns Hopkins, 1989.

Wright, F. *Northern Ireland: A Comparative Analysis.* Dublin: Gill and Macmillan, 1987.

Wuthnow, R. *Sharing the Journey: Support Groups and America's New Quest for Community.* New York: The Free Press, 1994.

Young, I. "Impartiality and the Civic Republic: Some Implications of Feminist Critiques of Moral and Political Theory," in Benhabib, S. and Cornell, D., eds. *Feminism as Critique.* Minneapolis: University of Minnesota, 1987.

Index